THE MACHINE AWAKES

Also available from Adam Christopher and Titan Books

THE SPIDER WARS

The Burning Dark

The Dead Stars (April 2016)

THE LA TRILOGY

Made to Kill (November 2015)

ELEMENTARY

The Ghost Line

ADAM
CHRISTOPHER

THE MACHINE AWAKES

TITAN BOOKS

The Machine Awakes
Print edition ISBN: 9781783292035
E-book edition ISBN: 9781783292042

Published by Titan Books
A division of Titan Publishing Group Ltd
144 Southwark Street, London SE1 0UP

First edition: March 2015
2 4 6 8 10 9 7 5 3 1

A CIP catalogue record for this title is available from the British Library.

Printed and bound by CPI Group (UK) Ltd, Croydon, CR0 4YY

For Sandra

GOD IS A NUMBER

"God*damn* it, I'm good!"

Chief Mining Engineer Ramin Klaus clicked his tongue and sat back in his chair. Stretching his arms, he interlocked his fingers behind his head and gave the planetary projection in front of him a satisfied nod. Pay dirt. Big time.

Around him, the usual quiet efficiency that characterized the huge circular control room of the Jovian Mining Corporation's refinery was broken by a smattering of applause and even an enthusiastic whistle. Two dozen mining engineers, clad in the high-collared magenta uniforms of JMC technical crew, were seated around the planetary projection in two long, curving, semicircular consoles. In the center of the minimal, white chamber was the planetary projection of Jupiter itself, a photoreal holographic sphere, ten meters across and filling the control room with swirling orange and red light.

Klaus accepted the congratulations of his colleagues as he watched the slowly rotating bands of Jupiter's atmosphere. Jupiter's rich, rich atmosphere. Holy *crap,* the bonus on this storm alone was going to be enough to pay off his indentured contract with the JMC. Klaus clicked his tongue again and let his sprung chair push him forward as he reached for his keyboard. A few taps later and the storm—a bluish oval a quarter the size of Jupiter's famous red spot, slowly sliding clockwise around the planet's upper latitudes—was outlined on the projection with a yellow computer overlay. Another tap, and a series of red lines were drawn—vectors from a scattering of bright green triangular icons that were spread out across the side of the planet facing Klaus's console. Klaus sat in the center of his row; on either side, the other engineers got back to work, murmuring into their comms as they studied their own holodisplays floating above each station.

Storm identified, vectors plotted, it was time to get to work. Klaus tapped at his controls, and hundreds of thousands of kilometers away, fifty of the largest robotic mining platforms—the Sigmas—changed course.

The JMC refinery floated in the upper atmosphere of Jupiter, at a zone where the external pressure was more or less Earth-normal, and the atmosphere, while still turbulent, was much more stable than the deeper levels. The Sigmas, each a factory bigger than the city-sized refinery itself, floated at varying depths according to need, their fully autonomous AIs programmed to search for and extract the richest belts of gas, processing the valuable product and sending it in solid, frozen shipments up to the refinery by automated cargo drone. At the refinery, the gas was further processed, the more exotic trace elements separated, and the product shipped out to the miniature planetary system of Jupiter's moons. There, safely out of the Jovian atmosphere, the JMC ran one of the biggest logistics operations in Fleetspace, packaging the product for sale to their primary customer: the Fleet.

Seated on Klaus's left, junior engineer Parker frowned, his hand held against the side of his head as he listened to something on his comms.

Klaus turned in his chair toward his colleague. "Everything okay?"

Parker nodded, but the frown remained plastered to his face. "Yes, sir . . . just . . ." He tapped at his console and squinted at his holodisplay. "Just an echo off of something. Sigmas Five and Forty are bouncing a transmission between each other."

Klaus shrugged. "Don't worry about it. This the first time you've been storm chasing?"

Parker's frown melted into a smile. *Good lad,* thought Klaus. The young man was no doubt thinking about his storm bonus. As they all should be.

"Right," said Klaus. He pointed to the planetary projection, to the green icons representing the Sigma mines as they slowly tracked toward the new storm. "The mines will coordinate between themselves for maximum efficiency. Storm like this, don't be surprised if you hear all kinds of chatter from them. They might even reconfigure their superstructures for maximum extraction."

"Eavesdropping on the mines again?"

Klaus and Parker both turned in their chairs, looking up to the high, railed gallery that ringed the control center. There a man leaned on the railing, looking down on the control center. "I'm not sure they like that, mister." Then he grinned broadly.

"Wouldn't dream of it, sir," said Klaus. He glanced sideways at Parker, who visibly gulped, then turned back to his station. Klaus laughed and looked back up at his boss. "All under control."

"Glad to hear it," said the refinery controller. "Send me a full storm projection for review, will you?"

"That's an affirmative, sir."

The executive tapped the gallery rail with the large ring on his right hand, the sound echoing across the control chamber. The gallery was dark—intentionally so, allowing visitors to observe the workings of the refinery control center without disturbing the engineers—but the exec was lit up in the reds and yellows of the huge Jupiter projection, his teeth and eyes glinting as he nodded. He tapped the rail with his ring again, then turned and vanished into the shadows.

Klaus spun his chair around. "Okay," he said, addressing everyone seated around the room. "You heard the boss. I want a full storm projection. Duration, yields, profit margins, the works. Get to it, folks."

There was a murmur of acknowledgment from around the

room as the engineers hunched over their stations, compiling the individual reports that Klaus would then check and assemble into a single document for the refinery controller.

Next to him, Parker pursed his lips.

Klaus raised an eyebrow. “Yes, Mr. Parker?”

“Are the mines okay?” he asked. He pulled at the earpiece in his left ear. “There seems to be a lot of *something* going on.”

Klaus shook his head. “That’s normal, engineer, like I said. Turn off your comms, and pull up your projects for the executive report.”

“Yes, sir.”

As Parker turned back to his console, Klaus allowed himself a small smile. Ah, was he ever as young as that? Maybe he had been. He couldn’t really remember. And maybe one day young Parker would be in his chair, as chief mining engineer on a JMC refinery.

But, in the meantime, they had a storm to catch.

An hour later, the chief engineer stood in front of the controller’s desk in the plush management office. Like the rest of the refinery, the décor was in corporate colors—all muted purples and white—but Klaus had to admit that he didn’t really like it. There was a clinical, almost medical atmosphere in the office.

Which, if he was honest, befitted its occupant.

His boss sat behind a smoked glass desk, dressed in the same magenta as the engineers. But instead of the pseudo-military tunic of the workers, his suit was an elegant designer piece, with a crisp high-buttoned shirt of the same color beneath the jacket. His steel gray hair, brushed back into a high pompadour, matched his eyes, which were small and hard. True, he was pleasant enough, but he represented a class of company employee existing in the rarified echelons of the JMC board that Klaus couldn’t really identify with. As the executive tapped at his datapad, Klaus saw he was wearing cufflinks studded with red gems as big as his thumbnail. Klaus might have had a comfortable job in the controlled environment of the JMC refinery today, but he was a starminer through and through.

He'd started his career digging herculanium ore out of slowrocks with nothing but a plasma pick, his thin spacesuit the only protection from the vacuum of space as he worked on one airless, low-gravity asteroid after another. But while his JMC boss knew his stuff, Klaus couldn't really picture him in the cramped confines of a mining ship, studying stellar mineralogy charts, plotting his course from one belt to the next.

Of course, that life was so long ago for Klaus that he couldn't even remember when he'd won the position at the JMC. Must have been, oh—

"Hmm."

The executive frowned, drawing a manicured finger over his top lip as he studied the report. Neither of them had spoken for some minutes. Klaus, snapping out of his reverie, rubbed the skin under one eye as he returned his thoughts to the problem at hand, running some possible explanations—and solutions—through his mind.

It seemed that Parker had been right. Two of the Sigma platforms were bouncing a signal between them, but after running diagnostics, Parker found that neither mine was acknowledging the other. Parker, on his own initiative, had drilled deeper into the status logs and discovered that the data stream from Sigmas Five and Forty—coincidentally, two of the very deepest of the Jovian gas mines—had been choppy for three cycles now. That wasn't necessarily a problem, or even unexpected, Klaus knew that. As he had explained to Parker, so far down in Jupiter's cloud deck conditions were difficult, to say the least. Besides the colossal atmospheric pressure and temperature—not to mention the frankly *insane* meteorology—there was electromagnetic radiation. A boatload of it, generated by electrical activity in the very storms the robotic platforms were supposed to mine.

And sure, the platforms were shielded and the communications network that linked the robots together, and the refinery to the robots, had enough automatic error correction to compensate. But this storm? Well, it was something special, a once-in-a-lifetime event that had brewed deep in the soupy layers of the planet before rising to the surface. The level of data loss was huge, although the JMC's central AI hadn't flagged it, content instead to let the mines—each an extension of the JMC AI anyway—get on with their jobs. Each giant mine was designed not only to overcome any routine problem on its own, but even to devise new techniques and methods, designing its own improved platform systems and using its factories to reconfigure their very own structures. Sometimes when a Sigma mine was later inspected by engineers, it bore little resemblance to the original design spec.

The controller flipped through a few more pages on his datapad. "Fascinating," he muttered, but he didn't look up. Klaus wondered whether he should answer, or whether his boss was talking to himself.

Klaus cleared his throat. There was something else about the signal bouncing between the Sigmas that he really needed to get an executive decision on.

"Strictly speaking, it's not outside normal operating parameters, but—"

"This is quite a storm, Mr. Klaus."

Klaus paused. He nodded. "That it most certainly is, sir."

The executive flipped through some more pages, nodding to himself. "Helium-3, tibanna, oxozone. Not to mention five percent vertrexan and zero-point-zero-zero-zero-zero-zero-five percent lucanol." He dropped the datapad onto his desk with a clatter and looked up at his chief engineer as he reclined in his chair. "Good work, Mr. Klaus. It's going to be a bumper payday for all of us."

Klaus gave a small bow. "Well, I hope so, sir."

"You hope?"

Klaus gestured to the datapad. "The behavior of Sigma mines Five and Forty, sir. We've run the signal they're bouncing to each other, but it's not a diagnostic code. To be honest, I'm not sure what it is. I've worked on these platforms nearly forty years and in all that time I've never—"

"Don't worry about the Sigma mines, engineer," said the controller. He steepled his fingers and looked at Klaus with narrow gray eyes. "They can look after themselves."

Klaus frowned, and locked his hands behind his back. "Well, sir, we can continue with the extraction, but I'd like to take Five and Forty offline for inspection. They're about due anyway."

The executive rolled his chair closer to his desk and leaned his elbows on the glass top. "Postpone that inspection, Chief. I want full extraction on this storm. I don't want a single molecule of lucanol to be missed. Understood?"

"If we take the two platforms out, we've still got forty-eight converging on the storm. There should be no impact on extraction."

"And there certainly won't be if all fifty are chasing it. Proceed as normal, engineer."

With that, the refinery controller picked up his datapad and began reading something else. The chief engineer's audience was over.

Klaus gave another small bow. "As you wish, sir," he said, but this time his smile was tight.

Dammit, this wasn't right. There was something wrong with at least two of the mines. And the timing was less than perfect—if they lost the storm, if they didn't extract every single molecule of value stirred up from the depths of Jupiter, then the boss would have his guts. Klaus had no doubt about that whatsoever. The mines *could* look after themselves, that was true—but even so, that didn't make them infallible. Machines could break down. Computers—even AIs—could glitch.

The chief engineer strode away from the office and headed back toward the control center. It was a fair distance, easily traversed by elevator, but Klaus wanted to cool his heels. He took the long way, a brisk stroll around the curving orbital corridor of the refinery. The exercise would help clear his head and give him a few extra minutes to think.

What the *hell* was the signal from Sigmas Five and Forty? It made no sense—just a string of numbers. It sounded like quickspace coordinates, but the sequence was missing two digits. And while the transmission was garbled by the magnetic interference from the storm, the constant repetition between the two mining platforms had allowed them to check and re-check the signal. They'd got the whole thing. It was just . . . strange.

Parker had shown initiative, digging it out from what should have been a routine observation. Klaus wondered what he would have done, had he picked it up before the junior engineer. Probably nothing. The machine code chatter between the mining platforms was just so much background noise that Klaus had learned to tune out years ago.

Maybe he was getting old.

Klaus huffed and kept walking.

The refinery's orbital corridor had a continuous curving window that looked out into the Jovian cloud deck. The glow from Jupiter's atmosphere was bright, but Klaus found the purple-orange cast gloomy, the way it bleached the color from his own purple uniform and stained the otherwise gleaming white interior of the refinery into a muddy, dirty hue.

Huh. Maybe it didn't matter. Maybe it was just routine. Maybe he'd made an issue out of it when there was no problem, the over-enthusiastic junior engineer casting unnecessary doubt into his mind. The robot mines knew what they were doing. Okay, so the engineers in the control room ran the entire JMC operation—in theory. But, the business of gas mining aside, the JMC's primary concern was really *automation*. Driven by pure profit, the corporation had pursued robotics and AI research to such an advanced level that its tech was way ahead of even what the Fleet itself—their primary customer—had. Gone were the days when the storms of the gas giants were chased manually, with pilots and their crews risking their lives aboard the giant extraction platforms. Hell, the Sigmas knew more about gas mining than even a veteran like Klaus. And he knew it.

But . . . it was bugging him. Something wasn't right, and Klaus was sure of it—forty years of gas mining had given him an intuition about things like this. The problem needed to be investigated and fixed, or something would happen and they'd lose the storm. And their bonuses. Let's see if the boss liked the sound of that.

Klaus nodded to another crewman passing from the opposite direction. Then he stopped and turned around.

The orbital corridor behind him was empty.

Klaus had stopped by an intersection, a point at which the wide corridor opened into a large, high-ceilinged atrium, complete with elevators and even seating. The space was designed to be open, something like a public square in a regular city, but the purple-orange Jupiterlight from the windows gave the whole place an eerie, dusky glow.

Klaus frowned. Whoever had passed him had vanished around the curve of the orbital corridor. He'd been distracted by his own thoughts, but it had seemed that the crewman hadn't been wearing the company uniform. Official visits from the Fleet were commonplace—there were always sales contracts to argue over—but, as far as Klaus knew, there wasn't a delegation due for several cycles.

Huh. It was nothing. His distracted mind playing tricks.

He turned back around and jumped in fright as he nearly ran into two people standing in the corridor—a man and a woman, dressed in black, their faces hidden behind featureless masks.

Klaus gasped, one hand reaching for the comm on the collar of his uniform even as he drew breath to ask the intruders who they were. But he was slow—the man raised a snub-nosed gun that spat a blue light with only a very high, short sound, and the chief engineer collapsed into the arms of the third intruder, who had reappeared behind him.

The murky corridor swam in Klaus's vision as he felt a deep, deep cold spreading across his body. He tried to focus, but saw nothing except whispering dark shapes looming over him.

A woman. "Quickly. Reboot. Use the data stick."

A man. "Got it."

Klaus felt something needle-sharp slide into his neck. He wanted to cry out in surprise, but he couldn't.

Someone else spoke, but their voice was a million miles away.

The woman replied, speaking, Klaus realized, into a comm. "Confirmed. Phase one initiated." Then, louder, to her colleagues: "One down, twenty-three to go."

And then the cold spread and the darkness grew, and Ramin Klaus's last thought was of the signal, and what the sequence *eight-seven-nine-one-two-two-Juno-Juno* could possibly mean.

And then . . . then he saw a light. A bright, bright light.

THE BATTLE OF WARWORLD 4114

The machines were still over the horizon, but even though the battle hadn't reached the marines hunkered down in the trench, the entire sky was lit by the fierce red-and-white aurora of suborbital bombardment.

Warworld 4114 was on fire.

In less than a cycle, the Spiders had swarmed over an entire hemisphere. Warworld 4114 was a hair smaller than Earth, an uninhabited lump of nothing, the surface alternating between thick forest and gray rocky plains. There was plant life aplenty. But animal life? Aside from the company of marines dug into the gray desert, waiting for the enemy war machines to arrive, Warworld 4114 was a dead planet.

A dead planet both sides wanted. The Spiders had moved first, as they always did, a Mother Spider seeding the world with millions of organo-mechanical babies, each the size of a dog, which landed and began consuming matter and growing and dividing and then *building,* until the machines now walking toward the marines' position were eight-legged monsters a hundred meters tall, their curved, knife-like legs carving the hard surface of the planet into rubble as they advanced.

The Spiders wanted the planet, which meant the Fleet wanted it too. The battle plan was simple: hold the machines back from suborbit—the U-Stars safely out of reach, the Mother Spider having departed as soon as its spawn had touched ground—until the psi-marines could dig in. Then, weakened and distracted by the aerial onslaught, the Spiders would be disabled by the psi-marines, their relentless march halted long enough for two smaller U-Stars—in this case, the *Seether* and the *Shutterbug*—to come in for the final, low-altitude kill.

So went the theory, anyway.

Psi-Marine Tyler Smith looked up, the HUD inside his helmet tracking the path of two more photonic torpedoes as they streaked across the sky, heading for the target. The U-Stars were doing a fine job, hovering in the upper atmosphere as they dumped munitions on the war machines. Tyler just hoped it was enough. There was no doubt the Spiders were getting toasted, but there were a *lot* of them. What they lacked in firepower and strategy was made up by sheer numbers.

The comms buzzed in Tyler's ear. Transmission incoming, battle command.

"Fireteam Alpha, Fireteam Bravo. Heads up, twelve o'clock."

An amber indicator appeared in Tyler's HUD. He glanced to his left and to his right, the other members of his seven-man psi-marine fireteam giving the thumbs up as they all squatted below the lip of the trench. Tyler pushed himself off the trench wall and, still crouching, shuffled around. The amber indicator slid around his HUD until it was dead center at the top of his vision.

Straight ahead. The Spiders were nearly here.

An alert inside Tyler's helmet told him that Fireteam Alpha was also ready, a few hundred meters farther down the trench. Tyler lifted himself up, until his eye line was at ground level.

Down the left side of the HUD, text began to scroll as the U-Stars somewhere above began feeding data to his combat suit's computer. As the night sky bloomed in brilliant color once more, the horizon exploding in flaring white, the HUD began drawing small red boxes—two, then three, then four, then a dozen, then Tyler lost count. The icons buzzed around the horizon like insects; then his HUD finally settled as the icons flashed, locking onto the targets.

The machines stepped over the horizon, still too far away to see any detail against the glaring whitewash of the continued aerial bombardment. But there they were—black shapes, as tall as skyscrapers, lumbering toward them. As Tyler's combat AI fed the view to the other marines, the comms clicked to life and filled with chatter—not from the psi-marine fireteams, but the regular troops dug in half a klick in front of Tyler's trench. There were two hundred heavily armed Fleet marines between them and the Spiders.

Once again, Tyler hoped it was enough.

He gritted his teeth and closed his eyes. Timing was key. He had to wait until the machines were close enough to make contact, but the Spiders were big, their giant legs covering alarming amounts of ground with each step. The window of opportunity was a small one.

Fireteam Alpha, confirm.

The communiqué came not over the comms, but inside Tyler's mind. With his eyes closed he saw nothing but dull shapes moving across blackness, as his HUD continued to shine its light against his eyelids.

Fireteam Bravo, he thought, linking minds with the other team leader. *Acknowledged.*

There was a moment of nothing, of silence, of stillness and calm borne both of training and experience, as Tyler closed his mind to the outside world and focused in on himself. Psychic battle with the Spiders was just as dangerous as a firefight. But the two teams were good, and while they weren't carrying anything more than small plasma rifles, they were very, *very* well armed indeed. The psi-marines had weaponized minds, and the battle was about to commence.

Then Tyler heard it and opened his eyes. His comms stayed quiet, but a blue triangle flickered in his HUD as the psi-fi router in his combat suit picked up the signal and amplified it, spreading the data load across all of the psi-marines. The sound in Tyler's head made his heart race and made him feel infinitely small. It buzzed and clicked, a staccato nonsense that was half white noise, half something else. Something rhythmic. Intelligent.

The language of the Spiders.

Contact established.

Engage.

Across the plain, ahead of Tyler's trench, the ground flickered with blue sparks as the embedded marines opened fire with their plasma rifles. Above, the two U-Stars continued to fire, the scrolling text in Tyler's HUD showing their descent path and a countdown.

The clock had started.

Tyler dropped down into the trench and rejoined his fireteam, their backs turned to the oncoming machines, their eyes—like his—closed behind the opaque visors of their helmets.

The sound in Tyler's head had reached a crescendo, so loud it felt like he was being physically crushed under the weight of it. Pain, hot and brilliant, shot through his eardrums, and then, behind his closed eyes, his optic nerve was lit by a wave of psychic feedback as his team opened up on the Spider communications web, throwing everything they had at jamming it.

But this . . . this was different. The pain, it was real. Tyler felt something warm and liquid roll down his cheeks inside his helmet. He screwed his eyes tight and screamed as he stared into the burning darkness.

The roar of the Spiders was agony without end. The screams of the psi-marines was pain beyond imagining.

The white light blazed, flaring golden, flaring blue—

Caitlin screamed and sat up, kicking at the damp sheets tangling around her feet, her drenched T-shirt slick against her skin. For a moment she could see nothing but golden light flaring and hear nothing but the roar of the ocean. But as she opened her eyes and blinked and blinked and blinked she realized the glow was morning light reflecting off the gold mirrored glass of the building opposite her own, the shard of light shining through the unfinished wall of her refuge and spotlighting her as she sat on her makeshift bed. The roaring wasn't in her head, either. It was coming through the ceiling, the endless screech and thud of music so heavy it sounded more like an unbalanced shuttle afterburner.

She kicked the sheets clear, then leaned back and reached under her pillow. It was the only place you could keep valuables, and her most prized possession was still in place. Likewise her watch, which never left her wrist, not in a place like this. She rubbed her face and glanced at it.

Five A.M.

Time to move. She swung her legs over the edge of the bed, then paused.

She'd had the dream, again. As vivid as a memory, a flashback from battle, as if it had been her on Warworld 4114, crouching in the trench, facing down the marching Spider army with her mind as her weapon.

But it hadn't been her. She had never served the Fleet—never gotten that far. The memory belonged to someone else.

Her brother, Tyler.

Cait sniffed the air. It was warm already, although the breeze blowing in through the open wall of her twelfth-floor hideout was starting to make her shiver in her sweat-soaked underwear. Getting undressed to go to sleep was a risk—a place like this, you had to be ready to move, quickly—but it had been so fucking hot the last few nights, she'd decided to take the chance. Not that she'd been able to sleep much. The dream had disturbed her rest for most of the past two weeks.

With the music still thundering from elsewhere in the half-finished building, Cait quickly hopped across the floor, the concrete cool on her bare feet as she crouched down near the plastic crate where she had stashed her gear. That was another risk. She really should have kept the crate within arm's reach of the bed. She chastised herself for being sloppy, but that was the last night she'd have to spend in this dump anyway.

For two weeks she'd been living—if you could call it that—high in an abandoned, unfinished skyscraper on the edge of Salt City. Despite the slum's overcrowding, the skeletal building was only half-occupied by squatters—perhaps, Cait had thought, it was the proximity of the building to the shiny clean world of New Orem, literally just across the street, that put people off. The construction—half-finished fingers of building poking into the sky like the rotting ribs of a forgotten animal carcass—had been halted who knew how many years ago, a symbol of the Fleet's complete indifference to the plight of the giant slum right on its doorstep. Maybe that was another reason she'd found a hideout so easily. The people of Salt City didn't want any reminders of how the Fleet had failed them. The construction site, and the shell of the building in which Cait had made her camp, was just that.

That didn't stop scavengers, of course. As Cait got dressed, she padded over to the open wall and looked down at the rubble-strewn ground far below. The body of the last one she'd fought off was still down there, lying in a particularly inaccessible half-finished foundation pile. She hadn't intended to kill him, but she hadn't been able to stop herself. Backed into a corner, fighting not just for her life but for the *mission,* and . . . it had happened again. Her wild talent had come to the fore, acting almost like it had its own intelligence, taking over to protect her when she couldn't do it herself.

The scavenger had screamed all the way to the ground.

And he was still there. And she really *hadn't* meant to kill him—her talent, her *power* impossible to control, no matter how hard she tried. But since then, nobody else had come to bother her. She guessed his corpse—his screams—had served as a warning. Stay away from the woman on level twelve, north side. She's a crazy bitch.

Cait pushed the memory away, focusing on the here and now, controlling her breathing as she felt her heart rate pick up.

Because her talent was a frightening thing. And not just for scavengers or the trainers at the Academy who had seen something different about her, out of all the thousands of recruits who enrolled.

She was scared of it too.

She blew out her cheeks to calm herself, and she sat on her bed and pulled her boots on. Her outfit wasn't black as instructed, but it was comprised of the darkest things she still owned. The pants and boots *were* black, but the hoodie was dark navy blue, and the T-shirt underneath was light gray—there was nothing she could do there except keep the hoodie zipped to the neck. She stood and pulled a hair tie from her pocket, scraping her still-damp bangs off her face as she looked out to the spires of the Fleet capital, New Orem, glowing in the sunrise. It was a beautiful sight, despite the ruined surrounds.

The morning sky was clear, and when the chill breeze dropped Cait could feel the real heat beginning to grow, the sunlight already reflecting off thousands of immaculate mirrored buildings opposite her own incomplete shell of one.

Today it was time to head back into the city, because today was her brother's funeral.

It would be a military service with full honors, to be held at the Fleet Memorial, a vast cemetery on the other side of the city. Cait had worked out a route, had run it a few times to make sure it was okay. It would take three hours to get into position, as instructed. The service was due to start at one in the afternoon. She had plenty of time, but she knew she needed to get in and set up before it got too difficult.

Cait turned from the open wall and lifted her pillow. Beneath it was a slim black backpack. As she picked it up, something hard clanked inside. She unzipped the top, made sure the objects inside were secure, and slipped it on.

She closed her eyes. Took a deep breath.

I'm ready, she thought.

The breeze picked up, pulling at her hair.

I'll see you soon, sis, said the voice of Tyler Smith inside her head, as real as her own thoughts.

Cait opened her eyes and smiled. She reached down into the plastic crate and took out a small canister of liquid. She flipped the cap, poured it over her bedding, and then walked backwards, splashing the liquid around as much as possible before tossing the container back into the crate. She took two steps down the open stairwell at the back of the room, then pulled a disposable lighter from her pocket. She flicked the flame and watched it for a moment, then threw the lighter. Immediately, her former accommodation was engulfed with thin, pale flames.

Caitlin Smith turned on her heel and jogged down the stairs.

She had a funeral to interrupt.

PART ONE

EARTH

1

The robot servitor bay was cramped, the air rich with the chemical tang of ozone and disinfectant. Von Kodiak did his best to ignore both discomforts as, balanced on one foot to reach the open access panel in the bay's back wall, he delicately touch-soldered an exposed circuit board while holding a bundle of wires between his teeth. The service bay was almost completely dark, but the HUD in his AI glasses amplified what little light there was, allowing him to get on with his work.

Kodiak was squeezed awkwardly in one of two channels, each a meter deep and a meter wide, that ran the full length of the bay on either side of the central platform. They were designed to allow humanoid crews—*vertically challenged* humanoid crews, Kodiak thought with a sigh—a minimal amount of space to work on the cube-shaped maintenance robot that would be parked in the center. There was just enough room to stand upright in the channel, but the space was narrow and Kodiak had to lean out awkwardly to reach the access panel at the back of the dock—the alternative being to crouch in the center of the bay itself, risking life and limb if the servitor should return to port, crushing him between it and the back wall.

Kodiak had been working for two hours now, according to the counter in the corner of his glasses. He had a sore back, and he had already paced the tiny channel twice to walk out a cramp. He was almost done, but the last couple of connections were a son of a bitch. But the work, the effort, would be worth it.

Because Von Kodiak's new plan was a damn good one, even if he said so himself.

The service levels of Helprin's Gambit, and the dozens of servitor docks they contained, were not on the usual visitor's docket. The station was a leisure facility, pure and simple, packed with spas and entertainment complexes, offering sensual delights both real and virtual, ranging from the family friendly to the borderline illegal as the facility lazily orbited a star just close enough to a major quickspace transit point to make it a tempting destination. But the station was famous for one thing above all else: the Grand Casino, which occupied almost the entire central spire of the torus-shaped pleasure palace. It was the biggest such enterprise in all of Fleetspace, privately owned and operated, a destination for the rich and famous and the poor and desperate alike.

It was also a front for one of the biggest criminal organizations in Fleetspace.

Kodiak tried to put out of his mind what they would do to him, and for how long, if he got caught. The new plan was a risk, but circumstances and the parameters of his mission had changed, and he'd had to come up with something else. And, really, the new plan was quite, quite clever. Okay, so it wouldn't have the same outcome as the original, but it was better than nothing. He was pretty sure the team would be pleased with the results.

Kodiak extracted one of the wires from between his teeth. As he held the bare end against the contact of his microsolder, there was a tiny puff of blue smoke, and the connection was in place.

The city-sized station needed cleaning robots. A *lot* of cleaning robots. The machines—*servitors*—were perfect cubes a meter and a half across, designed with the same aesthetic touch as the rest of the station. During the day, the army of machines was docked in their bays where they charged up, underwent maintenance, and, importantly, re-synced with the station's central computer via a hardwire link.

A hardwire link Kodiak was busy modifying. He hissed in annoyance as time ran on in the corner of his eye. He pulled another wire from his mouth and soldered it to the exposed circuitry on the panel in front of him. Just one more to go.

The service sublevels of Helprin's Gambit, sandwiched between the public levels, were monitored like every other part of the station—except for the inside of the servitor docks themselves. It was a security flaw that Kodiak had discovered months ago, soon after arriving and getting the lowly servitor technician job.

Of course, that wasn't the plan, but working as an anonymous tech was a great way to hide, especially after discovering his pre-arranged contact had been thrown out of an airlock by Helprin himself. Well, so the story went; he'd only got word secondhand, cycles later, while laying low and considering his options in one of the dive bars that dotted the outer rim of the platform, the less salubrious regions of Helprin's pleasure palace generally avoided by tourists but frequented by the poorer of his employees. Word was Helprin was looking for someone else too: a new arrival from Earth, his executed employee's co-conspirator.

Hello, Von Kodiak.

Every instinct in him had screamed to get the hell out, abandon the mission and make for the stars. Except he couldn't risk it, not until things had quieted down. Getting the tech job had been easy—now that the original plan had failed, Kodiak had an unfeasibly large amount of money on him with which to bribe the service controllers, who gave him a position, no questions asked. And, Kodiak told himself, it was just temporary. A few weeks, perhaps. He could use the job to hide in plain sight, and then when the coast was clear, catch the next transport off.

And then—thanks to his accidental employment—he'd found the security flaw and hatched a new plan. Because the servitor docks, which he was assigned to on a regular maintenance schedule, turned out to be the perfect place to discreetly hack the station's computer without being seen.

Last wire. Last connection. Job done.

Responding to his thoughts, his AI glasses ran a diagnostic over his handiwork, highlighting the solder points with a green indicator and matching the changes against a circuit diagram Kodiak had spent three cycles preparing. All good. Just another little touch-up here and there needed. Which just left another three cycles to continue his cover as the servitor tech, until the Grand Casino began its next Sentallion contest—his game of choice—and then he'd be off Helprin's Gambit in a shuttle loaded with credits before anyone, Helprin included, knew what had happened. And about time too. Six months of station maintenance was *more* than long enough.

It seemed that buying your way into anonymous employment within Helprin's organization was a fairly regular occurrence. His colleagues were a mixed bunch, to say the least. Some were fine, happy in their work and friendly enough. They included refugees and those forced by the war or circumstance to start over for all kinds of reasons. Helprin's Gambit was famous for second chances. If you had enough credits, you could buy a job, starting at the bottom and, with a lot of hard effort and a touch of luck, work your way up. No questions asked. No ID required. For those with an uncertain future, Helprin's Gambit was often the only option left, short of trying your luck in the lawlessness of a place like Salt City.

But there were others who took advantage of Helprin's unique hospitality. Deserters, criminals, outsiders. People on the run from trouble. People looking for it. Start at the bottom, get yourself—and your exploits—known by the right people, and maybe Helprin would recruit you to the somewhat less legal side of his organization.

Kodiak had done his best to avoid that crowd, but working at the bottom of the ladder wasn't quite a cakewalk. But at least it would be over soon.

And the new plan? Kodiak smiled to himself. The new plan was *good.*

All he had to do was win at the Grand Casino, and win *big.* Normally, this only happened to a very few lucky players—less than natural odds, given the games were all controlled by the station's AI, carefully maintaining a balance of wins versus losses that kept the rich and famous coming while lining Helprin's coffers rather handsomely.

But if he could somehow throw the odds—if he could win, and win *enough,* then it would hurt Helprin. In fact, with a little computer know-how, he might even be able to win so much that Helprin's whole organization would be crippled. Okay, so maybe the result wasn't quite as final as it had been with the original plan, which would have ultimately handed Helprin over to the authorities, but for second best it wasn't half bad.

Kodiak completed the last touch-up to his work, flipped a row of switches to reconnect the system to the main station computer, then closed the access panel. As he replaced the microsolder in the belt of his maintenance worker's uniform, he touched the side of his glasses. Scrolling text spun across the HUD, too fast to read, but all in green. The tiny device he had wired into the terminal was a work of art, even if Kodiak said so himself. It had taken him three of the six months aboard the station to build it, although most of that time had been spent discreetly pilfering the components he needed from the maintenance stores.

Kodiak concentrated, and a new display appeared in his glasses as his system hack came online. A simple indicator appeared, showing a red cross icon, and he heard a tone, transmitted directly through the bone of his skull from one arm of the glasses.

All good. The hack simply interrupted the games computer's algorithms, introducing a new element that would throw a round of Sentallion in Kodiak's favor, the tone—inaudible to anyone standing next to him—giving him the heads up if he didn't catch the cross indicator in his vision. It was so simple, Kodiak wondered why nobody had tried it before.

Because, Von, he thought, *you're a* bona fide *genius. Tales, my friend, will be told of your death-defying and quite possibly erotic exploits across the . . . well, across however many systems there are.*

Another tone sounded in Kodiak's ear.

"Shit!"

Kodiak ducked back down into the channel as the service bay door slid open and the maintenance servitor returned, flying into its nest with enough speed to crush Kodiak's arm against the back wall had he not moved fast enough. Just a few centimeters from his face, heat wafted off the side of the servitor, the whine of its antigrav piercing in the enclosed space.

Peering into the tiny gap between the cube-shaped robot and the back wall of the dock, Kodiak watched as a small, pencil-like connector extended from the servitor and mated with the port in the computer panel. The panel's LED display changed from red to green; then a white indicator flickered as the machine synced with the station computer and entered its dormant, daytime phase.

Kodiak smiled to himself and stood in the tight space of the service channel, quickly packing the rest of his tools up and stowing them away in the utility pouches on his uniform. Careful not to touch the hot surface of the servitor, he crabbed sideways to leave the bay. With a quick glance around the lip of the docking bay's door, he pulled himself out into the service corridor.

The service corridor was itself much narrower, the ceiling much lower, than the guest facilities over his head and below his feet, but the sudden feeling of space after working in the cramped servitor bay was a relief. He glanced up at the surveillance lens he knew was ten meters to his left—there was no point in trying to hide from it; if anything, that would look even more suspicious. For anyone watching, he was just one of the hundreds of station techs going about his duties.

As he walked down the corridor, he whistled to himself, watching a new timer in his glasses as the HUD counted down to the start of the Sentallion contest. Two point seven cycles—or sixty-four point eight hours, as a smaller line of text helpfully suggested.

Perfect. All he had to do was lay low, be his anonymous self, carry out his menial tasks as normal.

And then . . . well, then it was time to take down Helprin's Gambit once and for all. And if things worked out, more than just the facility.

Helprin's entire operation would be crippled, hurting him in his most sensitive place—his wallet.

Smiling, Kodiak rubbed his hands. There were a few hours before he was officially due back on shift. Time enough for a shower and something to eat and to consider how everything was going perfectly according to the new plan.

2

"This meeting of the Fleet Command Council is called to order."

Commander Laurel Avalon winced as Fleet Admiral Sebela strode into the huge council chamber, his face dark, eyebrows knitted together in a familiar expression—all *too* familiar recently, Avalon thought. She glanced around the elliptical table, its black obsidian surface reflecting the pale faces of the most senior members of the Fleet, distorting them, bleaching them of color, making them look even more miserable, if that were possible.

Avalon's eyes flicked up. Everyone was watching Sebela as he stood behind his high-backed chair at the head of the table, grinding his molars as he stared into the middle distance. Then he sat, the rest of the council following suit.

Avalon flicked her gaze to the chair opposite. Commander Moustafa stroked his thin black beard as he met her gaze and nodded a greeting. Moustafa and Avalon were the youngest members of the Fleet Council by at least a decade. They worked in separate areas of the Fleet—despite his relative youth, Moustafa was a talented psi-marine and had quickly moved up the ranks to head his division's Academy training program, while Avalon was the youngest chief of the Fleet Bureau of Investigation, the Fleet's internal affairs department, in the agency's history. Their positions granting them membership in the Fleet Command Council, the pair had gravitated together—drawn into friendship not just because of their ages, but because Moustafa was perhaps the only member of the council who didn't resent her presence. The Bureau dealt with internal matters, not the art of war. For most around the Command Council table, she had no place in their conferences. Some didn't even think the Bureau was part of the Fleet at all.

"Gentlemen," said the Fleet Admiral. Then he paused and looked at Avalon, before looking away without any correction. "As you are aware, the Fleet has been engaged on a mission in the Shadow system, coordinates eight-zero-eleven-zero by zero-zero-zero, theater designation twenty-eleven-six-two hundred."

Sebela paused and leaned back in his chair. Nobody spoke as the Fleet Admiral once again stared into the middle distance. Avalon glanced around the table; all eyes were on their leader. She used the pause in the proceedings to flip open the slim folder in front of her. Inside was a file, printed onto wafer thin plastiform sheets for security, each page embossed with Avalon's Fleet serial number. At the top were two lines.

SHADOW PROTOCOL
—PRIORITY 1 SECRET—

The mission the Fleet Admiral was describing was beyond top secret. So much so that as Avalon leafed through the flimsy pages of the report, she could see that instead of text, the file consisted of line after line of solid green blocks. The report—the entire briefing document for the Fleet Command Council itself—was redacted.

Avalon glanced up at Moustafa. His folder was closed, but he tapped the cover with his finger and nodded at her. There was no doubt in her mind that he had exactly the same questions as she did.

A mission too secret for even the Command Council to know the details of? Unless the redacted files were just for her and Moustafa.

Avalon's gaze moved around the officers sitting stiffly behind the conference table. Who *really* knew about the mission? Some here must have sufficient clearance. Perhaps Admiral Laverick, the Fleet Admiral's aide-de-camp? Or the Commandant of the Marine Corps, Vaughn, the man directly in command of the millions of Fleet troops spread out across the galaxy. That pair sat next to each other on Avalon's right. Neither moved nor spoke, their briefing folders lying unopened on the table in front of them.

Zworykin too. As Admiral and commander-in-chief of the Psi-Marine Corps—Moustafa's CO—he wore the same striking black uniform as his junior officer, and with his wavy dark gray hair brushed back from his forehead, he cut an impressive figure. As he sat with one elbow on the table, tapping a single finger against his lips as he watched Fleet Admiral Sebela, Avalon saw the corners of his mouth twitch into a slight smile.

He was the only person in the room who didn't look afraid. Whatever the Shadow Protocol was, it had the whole council spooked. Except Zworykin. In fact, thought Avalon as she watched the Psi-Admiral, he looked pleased. Like a cat, waiting to pounce.

Moustafa cleared his throat discreetly and the Fleet Admiral seemed to snap out of it. He looked around the table like he was surprised to find himself sitting there with a dozen senior officers around him.

"I must report," he said at last, "that Shadow Protocol has resulted in complete failure."

Now there were gasps around the table, mutterings from the other officers. Avalon frowned, unsure of what they were all talking about, angry at being left out. She glanced at Moustafa across the table from her, and this time he shook his head. Next to him, Zworykin hadn't moved, hadn't taken his eyes from their leader. Hadn't stopped smiling.

The shiny black surface of the meeting table flickered into a deep blue, and a three-dimensional holographic representation of a star system appeared in the air above it. It was sparsely populated—the star at the center, labeled as SHADOW, a few asteroid fields in a close orbit, and, farther out, a red cube indicating a Fleet ship or structure. Floating above the cube was a serial number, the official Fleet manifest designation, and then a name. It was a U-Star—but not a ship, a space station. Avalon leaned forward to see the tiny text a little better. It read:

UNION CLASS FLEET STARSHIP
RPOS ΨΥΨ
COAST CITY

The Fleet Admiral took a deep breath, his hands spaced out on the table in front of him. "I regret the RPOS station U-Star *Coast City* was lost with all hands."

Avalon leaned back into her chair, sinking into the padded leather, cold against the back of her head. The holodisplay changed, from the computer representation of the system to an actual three-dimensional image. It was beautiful, clouds of red and blue arcing symmetrically from a black central point, the star field beyond rich and colorful. The Shadow system was now home to a nebula.

"The star Shadow, an asymptotic technetium star, unexpectedly went nova mid-mission, destroying the *Coast City* and saturating the system with exotic radiation," said the Fleet Admiral. "The system is now classified Iota-Black. No Fleet access."

Then Sebela slumped in his chair and passed a shaking hand over his face. When his hand returned to the table, Avalon saw his eyes were closed. There were more mutterings around the table, but nobody seemed to notice his near faint.

And then someone started clapping. It was slow, mocking.

Psi-Admiral Zworykin.

"Congratulations, Fleet Admiral," he said, clasping his hands in front of him. He smiled again. "Well done on another glorious failure."

The officer on Zworykin's right—Commander Hammerstein, from some technical division of the Fleet that Avalon didn't remember—turned in his chair and stared at his colleague, a shocked look on his face.

"A little respect, please!" he said, gesturing toward Sebela. "The Fleet Admiral has been commanding this operation personally for months now, and—"

"Oh, shut up, Hammerstein," said Zworykin. "You have no idea what our beloved Fleet Admiral has been doing. None of you have. Do you know how far our glorious leader was willing to go to win the war? The kind of *deal* he had planned?"

Hammerstein's face was still red, but now his gaze flicked between Zworykin and Sebela. Sebela had opened his eyes, but was sunk back in his chair, deflated.

"What are you talking about?" asked Hammerstein.

Zworykin looked at Hammerstein with a cold, cruel expression. Avalon suddenly wished she were somewhere—*anywhere*—else. The atmosphere in the council chamber was electric, dangerous.

She met Moustafa's eye and he nodded. They should leave, the both of them. Avalon stood up.

"Sit down, Commander Avalon," said Zworykin, still looking at Hammerstein. Avalon froze. Moustafa was only partway out of his seat, and he slowly dropped himself back into it. All eyes were now on the Bureau Chief.

She turned to face the Fleet Admiral. "Sir, as an adjunct member of the Command Council, I only have limited security clearance when it comes to combat missions. This Shadow Protocol appears to relate to the Fleet at large rather than internal affairs, so if you will excuse me, I will return to the Bureau and—"

"Sit. *Down!*"

Avalon jumped. Zworykin was staring at her, his expression as dark as his uniform. Avalon, her mouth suddenly dry, felt compelled to sit.

Zworykin stood from his chair and touched the comm on his collar. At the back of the conference room, opposite the Fleet Admiral's position, the double doors slid open and two psi-marines marched in, their membership in Zworykin's corps indicated by the black triangles on the front of their uniforms. Without further orders, they raised their plasma rifles, aiming directly at Sebela.

Hammerstein stood and marched over to the two marines as the table erupted in protest.

What the *hell* was going on?

"Silence!"

The noise stopped as the arguing officers obeyed Zworykin's command.

The Psi-Admiral walked over to Hammerstein, leaning in close. "How far would you go, *hmm?* What would you do to stop the war, Commander?"

Hammerstein's jaw went up and down as he struggled for an answer.

"Well?"

"I . . . anything," said Hammerstein. "I would do anything. We all would."

Zworykin cocked his head. "Anything? Really?" He turned back around to the rest of the group. "Interesting answer," he said as he slowly paced around the table, hands still clasped behind his back. As he passed each member of the Command Council, Avalon saw them stiffen and look away.

They were afraid of him too.

"You would do anything, no matter the risk, no matter that victory against the Spiders might mean the creation of a new enemy, an unstoppable being that doesn't even belong in this universe?" The cruel smile returned to his face.

"What being?" asked Hammerstein.

"They don't know."

Avalon looked around. Fleet Admiral Sebela stood from his chair. Gone was the tiredness, the weariness that seemed to have suddenly fallen upon him. Avalon could see the fire in his eyes, the way he held himself. It was time to face this rebellion down.

Zworykin began to laugh. "Of course they don't! Oh, but they will soon. My dear, *glorious* leader, all of Fleetspace needs to know how you betrayed us. How you tried to sell us out to that *thing* from subspace."

Subspace? Avalon didn't know much about subspace, other

than it was one of the dimensions that underpinned their own, three-dimensional reality. But subspace wasn't used by the Fleet for anything.

On the other side of the room, Commander Moustafa was staring at Zworykin, his jaw slack.

Avalon frowned. What did *he* know?

Then she remembered a story—a legend, really—just one of many tall tales told by marines out on patrol on cold nights under alien skies. A story about the things that lived in subspace.

Monsters.

And the word Zworykin had used. His exact choice of description.

"A . . . thing?" she asked.

Behind her chair, Zworykin dropped his voice to a croaky whisper, like he was one of those lonely marines out on the front, weaving a story. "Yes, my dear Commander Avalon. You're the great-granddaughter of the woman who started it all, hmm? The namesake of our famous founder? Well, this thing has many names, but the Fleet Admiral here knows it best by one picked out of Japanese mythology: Izanami-no-Mikoto. You won't find that name in the Shadow Protocol, even if the text in your briefing was declassified."

He walked over to the Fleet Admiral. "But that doesn't matter. The Shadow Protocol failed. You failed, Admiral. It is just as well you did, otherwise that creature would be loose in our own universe. Your failure saved us, but it was failure nonetheless."

"I've had enough of your histrionics, Zworykin," said Commander Hammerstein. He shook his big head and turned back to the armed psi-marines at the door. "Out of my way. I'm reporting this back to my division. The Command Council will have to be dissolved so we can sort this mess out."

The psi-marines didn't move. Avalon could see Hammerstein's distorted reflection in their opaque visors as he looked from one to the other.

"I said stand down, marines. That is a direct order."

Zworykin chuckled. "You misunderstand, Commander Hammerstein. This council is already dissolved. The Psi-Marine

Corps has already established control of the capital." He turned back to the Fleet Admiral. "I am hereby relieving you of duty and will take interim command of the Fleet in your place. You will be held to face a Fleet tribunal in due course."

Avalon leapt from her chair. "You can't do that, Zworykin," she said. "Any charges brought against Fleet officers have to come through the Bureau. Through *me.*" She moved between the rebellious Admiral and the Fleet leader. "If you have a case, then *present it.*"

Zworykin smiled. "Oh, you're good, Commander. Very good. You'll be useful to me. Perhaps I'll bring you up in the ranks, give you a better position on my new Command Council. Now," he said, stepping back and addressing the room, "tomorrow is Fleet Day. An important and symbolic occasion for everyone in Fleetspace. For that reason, although I have assumed command and my staff have secured the capital, the Fleet Admiral—although under arrest—will fulfill his public duties, and will continue to do so until such a time as the change of leadership can be communicated to the public and to our forces in their combat theaters."

The members—*former* members—of the council looked at one another, then back at Zworykin.

"That is an *order,*" he said. "Failure to comply will result in court martial." He waved at the two marines. "Escort Admiral Sebela to his private office and ensure he remains there."

The psi-marines acknowledged and, lowering their rifles, moved around either side of the table until they stood next to Sebela. In unison, they reached for Sebela's arms, but he quickly lifted them, indignant.

"Please," he said, "I think I know where my own quarters are."

He marched himself out of the chamber, the two marines following close behind.

"The rest of you," said Zworykin, "will return to your divisions and continue the business of war. The council is dissolved. The Psi-Marine Corps are monitoring all transmissions. Any leak of the change of leadership to the public will be met with my *displeasure.*"

With that, Zworykin strode from the council chamber. As the

other officers milled around in confusion, Avalon and Moustafa drew together into a corner of the room.

Moustafa put his hands on his hips, eyes wide as he looked at Avalon. "So, is it just me, or did my CO just stage a coup?"

Avalon looked around the council chamber as the others filed out. The room was cavernous, all black, hard, shiny surfaces, glassy like the table. Everywhere she looked, she could see a dull reflection of herself and her friend.

"This is bad," she said. "Very, very bad."

"No kidding. What do you think Sebela was doing?"

Avalon frowned. "The Shadow Protocol? What was Zworykin talking about? A creature from subspace?"

Moustafa shook his head. "Whatever that is, it sounds like bad, bad news."

"I need to talk to him."

Moustafa paused. "Zworykin?"

"No, Sebela. I need to find out what just happened."

"And how do you plan on doing that?" Moustafa gestured toward the door. "They're not going to let you anywhere near him."

Avalon shook her head. "Didn't you hear what our new Fleet Admiral said? Until he says otherwise, it's business as usual. Which means . . ."

Moustafa's eyes widened as he joined the dots. "Which means you're still the Bureau Chief."

"Right," said Avalon. "And that means that any officer under arrest—like Sebela—is technically under my jurisdiction."

"Okay, but look, you have to be careful. I get the feeling our new CIC won't take kindly to you snooping around."

Avalon folded her arms. "We all need to be careful. This whole thing is very, very dangerous."

"As a coup, this was a pretty bloodless one."

Avalon felt her expression tighten. "So far," she said.

3

Avalon found the Fleet Admiral's official quarters in darkness, the main office lit only by the multitude of lights from New Orem shining through the floor-to-ceiling window. Sebela stood looking out at the city, arms folded, nothing but a tall black silhouette.

The Bureau Chief raised a closed fist to her mouth and was about to cough politely when the Admiral spoke.

"So they're still obeying the orders of some of us?"

Avalon joined Sebela at the window, her forehead creased in confusion. Sebela glanced at her, then nodded toward the door.

"Oh," said Avalon. "Well, under confinement you're officially under Bureau jurisdiction, sir."

Sebela gave a tight-lipped smile and turned back to the window. As Avalon looked out at the vast Fleet capital, she found her eyes drawn to a large section of even blue light, beyond the shining skyscrapers on the other side of the city from the Capitol Complex. The glowing space had no buildings and stretched to the horizon.

The Fleet Memorial. Where those who lost their lives serving humanity were interred. No matter where they died, no matter how far away. The Fleet always brought them home. Always.

"Five thousand, three hundred and twenty," said Sebela. Avalon glanced at him. He was looking toward the Fleet Memorial as well.

"Ah . . . yes, sir," said Avalon. Then she frowned. "Five thousand, three hundred and twenty what?"

Sebela unfolded his arms. "Personnel killed in action in the last cycle. Tomorrow is Fleet Day. I haven't even written my speech yet."

He turned to the Bureau Chief, a sad smile playing on his lips. "Somehow I'm not really in the mood." He chuckled and walked toward his desk, an antique made of real wood.

Avalon watched him, wondering what he found so funny. He was under house arrest, and what Zworykin had planned for the former commander-in-chief didn't bear thinking about.

"I imagine he'll be true to his word and keep *you* around in his new regime," said Sebela. He seated himself behind the desk and waved at the lamp to his left, which faded up, spilling a cone of warm yellow light over his workspace. Then sat back and ran his fingers along the edge of the desk, apparently studying the magnificent grain of the ancient wood. "You are as young as you are naïve, Commander Avalon. But Zworykin is arrogant. If he is to finalize his transition to power, he will need the Bureau on his side, and he thinks he can bend you to his will."

Avalon folded her arms. "I'm not such a pushover, *sir.*"

"Ha!" said the Admiral. He tapped an index finger on the edge of the desk. "There is the famous fire your grandmother had. You are young but *stubborn.* I think Zworykin has a battle coming. To him the Bureau is a distraction—he has always thought so. He thinks as little of it as he does of you. In a way, that is a good position to be in. He doesn't see you or your department as a threat. Remember that, Commander. That may be a truth that is useful to you if you are to survive what is coming. Perhaps here is a chance to live up to your name at last."

Avalon sighed. *Here we go,* she thought. "I'm sorry I can't live up to her legacy, *sir,*" she said, her eyes shooting daggers at Sebela. Zworykin didn't have a monopoly on arrogance at Fleet Command, that was for sure. But Sebela seemed to be on her side, at least, even if he was now showing it in his typically infuriating way. He was also right. In a way, she actually shared the view of the others on the Command Council that the Bureau wasn't really part of the Fleet, at least not its military command structure. The whole point of the Bureau was that it was an independent branch, tasked with policing the internal affairs of the Fleet and, where such tasks overlapped, handling local law enforcement. Sebela—and now Zworykin—were in total control of the Fleet, and therefore of the Bureau, but the Bureau was allowed to run autonomously under the chief's control.

Until today, anyway, thought Avalon.

Avalon changed the subject. "You seem remarkably calm about this, if you don't mind me saying."

Sebela smiled again, but this time the expression was sad. "Anything for a quiet life," he said. "And Fleet Day is an important occasion. I am duty-bound to honor those who serve the Fleet. Even Zworykin can't take that from me."

Avalon sat in one of the huge armchairs on the other side of the Admiral's desk. They were real leather, and the seat creaked pleasantly beneath her as she crossed her legs.

Sebela met her eye. "So, are you going to ask me about the Shadow Protocol or not?"

Avalon frowned.

The Admiral laughed. "Oh, Commander, I am a psi-marine. I can sense the question dancing at the front of your mind."

"Well," she said, "I apparently don't have the required clearance to know about it. But I do want to know what is going on. How could a single mission fail badly enough for Zworykin to gain the leverage to stage a takeover?"

"Perhaps it is just as well you don't have clearance," he said quietly. "I wish we'd never conceived of the mission. Never made contact."

Avalon took the bait. "Contact? The creature Zworykin was talking about?"

Sebela looked away, the light of the desk lamp casting the side of his face into a deep shadow, his eyes glittering in the gloom.

"Izanami . . ." he said.

Avalon watched him carefully. It seemed like he had stopped blinking, stopped breathing.

"Sir?"

Then he turned back to the light, and she saw tear tracks running down his cheeks. "If you don't mind, Commander, I have a speech to write."

He didn't move, didn't take his eyes from her face. She drew breath to speak, then thought better of it. She stood and snapped a salute.

He nodded in acknowledgment. "Commander."

"Sir," she said. Then she turned and marched out. At the double doors of the office, she turned around, but the Fleet Admiral had moved back to where she had found him, standing by the window wall, looking out at the city at night, the light on his desk dimming automatically to nothing.

There were two marines on guard outside the doors. Avalon glanced at the men who stood motionless, their rifles held crosswise in front of them, their faces invisible behind the visors of their combat helmets. On their chests were the inverted black triangles of the Psi-Marine Corps.

Avalon left as quickly as she could, unwilling to risk anyone else sensing her deepest, innermost thoughts.

4

Caitlin wiped the rain from her eyes and leaned back into the tree. The bark was rough but soft when she pressed the back of her skull into it. Her arms loose by her sides, she trailed her fingertips over the bumpy surface behind her, and she closed her eyes, focusing on the tactile sensations of the tree, of the rain on her face and the way the rain collected around her eyes, which felt hot.

There was silence in her mind. Her brother hadn't spoken to her since this morning. And she'd had no message from her contact either. But that was okay. The mission was still a go. She took a moment to focus, to center herself, like she'd been taught at the Academy. A warrior's mindset was as vital as their physical prowess. She had a job to do, a mission to complete, and complete it she would. The only difference now was that her orders weren't coming from the Academy instructors.

She opened her eyes and leaned around the tree to see down the hill, toward the Fleet Memorial.

People were gathered already on the tiered seating that stretched ten rows back, an undulating mass of blue and olive Fleet uniforms, most glinting with chrome and gold, rising up against the huge creamy stone wall that arced like a half-buried seashell, its surface inscribed in microtext with the names of the war dead. At the front center was a lectern, and in front of that the caskets were arrayed, each draped in the flag of Fleet Confederacy. There were just six, but the number was merely ceremonial. The annual Fleet Memorial culminated, after the Fleet Admiral gave his eulogy, with the interment of hundreds, if not thousands of fallen personnel, their remains repatriated from every corner of Fleetspace. These burials happened daily, of course, but once a year the routine became ceremonial and symbolic. Fleet Day was a day of remembrance for everyone.

In front of the caskets, the temporary stage dropped down, its edge lined with marines in full dress uniform. Then the dignitaries and invited families of the fallen, facing the lectern, their backs to Cait's position. Then the general public. And at the back, closest to Cait's vantage point, but still more than a kilometer away down the gentle slope of the hillside, were the media, reporters, producers, and technicians alike hustling for position as drone cameras hovered over their heads. The light drizzle didn't seem to be bothering anybody. It was just a heat shower and would pass in minutes.

Cait had watched this ceremony several times in the past from the comfort of her family home. She wondered if some members of that same family—members she hadn't seen for weeks now—were sitting down there, waiting for the ceremony to begin. If they were, it was unfortunate they were about to be eyewitnesses to history, but the mission was the mission.

Cait pursed her lips and exhaled, forcing herself to relax. She could feel a tingle on her skin, that ever-present buzz in the back of her mind ramping up a notch. That wild, uncontrollable talent, threatening to make itself known again as her stress levels rose.

Enough, she thought, clenching her jaw. And it worked. The feeling faded, not completely, but the power shrunk back, like a scolded pet. She was relieved, a little. She thought for a moment that maybe, one day, with help and training, she *could* control it. That's what her trainers had said, but at the time she hadn't believed them. There was something in their eyes, something in the way they looked at each other when they were talking about her that she hadn't liked. That was partly why she'd left, of course.

Partly.

Cait glanced up from the bustling proceedings at the bottom of the hill and cast her eye over the rest of the Fleet Memorial.

As a military cemetery, the Memorial was huge, a ten-square-mile zone crisscrossed with perfectly aligned headstones, with the giant wall of remembrance in the center at the bottom of a shallow basin, the edge of which was lined with trees—the perfect spot for Cait to set up. With a theater of war so vast, the front thousands of light-years across, the space was needed. Half of those interred here hadn't even been born on Earth, but all Fleet personnel were laid to rest at the Fleet capital, New Orem. It was a great honor.

Cait felt the bile rise in her throat, but swallowed it quickly and tilted her head back, opening her mouth a little to let rain water trickle in. Then she spat it out and rolled her neck.

Honor. Yeah, right. *That.*

They'd brought back the remains of her brother's psi-marine fireteam a month ago—they said. It had taken them that long to untangle and identify what was left of each marine—*they said*—so they could be officially returned to each family, including the one that Cait didn't belong to, not anymore. Not since the lies, the betrayal.

The Fleet had a lot to answer for.

Cait turned back to watch the build-up to the ceremony. Not long to go now.

She'd been waiting, planning, for weeks, ever since she'd run out from the Academy and hit the slums of Salt City, following the mysterious directions left for her and the voice of her dead brother in her head. Their family had been trying to find her, she knew that. She had watched them, making sure their efforts were for nothing. If Cait was honest, she'd thought that keeping out of sight, buried somewhere in Salt City, would have been a far more difficult task. But her family—and the authorities, including the Academy staff who had just lost a valuable asset and potential psychic warrior—hadn't been able to track her. It had seemed strange at first. After Cait had entered the Academy, she'd been tagged, effectively becoming Fleet property. The manifest tag at the base of her brain should have made it impossible to escape, impossible to avoid detection and capture. But they hadn't found her.

Then she'd realized it must have been her . . . *talent.* She'd wanted to vanish, to disappear. And she had. Her mind, that part of it she didn't understand, couldn't control, not willingly, was shielding her, jamming the broadcast of her tag like the psi-marines could jam the communications network of the Spiders. She hadn't chosen to do it. She just . . . had.

Cait lifted the telescopic sight to her eye and squinted down toward the Wall of Remembrance, moving from one end of the row of caskets to the other. She wondered what they contained, because she sure as hell knew her brother, Tyler, wasn't in one of them.

Because Tyler Smith was alive, and she knew he was alive because she could hear his voice whispering in her head.

She was doing this for *him.*

As she watched, the casket honor guard came to attention, and everyone stood.

Time for action.

Cait ducked down beside the tree and began unpacking black metal parts from her backpack. In just a few seconds, the sniper rifle was ready, the telescopic scope now slotted into the top.

Crouching, she braced the side of her long-barreled weapon against the tree, and once again looked down the sight.

"That's better," she muttered. Connected to the sniper rifle, the scope now displayed a mass of data, a series of independent crosshairs moving over the faces of the officers standing on the tiers as they waited for the arrival of their commander-in-chief, the Fleet Admiral. Then the rifle's OS glitched and the image in the scope broke up into jagged horizontal lines. Cait tapped the side of the sight, coaxing the device to work properly. First the data overlay reappeared, then the image settled, rolling for a second before re-stabilizing.

Cait tracked the sight across the front row, picking out the officers and identifying their ranks. They were all here: the entire Command Council, representatives of the Academy and the Psi-Division, even the Fleet Bureau of Investigation. All branches of the Fleet.

The Psi-Division had the whole front row. Cait bit her bottom lip in an attempt to kill the laugh that threatened to crawl up her throat, the crosshairs bouncing in her vision as she did.

Of course they had the front row. The psi-marines were the ones in charge. They were the ones doing the real fighting too. Everyone knew that, of course, even if the actual detail was lost on the citizens of Fleetspace. But Cait knew how it worked, because she'd enrolled in the Fleet Academy in order to join their fight. To join the psi-marines.

It was pretty simple, the way they taught it at the Academy. The Spiders were just machines of war, their operating system an AI. But this AI was different than those developed on Earth. The Spider OS was a *gestalt*, the individual components of the machine collective—the individual Spider war machines—all linked to one another to form a single hive mind. And the only way to break the laws of physics and connect every Spider machine with every other Spider machine across the whole universe was to use a *psychic* computer network. Like the Spiders themselves, there was no official name for this enemy communications network, but soon enough every cadet enrolled in the Academy's psi-program—Cait included—began calling it what it was: the SpiderWeb.

And so the psi-marines, psychic warriors picked from the Academy intake, their natural abilities amplified and honed with technology, training, and pharmaceuticals, were the Fleet's most valuable fighting force, because while they were highly trained fighters, like all marines in the Fleet, they had an extra weapon available to them—their minds. They could attack the SpiderWeb, cutting the war machines off from each other on the battlefield.

Bingo. Turned out uncoupling the Spiders from each other had some useful effects, like locking their CPUs into infinite loops as the individual machine AIs tried to clear the psychic jamming. That left the Spiders vulnerable.

So while the regular troops kept them safe, the psi-marines would reach out and fuck the Spiders up from the inside. Of course, what the Academy downplayed was the fact that while they were on the offensive, fighting in a battlefield that didn't even exist in the real world, psi-marines were effectively helpless. The mortality rate among Fleet Marines might have been high—the price of war, Cait knew—but among the Psi-Marine Corps it was even higher.

There was other stuff the Academy deflected attention from too, but as Cait's training had progressed, leap-frogging other recruits, her remarkably strong psi-ability fast-tracking her into advanced classes—Alpha One, baby—she began to think they weren't exactly *hiding* something, but they were trying very hard to ignore it.

Because if the physical risk of being in a war zone and unable to defend yourself at precisely the most dangerous moment wasn't bad enough, psi-marines had other dangers to face. Prolonged psychic combat could burn out your mind, no matter how well trained, or prepared, or powerful. And if you survived the missions, and dealt with the stress, the strain, the trauma that wasn't physical but *mental*, sometimes psi-marines were . . . *changed*. Came with the territory, said the Academy trainers. That's just the nature of psychic warfare, they said. Because during an attack, the psi-marines would actually *share* their minds, their consciousness, forming a gestalt of their own to amplify their powers and push back against the infinite force that was the SpiderWeb.

And that kind of thing changed you, forever. The price of war, right?

So maybe if you made it through Academy training without your brain melting, and then if you weren't blown up or eaten, and if your brain wasn't fried, or your mind broken, if you didn't get flashbacks and panic attacks or depression and anxiety and schizophrenia, then maybe—*maybe*—you could make it as a psi-marine.

Like Tyler Smith had. Like Cait Smith almost had, before she realized the truth.

Cait adjusted her grip on the sniper rifle. The moment was so close now.

Tyler had been a good psi-marine. One of the best, according to his Academy test marks. So good they'd sent him out too early, to the front line, and no sooner had his fireteam dug in than the Spiders came, and then—

Cait let out a held breath and stopped herself. There was no time to disappear down that rabbit hole. It was getting busy now, down at the stage. The buzz in her mind came and went, came and went, like the lapping of a tide. She focused down the scope, the image it showed flipping again a couple of times. She tried to clear her mind. The image stabilized. She was back in the game.

Any. Moment. Now.

Cait lifted her face just a little and checked the ammo counter on the top of the rifle. Full tank. She rolled her neck and repositioned her shoulder against the sniper's butt, and focused on slowing her breathing, relaxing her muscles.

If there was one psi-cadet who had scored better than Tyler, it was her—his beloved twin sister.

Twins were a gift, the perfect Academy candidates. And boy, did the tests show it—of course, *they'd* both known about the gift all their lives. There was a *connection,* a bond, link, call it what you want, something only twins had.

Only there was something else that Cait had that Tyler hadn't. He was strong, a powerful psychic warrior. But Cait . . . Cait had a talent that went beyond the norm. She knew it, and was frightened of it, and when the Academy saw it, her fear had only increased.

And then Tyler had been sent on tour, and Cait vanished.

A fanfare sounded, giving Cait a fright. She swore under her breath, then let that breath out, long and slow. Goddamn it, she had to focus and do her job. Her new job, the one given to her by her new friends. They'd seen another ability in her, a skillset they said was useful.

Caitlin, it turned out, was good at sneaking around, at being stealthy and shooting things from very, *very* far away. Sniper skills were not useful to the Psi-Marine Corps, but her brother had taken it as an elective course, telling her how much he enjoyed it. So she'd followed his lead, completing nearly all the advanced training before she ditched New Orem.

And she enjoyed it too. The quiet, the secrecy. To be a good sniper you had to be a certain kind of person: you had to enjoy your own company (check); you had to enjoy silence and stillness in a world that was full of noise and movement (check check); you had to be a very, *very* good shot, no matter how augmented your performance was by the computer systems and low-level psi-fi field of your weapon (check check and check again).

She wondered, not for the first time, whether her *other* talent had anything to do with it, the power nudging her accuracy into the highest percentiles. It was impossible to tell. Maybe they were linked, maybe they weren't. All she knew was that she was a good shot with a long rifle. Then again, so was Tyler.

Cait blinked and then the Fleet Admiral was standing at the podium, right in the center of the scope, all of the moving crosshairs now locked on. He was talking, making his speech, looking left and right and center, then down to his notes—he would have learned his speech by rote, but the notes were a useful prop, giving him moments to pause, the rhythm of his speech carefully rehearsed.

It was such a scam, Cait thought she might throw up, there and then.

Because she knew other things about the Fleet. About what the Fleet was doing.

She felt the heat rise in her cheeks, the tingle on her skin, the buzz in her mind. Fuck it. Let it out. Let it all out. Let them see what they had tried to control. Let them see what they had helped fashion.

Her finger moved from the safe position to the trigger position. In her scope data flowed: wind speed and direction, distance, time, angles, options for different shots, different targets. All she had to do was think it, and the scope, loosely linked to her mind, would refocus, pick a different mark, suggest better ways of taking it out.

She zoomed in until the Fleet Admiral's face filled her vision. The crosshairs changed from green to blue, and a dot was painted onto his forehead.

Target locked.

Cait thought for a moment. Thought that this should feel like the end. Closure. Punishment, revenge, whatever the fuck you wanted to call it. Justice, maybe.

But she knew that wasn't the case. This wasn't any of those things, because her twin brother Tyler was alive, the casket was empty, and the Fleet was lying about what was happening to their war dead. If Tyler's casket was empty—and she knew it was, he had told her himself—then what about the others? Of the thousands being interred today, was it *all* a fraud? They weren't all alive, were they? They couldn't be, because the Fleet was at war and war meant death and the Fleet was losing. Badly. The Spiders were chewing through the Fleet out there on a dozen fronts, on a thousand Warworlds.

But Tyler was alive.

The others too?

More heat, more anger. What was the Fleet doing, out there on the Warworlds? What were they hiding from everyone? She was determined to find out. Her new friends had some of the answers, but not all of them. What they needed now was a demonstration of their power, a demonstration that the Fleet was vulnerable. Here, at the heart of the capital, with the world watching.

The Fleet Admiral kept talking, the blue spot fixed to his forehead. Cait's finger curled over the trigger.

A shot rang out. It was dull, somehow—the sound of heavy metal striking heavy metal on the other side of the city. The Fleet Admiral fell, and behind him the assembled Fleet brass swarmed into action, most on the higher tiers ducking down as the front row rushed for their fallen leader. The scope zoomed out and Cait could see the panic ripple through the crowd as the honor guard began waving at people to keep down even as they lifted their weapons and began scanning the horizon for the enemy.

Cait ducked back behind the tree, more by instinct than conscious decision, her trigger finger slipping back to the safe position. She pressed the back of her head into the soft bark of the trunk, her eyes squeezed tight, her heart punching against her ribcage so hard, so fast it hurt.

Whatthefuckwhatthefuckwhatthefuckwhatthefuck?

She opened her eyes. She felt dizzy. She felt the buzzing in her mind like a physical thing, pressing on the world around her.

Then, almost as an afterthought, she thumbed the readout on the top of her rifle. The blue display flicked on, showing the weapon status and ammo count.

She hadn't fired a single shot.

Her earlier anger, hot and sharp, had been replaced with something else, something cold, something that made the world swim around her.

Fear. Panic.

What the fuck just happened? *What. The. Fuck?*

Someone had assassinated the Fleet Admiral. Someone *else.*

Fuck fuck fuck.

She stood, the muscles in her arms and legs suddenly weak. She fell onto her knees and stared at the grass under her. It looked weird, pressed down in a circle around her like she was kneeling on a circular plate of glass.

Because there was an invisible force, and it was coming from *her.* Her skin prickled with heat, the noise in her head nearly deafening.

And she was floating an inch from the ground. As soon as she realized, it stopped, and she jolted to the ground.

She had to leave. *Now.*

She began regulating her breathing, like she did when things started happening around her, trying to calm her unconscious mind. Letting her hands work on automatic, the result of ingrained routines learned by rote, she disassembled her weapon and slid the parts into her backpack.

And then she ran.

5

>> . . . please wait . . .
>> SECURE_COMMAND_CHANNEL_IPSILON
>>PRIORITY_ONE
>>~avalon_L_199900
>>password: *************************************
>>WELCOME BACK, COMMANDER

FROM: Commander Laurel Avalon, Bureau Chief of Staff
TO: Special Agent Michael Braben, Field Operations
SUBJECT: Extraction of primary asset
LEVEL: Priority 1 Secret

AUTHORIZATION ORDER GAMMA TWELVE. PRIORITY 1 OVERRIDE. EXTRACT PRIMARY ASSET USING PREPARED COVER. RESOURCES ASSIGNED AS BRIEFED.
AUTHORIZATION GRANTED, AVALON L 199900

P.S. Discretion is the better part of valor, Mike. Don't take any risks, and make sure you bring him back in one piece

6

The Sentallion contest at the Grand Casino on Helprin's Gambit had been running for four hours, and Kodiak's hack was paying off, and paying off well.

"Fifty-thirty on thirty-thirty," he said into his glass as he took a swig of whatever-the-hell the vicious red liquid was and slid a pile of chips across the table. He'd been practicing for several cycles too—the casual laugh, the easy smile. He'd even prepared a backstory—the spoiled son of a starminer, left to his own devices while daddy-O suffocated on some chunk of herculanium spinning out there in deep space. It was a bit of a stretch, given he was pushing forty, but he thought that actually might help with the story. A charming, if greasy, little rich kid who refused to grow up, dressed in a tailored suit of crimson silk, shirt and tie to match, the height of Fleetspace fashion among those rich enough not to worry what other people thought of their taste in clothes. Out of the technician uniform, hair artfully styled, stubble trimmed just *so,* he wouldn't be recognized by anybody who worked on the service levels. Not that any of the station's crew would have been able to afford entry to the casino anyway. Lucky for Kodiak, the credit stick in his pocket still had plenty of money left over after buying his way into his tech job and collecting the gear for this little disguise—although, damn, did people really pay this much for bright red suits?—and Kodiak was adding to his fortune at a steady rate.

The game he'd selected was also helping with the image. Sentallion was an obscure favorite of starminers, big in the ports of Arb-Niner and a dozen other industrial colonies, those unlucky in the asteroid fields drawn to the complex game that married advanced mathematics with pure random luck. The puzzles made you feel like you were actually doing something, that your years of interstellar navigation gave you some kind of edge on the calculations, while there was enough blind chance to make it dangerous. Kodiak had been familiar with the game long before he had arrived at Helprin's Gambit, but it was here that he had learned just how popular it was among the nouveau riche, who threw nauseating amounts of credits at it, even if most of them didn't really understand the principles behind the game. Any opportunity he'd had over the last three months, he'd read up on the game and its rules, downloading a version to his maintenance datapad and playing as often as he could. He'd never got *that* good at it, but he knew he didn't need to be. For the big game, he had a little help.

The dealer accepted his bet. There was a smattering of applause, which Kodiak saluted by draining the fiery liquid in his glass and lifting the empty tumbler high above his head. Holy smokes, what *was* that stuff? It tasted like sweet wild strawberry, with just a trace of shuttle engine coolant.

While he grinned at the crowd around him, the HUD in his glasses spun as a face recognition algorithm ran matches on everyone in sight, comparing the casino guests with the central register of employees held by the station's computer. That was a little add-on Kodiak had thought of only yesterday, along with a quick little screening override that prevented the AI of his glasses—and the HUD it powered—from being picked up by any security scanners in the room. Both additions were, he now realized, absolutely essential. While the screening jammer went on in the background, the facial would alert him immediately if any undercover security agent came within his eye line.

The three-dimensional projection of the Sentallion game board hovering over the table shuffled the players' pieces; then the thirty-thirty square came up with a score of 93 percent on Kodiak's last calculation. He'd won. He laughed as the dealer pushed a large pile of chips toward him, the shocked look on his face not entirely fraudulent, while his AI glasses chimed, indicating that the next bet would go against him so as not to create a suspiciously long winning streak.

To the cheers of the spectators, Kodiak selected a single chip—a sliver of clear blue plastic, the logo of Helprin's Gambit embedded within in glittering gold—and slid it forward on the table. One hundred thousand credits. It was a lot of money to lose on the next play, but two more rounds after that he would win it back, and more besides. A couple more plays after that and it would be time to high-tail it off the platform and hide in the shadow of an asteroid, watching while Helprin's empire suffered a financial meltdown.

The holographic Sentallion game board realigned itself, presenting a new challenge to the players. There were three seated on Kodiak's left. They were all men, each dressed, like him, in scarlet evening wear. Two were young—younger than Kodiak by something close to twenty years, he thought to his own chagrin; exactly the kind of annoying rich kids he was pretending to be. The third man was much older, sixty at least, the tattoos covering his face and bare arms—and the jewelry studding his nose, ears, eyebrows—suggesting he was, or had been, a starminer. The real deal.

The first young man reached forward into the air in front of him and traced some lines on the puzzle board, solving his equation. The grid tilted toward player two, who did the same. Then the grid aligned itself to the older man with the tattoos. The mathematical puzzles on the grid were randomly generated—when Kodiak's hack wasn't at work, anyway—and the level of difficulty fluctuated. The game might have been created by starminers as a useful way to stretch the mind as their ships' automatic systems processed tons of ore, but that didn't necessarily mean the tattooed man had a natural advantage. Kodiak winced as he saw the equation presented to his fellow player. The poor guy had drawn a very difficult calculation indeed.

The gnarled player had already pushed a large pile of chips toward the dealer, an early gamble that now looked like a gigantic mistake. He frowned at the grid, reaching out with a finger, ready to drag his solution through the air in front of him. But then he quickly drew back, like he'd got a shock. He wet his lips and tried again, slowly drawing a series of lines over the puzzle as he linked formula and mathematical functions. Kodiak watched, trying—failing—to solve the problem in his own mind. Tough luck.

The tattooed man hissed in annoyance, dropping his hand and pushing his chair away from the table. He couldn't solve it. He shot the other players a dirty look, his lip curling into a snarl, and pointedly picked up his remaining chips—just six small yellow pieces, a fraction of the teetering stack he'd gambled and lost—before walking away from the table, mumbling under his breath.

Kodiak's turn. The equation appeared in front of him, and it was just as bad as the one the third player had drawn. Kodiak took a breath and did his best to solve it, but it was impossible. There was a tiny error, introduced by his hack, that made it unsolvable. Kodiak glanced at the other two remaining players, but they were expressionless, as any good gambler would be. He turned back to the equation, tried a couple of options, but then—all according to plan—had to concede defeat.

The holographic board dissolved as the game was reset for the next round, the dealer sweeping Kodiak's bet back into the bank and counting out the winnings of the other two players. While he waited, Kodiak drained his glass and scanned the room, pretending to look for a top-up from one of the wandering hostesses. Green squares flew around in his vision as his AI glasses crosschecked faces, but no flags popped up.

No sign of a hostess either. Kodiak sighed, licking the last remnants of the sweet, sticky liqueur from his teeth as he turned back to the game. The Sentallion dealer, a young woman about the same age as the two young men seated next to Kodiak, smiled at him as she invited him to place his bet.

Kodiak blinked. The HUD in his eye line flashed. Time to start making waves.

He shoved his entire pile of credits forward. "Double-up," he said.

The crowd gasped in awe. Kodiak smiled to himself. Were they in for a show or what?

The two other players glanced at each other. Then one laughed and shook his head, slapping Kodiak on the shoulder as he got up from his chair. The other man looked more annoyed than happy, and the pile of credits he then bet was, in comparison to his earlier plays, very small.

The game board shuffled. Kodiak watched the HUD in his glasses spin as his hack fixed the equation. He quickly dragged the formulae around and solved it. When the board tilted toward the other remaining player, Kodiak felt his chest begin to tighten. He'd worked it out, calculated the risk—well, okay, *guesstimated* it—figuring out how much he needed to lose and how much he needed to win. The hack in the servitor dock far beneath his feet would not only throw the games computer, but block any failsafe, preventing alerts being sent to casino security, keeping the games floor open even when the monetary losses became too heavy.

And it would work. Of course it would work. But that didn't stop him from being nervous. Kodiak reached for his glass and went to take a sip before remembering it was empty.

At the other end of the table, the other player sat and stared at his equation, not lifting a finger to try and solve it. Ten seconds. Twenty. Thirty. Still he didn't move. A minute.

Then, without a word, he got up and walked away. Kodiak watched him leave, his throat suddenly dry.

It *had* worked. He turned back around on his stool and blinked as the dealer gathered up the other player's bet with his own, added a sizeable stack from the bank, and slid the whole lot toward him with a clear plastic paddle.

"Congratulations," said the dealer. "Double-up, winner takes all."

The games room erupted into applause, and Kodiak realized he'd just won five million credits. He whooped at the top of his lungs and, grinning wide, pulled the credits toward him with both arms. "Come to daddy!" The exhilaration he felt wasn't entirely faked.

But there was still that tight feeling in his chest. Fight or flight. Even if the games computer was unaware of what was going on, there *were* people watching, weren't there? Kodiak looked around again, acknowledging the applause of the sizeable crowd, noticing for the first time that his table was the only one still running, the other gamblers having abandoned their own bad luck to watch him haul in the credits. The plan might have been working, but it was hardly discreet.

But there were still no flags in his HUD. According to his AI glasses, there were no undercover casino staff in the room. Not even the usual security.

Wait. No security? That wasn't right. Even on a quiet night the casino floor was patrolled by the station's private police force.

"Excuse me," said a low voice in his ear. Kodiak flinched and turned around to find a man smiling at him. He was dressed in the crisp white tunic of the station security service. Behind him were two more officers, similarly attired.

As Kodiak watched, the green face recognition overlay in his glasses moved over the three officers, mapping key features and characteristics. Then the overlay faded away.

No match.

"Shit," whispered Kodiak. His crosscheck algorithm was bugged. *Dammit*, he should have taken more time over the coding.

The security officer closed his eyes and bowed his head, as though tacitly acknowledging Kodiak's unspoken summary of the situation. "Mr. Helprin would very much like to meet you," he said.

"Yeah, right," said Kodiak. He returned his attention to the table and began sorting his credit chips into a more manageable pile. "Maybe some other time, pal."

The man gripped Kodiak's right biceps, hard. Kodiak froze. He was held fast.

The security officer smiled again.

"That was not an invitation," he said. "Mr. Helprin wants to see you. *Now.*"

"Shit," said Kodiak as he was led away to the hushed gossiping of the other players, his pile of credits abandoned on the table.

So much for his grand plan.

7

The holding cell was cold and uncomfortable, and Kodiak had been in it for hours. So when a white-clad security officer came to take him to an interview room, the change of scenery—the *company*—was a blessed relief. Still clad in his scarlet evening suit and feeling a little ridiculous in the expensive, shiny silk, Kodiak followed the officer down a featureless corridor that seemed to stretch halfway across the station. Hands cuffed in front of him, Kodiak could do nothing but follow his guide.

The fact that the officers hadn't been flagged by the facial recognition algorithm of his AI glasses—glasses sadly confiscated as evidence—bugged Kodiak. He couldn't have got it *that* wrong, could he? Compared to the hack of the casino games computer, the recognition system was a piece of cake.

Unless . . .

The security officer punched a keypad next to a door indistinguishable from the dull gray wall except for a narrow red outline. He stepped to one side, then gestured for Kodiak to enter, as though he were a guest, not a prisoner.

Kodiak stepped inside.

Unless, he thought, the security officers weren't employees of Helprin's Gambit at all.

The man sitting at the table in the interview room was wearing a dark gray suit with a dark blue shirt underneath and black tie. The tone of his skin was somewhere in between, his dense, closely cropped hair and chinstrap beard almost mathematically precise. In front of him on the table was a slim datapad.

Kodiak turned on his heel, but the door had closed. He turned back, and the man gestured for him to take a seat. Before he did, Kodiak couldn't stop his mouth curling into a lopsided smile.

"Special Agent Braben. Fancy meeting you here."

Braben said nothing, but one eyebrow went up as he looked Kodiak up and down. "Nice suit."

Kodiak lowered himself into the chair. "You come all this way to offer me fashion advice, or is there something else I can help with?"

Braben pressed a finger to the datapad on the table, then turned it around to face his prisoner. Kodiak leaned forward to look.

The datapad showed a profile, an official identity record. Kodiak recognized it immediately, because it was his. On the left side was his official Fleet ID picture, his shoulders turned three-quarters as he pointed his clean-shaved jawline at the lens. Underneath the picture were his vital statistics, including employment history. Down the right side of the page, most of the text was blacked out. Redacted.

Kodiak laughed. "What, they didn't give you clearance to read my whole profile?"

Agent Braben sighed and thumbed the datapad to display the next page.

Kodiak's smile dropped. His photograph was still there, but now there was new text superimposed over the top.

WANTED

It was an arrest warrant.

Kodiak shook his head as he scanned the rest of the page. "Mike, come on, you don't want to do this," he said, lifting his cuffed hands from his lap, reaching toward the agent. "I can explain."

Braben pulled the datapad back toward him. "Special Agent Von Kodiak, you're under arrest—"

"Look, buddy, there's been a mistake here. You just need to call the chief. Talk to Avalon. She'll clear it up."

Braben sucked on his top lip and held up his hand. "It's not that easy, Von."

"No, seriously, listen—"

"Kodiak, *please,*" said Braben. He adjusted himself in the chair, looking around the interview room like he was afraid the walls were about to come crashing down.

Kodiak banged the table with his cuffs. There'd been a mistake. A big, *big* mistake. Braben clearly had no clue what was going on. Dammit, he should have been told. Of all people, he should have been told.

The agent straightened his tie and cleared his throat. "Special Agent Von Kodiak, you are under arrest for treason. You have been found guilty and sentenced in absentia. The penalty is death. I am authorized by Fleet Command to carry out the sentence."

Kodiak's stomach did a somersault. Now *here* was a mistake. Big time. Theft? Sure, he was guilty. Officially, anyway. But . . . treason? Death penalty?

"What the hell is this?" he yelled, leaning across the table, the sound of his blood rushing in his ears nearly drowning out his thoughts. "I stole some money. That counts as treason now?" He could feel the pulse in his neck, the sensation sickening.

Braben glanced sideways at nothing, then licked his lips. Then his eyes met Kodiak's, but still he didn't speak.

"Talk to me, Mike," said Kodiak. "What the *fuck* is going on? What did Avalon tell you, huh? You know I didn't *actually* steal those credits, right? You do know why I'm here?"

Braben opened his jacket and pulled a gun out of his body holster. Kodiak's eyes widened at the sight of it—it was new, shiny, half a translucent blue plastic, the rest brushed metal. He hadn't seen this kind of pistol before. Must have been a new Bureau issue.

"I'm sorry, Von," said Braben. "I'm just following orders."

Then he pointed the gun across the table at Von Kodiak and pulled the trigger.

8

Cait—head down against the stiff wind, hood up against the evening rain—headed through the poorly lit night streets of Salt City, grateful to have gotten out of the virtual daylight of New Orem just a few miles behind her. It had taken hours to get out of the Fleet capital, her flight from the Memorial a series of double-backs and dead-ends as marines flooded the city streets, rolling out a lockdown with terrifying speed. That she'd managed to keep ahead of them was a miracle, but once within the bounds of Salt City itself, it had gotten easier. The security forces in the city seemed more intent on locking down the good side of the city, turning the slum into Cait's haven. Normally there was little surveillance, only the occasional monitor drone soaring high overhead, and few cops bothered to venture very far into its labyrinthine streets. Tonight seemed no different—if anything, with the attention being focused on the streets of New Orem, Salt City felt ever safer somehow. The clouds were low and thick, the rain heavy, and Cait's dark clothing melted into the shadows admirably. Throw in her stealth training, and she made good progress, putting as many blocks between her and the Fleet capital as possible.

She pulled into an alley, adjusted her pack, and peeked out from the under the brim of her hood to check her bearings.

Then a light-headedness came over her. She crouched down against the wall and took a series of deep breaths as the events of the day finally began to catch up with her.

Because while she had managed to get out of the city, she had no fucking clue what to do next. The Fleet Admiral was dead, but it hadn't been by her hand. The instructions she'd been given, the plan outlined to her, was out the fucking window.

So what was going on? What had happened back there? There was another assassin—that much was obvious. Had they sent multiple shooters, without telling any of them that there were others? That didn't make sense—they'd be as confused and scared as her, and while she'd been lucky in her escape, the more agents they had on the hill overlooking the Wall of Remembrance, the more chance one of them would have been caught, blowing the whole operation wide open.

Cait's mind raced. Wasn't it more likely there was another group who wanted the Fleet Admiral dead and had seen the same opportunity her own employers had? If one such group could plan an attack like that, couldn't another?

Cait closed her eyes, focusing on the tingle that sparked across her skin, willing the power to fade, to leave her the fuck alone so she could think.

What could she do? The plan was to carry out the mission, then rendezvous back in Salt City at a predetermined location, and then they would fulfill their part of the bargain. The thought of seeing her brother again lifted her spirits, but was that even going to happen now?

A cold feeling grew in her chest. They'd know it wasn't her, that she hadn't pulled the trigger. The Fleet Admiral was dead but she wasn't the killer. What would they do when they found her? Even without thinking about it, she'd been heading toward the rendezvous. But what was she going to walk into?

What would they do to her? To her brother?

"Fuck," said Cait, then she said it again, and again, standing and kicking the alley wall with her toe until it hurt.

Then she turned and pressed her back against the wall. She tilted her head up, allowing the rain to patter on her face.

She needed answers. She needed a plan of her own.

Cait checked the street from the alley. It was quiet except for the steady hiss of rain. She was pretty close to the rendezvous. She could still make it in time.

But was that the right thing to do? The *safe* thing to do? Possibilities, scenarios ran through Cait's mind. Maybe they had changed their minds. Maybe they didn't trust her, had sent someone else in to carry out the mission. So, did that make her disposable? She was part of a plot. They hadn't told her much, but probably enough for her to be a threat to them now, to make her a liability. If she made it to the rendezvous was she just walking into a trap?

Or had some other group moved in—not just taking out the Admiral, but taking out Cait's employers? She'd had no contact with them in several days, which *was* part of the plan . . . but maybe it wouldn't be her contacts waiting for her. And chances were they—whoever "they" were—would be just as likely to want to clean house as well.

Cait's fingers pulled at her hair under the hood. There was only one thing she was sure of: the Fleet Admiral was dead. That had been the primary mission goal—maybe something she could use to her advantage.

And . . . if she was honest with herself, she was relieved. Could she have pulled the trigger? She told herself she could have. She'd been telling herself she could for weeks. She was a warrior, a psi-marine in all but name. But, as she remembered crouching by the tree, it all seemed hazy, like a dream.

Could she have done it? *Would* she have? Now she wasn't so sure.

She rolled her neck, took deep, controlled breaths.

She needed *answers*. She needed to see her brother. She needed her employers, if they were still around, to keep their part of the bargain.

Which meant continuing to the rendezvous. Which meant facing whatever dangers lay ahead. She was a fighter, she told herself. She could handle it, she told herself.

She was strong.

Wasn't she?

And if anything, she would get those answers. Whatever they meant for her, now that everything had gone to shit.

Cait pulled herself up and stepped back out into the street, keeping her head down as she walked through puddles, splashing her legs with black, dirty water as she headed deeper into Salt City. She'd picked the route deliberately, skirting the busy central thoroughfares of the slum and instead tracking along a strip of abandoned industrial buildings. She was alone, and that was the point. If anyone approached her, from any direction, she would know it.

She walked on, lost in thought.

Salt City wasn't a city at all. It didn't even have a real name. It abutted the Fleet capital, New Orem, with no border or barrier, just a steadily crumbling zone of half-finished construction, relics from when someone had tried—and failed—to spread the prosperity of the capital northwest, absorbing the slum that occupied the bed of the great salt lake that had once made the region famous. Salt City was a mid-sized patch of nothing in the heart of the Fleet, an expected side effect of the Fleet being the planet's primary employer. The conglomeration of humanity that stretched from one side of the Confederated Utah Territory to the other was a near unbroken metropolis home to thirty million people; as the Fleet capital, New Orem had more gravity than a supermassive black hole for those looking for work.

Salt City was a refuge for those drawn to the promise of a dream-like career in Fleet service—most from South America, having crawled up into the northern continent after most of the land masses south of the equator had been eaten by a Mother Spider—only to find that, really, the Fleet didn't want them. So, with their homelands now a smoking, radioactive wasteland, they had no choice but to stay, camping out on the salt plain.

Salt City was born, and the Fleet didn't care. There were more important things to worry about. Things like Spiders. Things like war.

So Salt City grew alongside New Orem, a virtually independent state: unrecognized, disorganized, but autonomous. It developed its own economy. It was a place Cait had grown to know these past few months, ever since she had left the Academy, ever since she had been contacted by a group that told her that everything she knew about the Fleet, about the war itself, was a lie.

That everything she knew about what had happened to her brother was a lie too.

The group that had entrusted her with a very special mission, one requiring her specialized skills, one that would start a chain reaction that would reveal everything—*everything*—about what the Fleet was really doing.

Cait slowed, looking up from under her hood. She tracked toward the flat, featureless wall of a factory, then slid into another alley, diving into the deep shadows. She held herself against the damp wall, and she waited.

She was being followed. It hadn't required psychic powers to sense the presence that had been trailing her through the last few empty blocks of the industrial zone.

This was *not* part of the plan. The plan was to head to a prearranged place, the rendezvous, where she would be met. Then they would take her to her brother.

But now she was being followed.

Shit. It was them, wasn't it? They knew she had failed—no, no, that wasn't it. They had sent the other shooter, because they had lost their trust in her. And now she was being stalked. They were going to take her out, before she reached the rendezvous.

Cait cursed inwardly. Of course. The route she had chosen through the backwater industrial zones. The perfect place for an ambush. Nobody would see. Nobody would hear.

Oh, God. This was it.

Her tail was getting closer and the world buzzed in Cait's ears as she crouched down in the darkness.

Across from her in the alley was a pile of rubble. There was a clicking sound, a ceramic tap; Cait jerked her head up at the sound and, almost without thinking, reached out her arm to receive the triangular shard of concrete that lifted itself off the top of the pile and flew toward her. The block was heavier than she had expected, jarring her arm as she caught it. She looked at it in her hand, trying to focus on the here and now while her vision clouded with spinning stars. She hefted the block. Heavy, awkward, but she would still be able to get a good swing with it.

Or maybe she wouldn't need to swing it at all. The block was suddenly lighter; Cait opened her fingers and watched as the shard floated a centimeter in the air over her open palm.

Out on the street, the tail had slowed, perhaps realizing they'd lost their mark. Hard footsteps sloshing through puddles stopped, shuffled, stopped. Boots turned on the rough road; then the person headed off toward a dark street directly across from Cait's alley. She peered out from the shadows, watching the man's receding back. He was wearing a long pale coat that trailed out behind him as he walked. It wasn't very discreet, not for a tail, not for an assassin sent to kill her. Maybe he was the one who had shot the Fleet Admiral.

Cait wobbled on her haunches as a dizzy spell hit. The man was gone. Maybe . . . maybe he *hadn't* been following her. Maybe he was up to crimes and conspiracies of his own. This was Salt City, after all.

The concrete shard dropped to the ground, the clinking sound it made helping Cait to snap out of it. She sighed. She felt ill. She slid down the wall a little more and sat on the damp ground as she waited a few moments, counting time, eyes scanning the street, waiting for the sick feeling to pass. The rain eased, leaving behind huge, still puddles in the rutted pavement, the pools reflecting the underpowered street lighting.

Cait licked her lips. Her mouth was dry. That power, that *talent* . . . it took it out of her. But, she thought, that was what it was. A *power*. She might not have been able to control it, but she took strength from what had just happened.

She was a warrior. She was on a mission. She had to see her brother again and maybe, just maybe, she was strong enough to survive whatever was coming next.

Cait counted in her head again, then, satisfied that she was alone once more, stepped out of the alley to continue her journey.

9

"Rise and shine, sweetheart."

Kodiak opened his eyes and saw a dark shape looming over him. The world was nothing but fuzzy shades of gray. Something moved in front of his face. Another face, just a dark oval. He blinked and coughed and tried to speak, but his mouth and throat were dry. He felt like death.

And then he remembered.

"Here." A familiar voice. Braben. The dick who shot him. Kodiak tried to sit up, to get into a better position to throttle the Bureau agent, but his limbs refused to move. He could feel them all right. They were all there, apparently intact, but they were immobile. He was lying on a hard surface, completely paralyzed.

Something warm and clammy touched his lips—the lip of a plastic bottle—and although his mouth didn't open as much as he really wanted it to, the cool water that filled it was *glorious.* He took four sips, each increasing in size as Braben held the bottle. Then he sighed and slumped back, realizing that he'd managed to lift his head a little. After a few moments, he felt better—*much* better—although as his heart rate kicked up it banged a matching rhythm inside his skull. Kodiak sighed and winced as the headache took hold.

"Yeah, you'll feel lousy awhile." The shadow that was Braben appeared to shrug. "Side effects I guess. What do I know?"

Kodiak coughed. "You shot me," was all he could croak out before he let his head rest against the table again.

Braben laughed. "Drink some more," he said, this time offering the bottle to Kodiak instead of feeding it to him. Kodiak let his head roll to the side to see, and then he lifted his arm and grabbed hold of the drink. The bottle felt like it weighed a ton. Kodiak quickly rested it on his chest, then craned his neck up to drink. He coughed, mid-gulp, and turned his head to cough up a mouthful of water.

Braben's shape took a step back, and it seemed like he was looking down at his shoes.

"You're doing this deliberately," he said.

Kodiak smiled and drank again, this time taking big, clean swallows. Then he pushed himself up on his elbows. The thump in his head reached a crescendo and he gasped in pain, but then the feeling subsided. He shifted on the table, taking stock of his situation.

He was still wearing the scarlet evening suit from the casino, although it was creased to hell, the bright fabric dirty, smudged. He was lying on something black on the hard table. The material was stiff plastic, almost waxy to the touch. There was a zipper near his feet.

He was lying in a body bag.

The realization sent Kodiak into a coughing fit. He held the drink bottle out and Braben took it from him. Then Kodiak leaned forward, trying to control the cough, pushing the heels of his hands into his eye sockets. His eyes were sore and filled with tears. For a moment he reveled in the darkness behind his hands; then he dropped them and turned to Braben.

Special Agent Braben. His former partner stood beside the table, looking like he'd just come from a relaxing weekend away. He was wearing the same suit as on Helprin's Gambit, but the shirt had switched to brown and the tie to metallic silver.

Kodiak looked around the room. It was well lit but somehow remained dingy, all concrete and steel. Cold too, although Kodiak wondered if that was just him. He pulled the edge of the body bag away from the table, the stiff plastic rustling. Underneath was chrome steel.

They were in a morgue.

He looked up at Braben. "How long have I been out?" he asked, reaching for the water bottle again. Braben handed it over, then he stuck his thumbs around the top of his belt and swayed back and forth on his feet.

"About ten hours."

Kodiak shook his head and drained the bottle. "No wonder I feel like shit. What the hell did you drug me with?"

"No drugs."

Kodiak wiped his mouth with the back of his hand and raised an eyebrow. Braben grinned and flicked the edge of his fancy jacket to one side. The lining was red, the same color as Kodiak's crumpled suit. The same strange-looking weapon Braben had drawn at the station now hung on a belt holster instead of one concealed against the agent's side.

"Took us that long to get back to Earth, and we couldn't risk anyone finding out you weren't dead," said the agent. "Helprin's men were watching us from the moment we entered his domain, and he had scanners on us for a long time after we left. Business like his, I guess he likes to keep an eye on people coming *and* going. So anyway, I just kept shooting you every now and again to keep you under."

Kodiak blinked in disbelief. "You just kept shooting me?"

"Yeah, every now and again," said Braben. He looked down at the gun on his hip. "Staser, new thing." He let his jacket fall back into place. "Think they were rolled out just after you left. Got a great stun setting on them."

Kodiak pulled his feet out of the bottom of the body bag and swung his legs over the table. Braben stepped forward, ready to help, but Kodiak brushed him off. "I can manage, you trigger-happy asshole."

He squeezed his eyes shut as the world went gray and wobbly. Some extraction plan. Who knew being executed for treason would hurt so much? Then he opened his eyes, glanced around the morgue at the other tables. They were occupied. With a frown he quickly slipped off his table and rubbed his face. He was annoyed at the interruption of his grand plan, his one chance at hurting Helprin. But they wouldn't have pulled him out without good reason. He felt his natural curiosity piqued.

He dropped his hands. "So why did you bring me out of there?"

Braben looked at him. Kodiak shrugged. "What?"

"You really don't know?"

"Know what? I've been locked in that casino for hours."

Braben gave a low whistle and buttoned his jacket. "Okay," he said slowly. "The Fleet Admiral has been assassinated. It's a red ball, all hands on deck. The chief will give you a full briefing." He headed toward the door.

"Assassinated?" Kodiak's head cleared immediately, a surge of adrenaline giving his tired body new life. He pushed away from the slab and walked over to Braben, waiting by the door. Kodiak stared at his partner, but Braben's expression was set.

Kodiak parsed Braben's statement through his mind again. Assassination of the Fleet Admiral. A thousand other thoughts suddenly fought for attention—was it terrorism? Some kind of attack? Was it a precursor to . . . what? *Another* assassination? *Another* attack? Was this just the first move in a new kind of conflict? Like they didn't have enough, fighting a war with the Spiders. But there were a lot of organizations who didn't like the way the Fleet was running things, who had threatened just this kind of action.

Braben cocked his head. "Von?"

Kodiak rolled his neck, trying to clear his mind. "Holy *shit,*" he whispered, shaking his head.

Braben nodded. "My thoughts exactly."

Kodiak stepped past his partner, pushing open the doors and striding into the corridor. Then he stopped and turned, holding the door open. "You coming or what?" he asked. He was impatient to talk to the chief, get the full picture of what had happened.

Braben adjusted his tie and followed.

10

By the time the two agents reached the corridors of the Bureau proper, Braben was back in the lead, Kodiak at his heels.

Nothing had changed, as far as Kodiak could see. Then he wondered why he thought anything would have considering he'd hardly been gone a year. Same building. Same corridors. Same carpet and same lights and same coffee machines and water coolers. The walk from the morgue was a long one, a walk he remembered too. So far the only thing that was new was Braben's fancy gun.

That, and the mood, the atmosphere. Braben had said it himself: this was a red ball, an emergency so bad they'd called everyone in—including him, pulling him out from a long undercover mission, throwing away months of planning and preparation.

Red ball.

They walked on, Kodiak's expression grim. The Bureau was busy, filled with agents, some of whom Kodiak recognized and some of whom he didn't. The Bureau was buzzing with energy, none of it positive. It felt cold, fearful. Like something dangerous just below the waterline. Like something else was about to happen, like the Fleet Admiral's assassination was just the start of something new and terrible.

As if to underline that point, Kodiak and Braben stopped in the corridor and moved to either side as a line of marines in full combat armor marched past. When they were gone, Kodiak turned to watch their plated backs.

"This is going to take some getting used to," he said.

"That it is."

Kodiak tried to remember the last time he'd seen the heart of the Fleet at real battle stations. There was a war on, but here in New Orem that was almost an abstract concept, something happening somewhere else. The front lines were light-years across, but they were a very long way from the Earth.

Thankfully.

They walked on. Kodiak nodded at those agents he knew as he passed them. Some returned the gesture; most looked the other way. Kodiak started to wonder how many people actually knew what had happened to him. He was an agent gone rogue, one who had broken into an evidence server and lifted a whole heap of money before disappearing. He was a wanted man.

So the official story went, anyway. He just hoped that the Bureau staff would at least be briefed on his status by the chief. The last thing anybody needed was that hanging over his head, distracting not just himself but those he would need to give orders to. They'd brought him back to work, after all.

Soon enough, they reached the Bureau bullpen, the command center of the whole operation. It was a large circular chamber, the main floor sunk down to separate it from the six glass-walled planning rooms that ringed it. From the outer ring, eight short flights of steps were spaced out evenly, leading down to the operation floor.

The bullpen proper was a chaos of desks and tables and agents, the air thick with so many spinning holodisplays that Kodiak could hardly see to the other side of the room. He paused at the top step, getting his bearings. Braben, walking ahead, stopped and turned around.

"You coming, Von?"

The bullpen went quiet as every agent stopped what they were doing and turned to watch Kodiak. Kodiak cleared his throat, feeling his face turn the same shade of red as his crumpled suit. Then he gave a little nod with a tight smile he hoped looked more like grim determination than the nervousness it felt like, and jogged down the steps to join his partner.

Braben licked his lips and then turned back around and kept walking, heading across the center of the room and toward one of the planning rooms on the opposite side of the bullpen, the glass walls of this one opaque gray, the room set to private. Kodiak followed Braben, very aware that everyone was staring at him as hc walked.

Braben stopped at the planning room door. He nodded over Kodiak's shoulder at the bullpen behind them. "Don't worry, there's a briefing set for later today, once the chief has filled you in."

Kodiak frowned, nodded. "Glad to hear it."

Braben pushed the door open and gestured for Kodiak to enter.

The planning room was filled with a long table, lined with chairs. As Braben closed the door, Kodiak felt a slight pressure on his eardrums as the sound-canceling surfaces clicked on. Whatever was said or done in this room was now completely secret.

"Welcome back, Von."

Bureau Chief Laurel Avalon sat on the other side of the table. She tilted her head, watching him.

Kodiak glanced at Braben, then walked around the table and pulled a chair out in front of Avalon.

"Chief," he said, sitting down. Given the circumstances of his return he tried not to smile, but it was surprisingly difficult. Avalon, like everyone else, was the same as before. Exactly the same. Red hair the same scarlet as his suit. Piercing green eyes. Immaculate uniform. She exuded authority, thanks in no small part to her being part of a great Fleet dynasty. She carried the Avalon name, and everyone knew it.

Suddenly self-conscious, Kodiak shifted in his chair. He looked and felt like a wreck. He glanced at Braben, who was still by the door. "Sit down, for crying out loud. You make me nervous, loitering around where I can't see you."

As Braben pulled up a chair next to him, Kodiak turned back to the chief. "I must admit I didn't expect to be back here so soon," he said.

Avalon nodded. "I'm sorry we had to cut the mission."

"That's a lot of planning out the window."

"We'll get Helprin sometime," said the chief. "Trust me. But we need you here now."

Kodiak sighed and caught sight of his reflection in the glass of the table—he'd been right, he looked terrible. Messy, greasy hair, his face dark with stubble, bags under his eyes. His suit looked like he'd been sleeping in it, which, actually, he had been. He nodded at Braben. "Your agent here shot me with his stun gun."

The corner of Avalon's mouth curled up. "I'm sure he didn't enjoy it, Von."

Braben brushed a finger along his chinstrap beard. "No, ma'am, I did not." A pause. "Actually, maybe a little bit."

Kodiak pointed at the agent. "See? This is abuse of authority. Revoke his badge before he hurts somebody."

"We had to get you out of there somehow," said Avalon. "For the moment, Von Kodiak is going to have to stay dead."

Kodiak raised an eyebrow. Braben leaned forward over the table. "Helprin has people in the Fleet. Word gets out that we faked your execution and brought you back—that you were an undercover agent from the Bureau, working in his little empire—he'll send someone after you."

As Braben spoke, Avalon's fingers moved over the table in front of her, which lit up at her commands. On the surface in front of Kodiak appeared his own face—not a reflection, but his official ID photo. It was the same warrant Braben had shown him before stunning him with the staser, only now it was amended to indicate that the sentence had been carried out.

"Even that crazy old man won't go chasing a corpse for revenge," said Braben.

Kodiak rubbed his chin and sighed. He gestured to his image on the table. "How long do I stay dead for?"

Braben and Avalon exchanged a look. Kodiak saw it. He didn't like it.

"Awhile," said Avalon.

Kodiak screwed his eyes tight. He knew his mission had a price, but it still stung. He jerked a thumb over his shoulder.

"How am I supposed to work when I'm dead?"

"Bureau staff will be briefed. You'll have security clearance within the Fleet capital, but you won't be able to leave."

"Didn't you just say Helprin had people in the Fleet?"

"In the Fleet, yes," said Avalon, "but not the Bureau, as far as we've been able to screen." She sighed. "Look, it's not perfect, but it's going to have to work. Things are bad, Von."

Kodiak frowned. He glanced at Braben, but his partner's expression had darkened too. "Okay," he said, turning back to the chief. "Tell me what happened."

Avalon nodded at Braben. Braben adjusted his tie, then took control of the table display. As he typed, Kodiak's official picture was replaced with new data: the portrait of the Fleet Admiral, Leo Sebela; maps of New Orem; a schematic of the Fleet Capitol Complex itself, and one of the Fleet Memorial.

Kodiak furrowed his brow as he studied the images.

"Sebela"—Braben tapped the late Admiral's picture—"was assassinated at the Fleet Memorial, as he gave his official Fleet Day speech, in front of thousands of people. As soon as he dropped, emergency protocols kicked in and the city went into lockdown."

Kodiak looked up. "He's killed in public, surrounded by marines, and the shooter gets away? No surveillance?"

Braben and Avalon looked at each other. "All footage cuts out just before the Admiral is shot," said Braben. "Likewise all public media streams."

Kodiak rubbed his chin again. "How is that possible?"

Avalon shrugged. "It's like everything was jammed, scrambled."

"Deliberate, then."

"Has to be."

Then Avalon reached forward, moving the images around on

the table. She brought up a new picture, one of an officer in a black uniform, his eyes narrowed at the camera like he was angry.

"It's not public knowledge," said the chief, "but Sebela was deposed by Admiral Zworykin the day before his assassination."

Kodiak stared at the new picture. He thought he recognized the officer. "Zworykin? Isn't he in charge of the Psi-Marine Corps?"

"Yes."

"And now he's the Fleet Admiral?"

Avalon gave a single nod. "He is."

Kodiak pursed his lips. "And then the guy he kicked out is murdered. Seems pretty convenient." He leaned over the table, examining the images. "New guy stages a coup and takes over. Keeps it a secret while he moves his own people in. Then old guy is eliminated, and new guy suddenly appears to step in as the legitimate successor. Uses the situation to his advantage, strengthening his own position. Shows himself as a responsible, courageous leader in a time of turmoil."

"Yes," said Avalon.

"Which means," said Kodiak, tapping the table, "new guy is behind it."

"Seems most likely," said Braben. "But that's what we want you to find out."

Kodiak shook his head, trying to piece things together. "But he knows the Bureau will investigate and rat him out, right?"

"If he's responsible, then yes," said Avalon. "Which is why I want you to lead the investigation."

Kodiak shrugged. "Because?"

"Because you're dead. I'm going to grant you personal security clearance inside this building, but even that won't lead back to you directly. If there is a cover-up, a conspiracy, if Zworykin is responsible and is working to hide his tracks, then you're the one to find out. Your investigation won't leave a trace."

Kodiak shook his head. "But he'll be *waiting* for an investigation. He'll be following it, making sure he stays ahead of us. We can't run a covert op. If we're not seen to do something, he'll realize we're onto him from the start."

"There will be an official investigation," said Avalon. "Braben will be the lead. You'll have a cover ID—to Zworykin you're a Bureau analyst assigned to the case, nothing more."

At this, Braben reached under the conference table and extracted a black case. He placed it on the table and turned it toward Kodiak.

Kodiak glanced at Braben. "What's this?"

Braben just nodded at it. "Open it."

Kodiak pulled the case toward him. It was featureless, the surface matte save for the shiny Bureau logo on the top. He felt along the edges until he found the catches. The case beeped as it recognized Kodiak's DNA and unlocked.

Inside, nestled in shaped foam packing, were two items. The first was a Bureau ID badge, a mirrored square of metal on a clip backing, the Bureau emblem etched into the front in gold.

Next to the badge was a pistol. It was small, thin, the upper half translucent, the rest brushed silver.

Now Kodiak allowed himself a smile as he slid his hand around the grip of the staser and lifted it from the case. It was very light. By his thumb were a series of simple switches.

"You'll need to pass the Bureau training on the staser," said Braben.

Kodiak *hmmmed.* "Yeah, not sure I need that." He thumbed one of the controls, pointed the gun at Braben, and squeezed the trigger. The gun spat something white and fizzy and the agent cried out, sliding sideways off his chair.

Avalon was on her feet in a second, her hand reaching for her own staser on her belt.

"Von! What the *hell?*"

Kodiak flicked the safety back on and put the gun back into the case. He rolled his chair back a little and nudged Braben with his foot. The agent rolled on the floor, moaning in pain.

"I'm just returning a favor," he said. Then, ignoring Braben's semi-conscious form, he pulled himself back to the table. He locked the case and placed it on the floor beside his chair. Then he tapped at the table display, bringing up the image of the deceased Fleet Admiral and the maps of the city.

Avalon slowly lowered herself back down, her hand moving away from her gun, her eyes darting between Kodiak and Braben on the floor.

Kodiak looked up at her and waved his hand. “He’ll be fine. Now, let’s get to work.”

11

The farther Cait walked, the faster her pace. After a couple of hours she pulled up by a railing that circled an empty yard in front of a warehouse, hand on her chest as she caught her breath and realized she'd practically sprinted the last block. The confidence she had felt earlier had been short lived. Right now, she felt alone.

She felt afraid.

She checked her watch. She was still on time. In fact, she was *ahead* of schedule. She could afford a moment to stop and collect herself before continuing to the rendezvous. But not here, not in the open. She needed darkness and shadow, because while she was alone in the deserted streets, she also knew that they were watching. Surely, they were watching. Waiting.

Half a block on was a large intersection, a number of narrow, tall buildings offering myriad hiding places. She stuck to the side of the building behind her, checked that the coast was clear, then darted across the intersection and into another alley, thanking the universe that Salt City was a disorganized, organic mess of buildings and architectures.

Lost again in the dark, she sank to the ground. She closed her eyes, reaching out. Calling to him.

To Tyler.

Nothing. Nothing but the rush of blood in her ears and the cool night breeze. And the faint sounds of people, lots of people, brought to her on that wind.

Cait opened her eyes, and listened. She was on track, getting closer to her destination. The stretch of industrial warehouses and abandoned factories would soon come to an end, the streets already becoming brighter as she approached a night market. The sounds were carried on the breeze and echoed off the walls of the alley, but they were close—perhaps just on the other side of this block of warehouses.

The night markets of Salt City were famous and popular, not just among the refugees who lived and worked in the slum, but even among upstanding citizens of New Orem, the more adventurous of whom were known to venture out to see what exotic bargains could be found. Those were a different kind of night market, arrayed on the outskirts of Salt City, safe enough for New Orem tourists and with artificially raised prices to match their comparatively rich clientele.

It was sickening, the people of New Orem content to patronize the markets while turning a blind eye to the plight of Salt City itself. But tonight, of course, those markets would be closed, the citizens of the Fleet capital held under curfew.

But here, farther in, deep enough for outsiders to never reach, were the *real* night markets of Salt City. Here there was more on sale than overpriced knick-knacks and badly cooked street food.

In the heart of Salt City, you could buy almost anything, from art—smuggled, crumbling artifacts from the ruins of South America—to *people,* likewise smuggled, likewise crumbling. To passage off planet. Even to weaponry, stolen from the Fleet, serial numbers etched off and fire control CPUs hacked with a buggy, pirate OS. Like the sniper rifle in Cait's pack, she supposed, with its glitching computer. She'd collected it from the pre-arranged hiding place, in a difficult-to-reach water conduit below one of Salt City's main thoroughfares. She'd been impressed that they'd gotten her almost exactly the same kind of rifle she had trained with in the

Academy. The weapon appeared to be new, as well. They must have hit a weapons dump to steal it.

Of *course*. The gun.

Cait listened to the sounds of the market as she ran an idea around her mind.

Her plan was to hit the rendezvous right on time and demand some answers, trusting her training and her talent to keep her alive. Even as she thought of the plan again, she felt the nerves return. It sounded simple—too simple. She was walking into the unknown, and she knew it, and she wasn't even able to reach out to her brother's mind anymore.

But he was out there. He was alive. He *had* to be alive. This is what she was doing it for.

And there was a chance, a slim one perhaps, that her employers *weren't* behind the Admiral's assassination. Perhaps all they knew was that the Fleet Admiral was dead—proof enough that Cait had fulfilled the task assigned to her.

Perhaps to get the answers she wanted, she needed to walk into the rendezvous like nothing was wrong. Like everything had gone according to plan.

She needed to bluff. And to bluff, she needed a little bit of evidence.

The alley was dark and smelly, the ground wet not from the recent rain but with something thick and sticky oozing from the garbage stacked high at the far end of the narrow passage. Cait headed toward it and crouched down on the other side, the fetid heap of refuse providing ample cover. Then she slid her backpack off and began taking the pieces of the sniper rifle out. In less than a minute, the gun was assembled and ready.

Hoping that the death of the Fleet Admiral was all that mattered, hoping—perhaps foolishly, perhaps not, there was no time to second-guess herself now—that her employers were just as much in the dark as she was, Cait raised the sniper on her hip, pointing it at a sharp angle toward the sky, and pulled the trigger.

There was no flash. For a sniper, detection meant death, so the gun released only a muffled *crack* as the invisible energy bolt flew skyward. Despite just a row of buildings separating Cait from the night market, no one would have heard the shot.

Cait lowered the weapon, relieved that the gun had worked, glitching OS and all. Shielding the display with her hand, Cait thumbed a control on the top of the weapon. The gun had been fired—and now there was the log to prove it. More than that, for once the glitching OS would be to her advantage, the log's scrambled timestamp making it impossible to pinpoint the last time the weapon had been used. Now, if they checked the gun, they'd think she had been the one who had downed the Fleet Admiral. All according to the plan.

Cait found herself smiling as she pulled the weapon to pieces and slid them into the compartments in her backpack. She had no idea if her plan would work, but she felt good just doing *something*. It was better than staying hidden, or running away. And if things went south, she could fight—for herself, and for her brother.

Caitlin Smith was a *warrior.*

She stood, swung the pack onto her back, and walked out into the main street, turning toward the sounds of the crowds ahead. All she had to do was reach the market and cross it, enter the dark streets in the next quarter, and she would make the rendezvous.

She walked for a few minutes, to the end of the block, then turned into a wide thoroughfare. Ahead of her, the street was filled with people, the crowd increasing in density farther along as the night market proper began.

"Excuse me, Ms. Smith."

Cait froze, eyes wide. Then she turned to face the voice behind her.

It was the man in the pale coat. He stood with his hands clasped in front of him. He was middle-aged and wore glasses and his hair was brown and short. His expression was flat, still.

Oh, shit. She *had* been followed, and now they had found her. She was still a kilometer or so away from the rendezvous. Whoever the man was, he wasn't—*couldn't*—be with her employers.

A rival organization. They were behind it all. They'd taken out the Admiral, and now they were taking out everyone else.

Or . . . the Fleet. The Fleet *Bureau.* She'd been tracked from the Memorial, despite her jammed manifest tag. She'd been tracked, and now this guy, this agent, was going to take her down.

Cait felt her throat close, a shiver passing over her skin as *it* started to happen. She watched the man in the pale coat hesitate, his eyes widening as he looked at her.

She could fight. Or . . .

The night market behind her, toward the other end of the thoroughfare, was huge, a sprawling collection of stalls and tables, funneling customers, drinkers, and diners into a maze of brightly colored passageways, disgorging them into large squares and plazas, then bottlenecking them back into narrow streets packed with wares for sale. The perfect place to get lost.

Or to lose someone.

Cait turned, ready to run, then swallowed a cry of surprise. Standing in front of her was another man, this one dressed in black and wearing a hard, flat black mask, smooth except for two inset goggles.

Cait curled her fists and drew her chin up. "I don't know who you are, but you're going to have to get out of my—"

The man drove a fist into Cait's stomach, the blow driving the air from her lungs. She doubled over, her arms instinctively folding over her middle before they were grabbed from behind and twisted behind her back. Cait wheezed, tears streaming down her face. She looked down at the road, watched as the puddles beneath her began to move, water streaming *away* from her like they were being blown by a fan. She looked up, willing the power to obey her, trying to find some way to control it, to *direct* it. She saw a tiny reflection of herself in the man's goggles.

And then something sharp and cold was slipped into her neck, and a black bag was slipped over her head and her world was nothing but musty chemical darkness.

12

They'd been going for hours: Kodiak sat in the front row, beside him an empty seat left by Braben as he got up to lead the team through the next section of the briefing. On his other side, Commander Avalon, datapad on her knee, making notes.

The planning room was packed, standing room only. So many agents had been called in—more than ever worked in a regular shift, that the situation briefing was being repeated three times that day. Braben and Avalon shared briefing duties, while Kodiak sat, ready to field questions and pick up anything useful that might come up from the other agents. But, really, he needed this briefing as much as anyone else. He'd been out of touch for a year and was now dropped right back into the middle of a genuine crisis.

At least he had managed to grab a few fitful hours of sleep before they'd started. After meeting with the chief, he'd started to feel the effects of his "capture" on Helprin's Gambit and his subsequent unconscious transit back to Earth. The chief had seen he was running on adrenaline and little else, and arranged for him to take one of the Bureau safe houses within the precincts of the Capitol Complex. The apartment was basic, to say the least, but comfortable and within easy reach of the office itself. Permitted a scant few glorious hours of rest, Kodiak had ditched the dirty scarlet suit, stuffing it into the trash disposal chute in the apartment's tiny kitchen, and had then stood under the piping hot shower for what felt like a lifetime. Then a nap—just two hours, enough to recharge while Braben got the briefings organized.

When his alarm woke him, Kodiak realized to his chagrin that he'd thrown out the only garments in the apartment. Cursing his own lack of foresight, Kodiak had grabbed the shrink-wrapped bathrobe that was in the closet and, using it as his sole item of clothing, he'd padded down to the Bureau uniform store, requisitioning himself a set of gear from the bemused officer on duty.

He now sat in the planning room wearing a black combat jumpsuit, over the top of which was a lightly armored gilet with the words FLEET BUREAU spelled across the chest in big white letters, the same on the back. It was functional and comfortable, and allowed him to focus his attention on more important things than his wardrobe.

Like who was responsible for the assassination of Fleet Admiral Sebela, the leader and commander-in-chief of *all* of humanity, spread out across what was referred to as Fleetspace—the portion of the galaxy that belonged to the Earth, rather than the Earth's enemy, the Spiders.

Kodiak crossed his legs as he listened to Braben, immaculate as ever in a steel gray suit that matched the color of the walls, give a rundown of another terror group profile—the Spiders may have been the Fleet's combat enemy, but there were plenty of organizations within Fleetspace that rejected the leadership and directives for war issued from Earth. Some were little more than small gangs, their members only loosely affiliated, their activities limited to crime and black marketeering. Some were larger, more organized—others still had hierarchies, mission statements, even uniforms and logos. What they all had in common was a disregard for the Fleet's authority and a desire to impose their own order on things—whether that threat was credible or not was what they were in the briefing to discuss.

None had claimed responsibility for the crime—but that didn't mean none of them was involved. Some organizations loved to broadcast their exploits, their demands. Others operated in shadow, causing trouble where they could but not reveling in some twisted glory, at least publically.

Kodiak sighed. Braben and Avalon had run through a lot of groups—Black Five, the South American Congress, the United States Liberation Front—and individuals too. Red Chandler, wanted in the Akcur system for bombing education facilities on three of the four colony planets. William and Hilzer Dazizen, a husband and wife pair who had led public protests against the Fleet's treatment of refugees from South America before killing two Bureau agents in the streets just outside the Capitol Complex and fleeing. John Simon, who liked to hijack unarmed civilian transports out near the Omoto trading belt.

All of them, wanted men and women. Banned organizations.

None of them, Kodiak's gut said, responsible.

He sighed again and re-crossed his legs.

"Okay," said Braben. "Two more on the Bureau watch list. First up, the Morning Star."

The holodisplay next to the agent shimmered as a head-to-toe image of a woman appeared. She was dressed in a long white robe with a hood, and beneath the hood she was wearing a red headband.

Braben glanced up at the image as he read the information off his datapad. "The Morning Star claims to be a religious order on a holy mission to seek out their god, which they call Lucifer or the Fallen One, who they believe is lost somewhere out there."

"What happens when they find him?" asked someone from back in the room. Kodiak craned his neck around. Agent Braffet, a young woman with blond hair tied back in a tight ponytail, was leaning forward on her chair, back straight as she waited for the answer. Kodiak turned back around, his eyes on the image of the woman on the holodisplay. If the Morning Star was a religious group, the woman, whoever she was, certainly looked the part.

Standing at the front, Braben shrugged. "I'm not sure they've thought that far ahead. We don't know much about them, but they're a low priority for us. Their quest has taken them out to the edges of Fleetspace. Last report we have was of one of their leaders"—he pointed to the image with his datapad—"buying a secondhand freighter on Rayner-79 and heading out of Fleetspace with a group of four acolytes."

Kodiak frowned. "Rayner-79 is a long way out." He nodded at the image in front of him. "So why are they on our watch list if they're harmless?"

Braben cast his eyes down to his datapad. "A few years ago, they were stirring up anti-Fleet sentiment in the Belec and Ogelo systems. This woman, Samantha Flood, was arrested as a stowaway on a U-Star. When they caught her, she had two sticks of TenTen strapped to her body."

Kodiak whistled; behind him, a few of the assembled agents murmured to each other. TenTen was an industrial explosive, used for demolition out on the Warworlds. More than enough to down a U-Star.

Next to him, Avalon cocked her head. "So Samantha Flood escaped custody?"

Braben nodded. "Apparently so. No idea how, the report doesn't say. That was five years ago. Next sighting was on Rayner-79 two years later, and that's all we have." He lowered his datapad and gestured to Avalon. "Chief?"

Avalon nodded and stood, swapping places with Braben.

"Last on our watch list are the Independent Loyalists," she said, addressing the room. The holodisplay changed to a series of mug shots: six men, two women. Five of the images were official portraits, the people in them in a variety of uniforms that were military in style, but nothing that the Fleet used. Two of the other images were candid shots, personal pictures showing smiling faces. The final image looked like a shot from surveillance of a man half-turned toward the camera in a city street.

"IL are by far the largest and most organized terrorist group on the Bureau watch list. They claim to have several thousand active agents and operate within a military hierarchy. They were formed in the Portia trading belt by the governments of Lehane and Toliman, who illegally declared themselves independent from the Fleet."

Kodiak sat back as Avalon gave brief profiles of the eight people on display and ran through IL's operations. This group had positioned themselves as a rival power bloc to the Fleet itself, although smaller by several orders of magnitude. But they had something the other groups didn't—ships, including Fleet U-Stars confiscated from the starports on the twin planets and the backing of the two governments that had declared independence.

IL were big, and they were dangerous.

But, as Avalon explained, they had never carried out any attacks on the Earth. They were against the Fleet—had declared war on them, even—but their activities had been confined to the Portia trading belt and neighboring systems.

Well, thought Kodiak, until *now* anyway. Of all the groups, they were the ones who had the most resources, the best organization.

But still, it didn't feel right. The circumstances of the assassination were weird, coinciding as they did with the power games being played by Admiral Zworykin.

Kodiak remained in his seat, considering this as the briefing room emptied, leaving just himself, Braben, and the chief. In one hour the room would be filled again, the briefing repeated.

"Von?"

Kodiak blinked as the commander spoke to him. "Chief?"

"Thoughts?"

"Oh," said Kodiak. "Lots of those. None of them particularly useful, I suppose."

"What do you mean?" asked Braben.

Kodiak stood and went to the holodisplay, which was still showing the images of the IL leadership.

"May I?"

Braben nodded, handing him the datapad. Kodiak began flipping through the briefing notes, the holodisplay changing as he cycled through the watch list. IL, the Morning Star, Black Five, the rest.

"The watch list is longer than I remember," he said. He continued to cycle through, unsure of what he was looking for, all the while aware of the nagging doubt in his gut.

Braben folded his arms and stepped closer to the display, watching it as his partner flipped through images. "A lot of people don't like the Fleet."

"Including people inside the Fleet itself?" Kodiak lowered the datapad, the holodisplay now showing an empty silhouette, a placeholder for someone known only as "Neubaum." He looked at the silhouette—they'd discounted Neubaum already, the criminal rumored to be dead, but the blank image seemed an appropriate visual to accompany Kodiak's thoughts, representing the shooter, the assassin. The unknown perpetrator they were trying to catch.

The perp, he suspected, who was working for someone inside the Fleet.

"We'll have full manifest access shortly," said Avalon. "I put the order through earlier this morning."

"You really think this is some kind of Fleet conspiracy?" asked Braben.

Kodiak and Avalon exchanged a look, then Kodiak said, "We have to consider it. The manifest is a good place to start looking."

"If they're using Fleet personnel in the first place," said Braben. "Even if it was an inside job, they could have used contractors to cover their tracks."

Braben was right, and Kodiak knew it. The Fleet manifest was a complete record of everything the Fleet owned and where it was currently located, anywhere in Fleetspace. Within the bounds of the Capitol Complex, this would range from every office chair, every coffee cup, computer terminal, every single piece of equipment or asset.

Including personnel. Every member of the Fleet, past and present, was electronically tagged. Personnel were more valuable than office chairs, so the manifest tag was buried deep, near the medulla oblongata, where it could never be extracted without killing the subject. That was the whole point.

If the assassination was some kind of inside job—*if* Fleet personnel were involved—then their movements would show up in the manifest.

Whether there was anything useful there or not, Kodiak couldn't say. They had to see the data first. Accessing the manifest was standard procedure in a major crime, but not an automatic one. It still required the Bureau Commander to get clearance from the Fleet Command Center, given that the manifest showed the location of everything that belonged to the Fleet. It was sensitive, secure information.

"We have to start somewhere," said Avalon. Then she checked her wrist computer. "Okay, after the next briefing, Admiral Zworykin wants to see us for an update."

Kodiak nodded. "Actually, I want to see him too. I have a whole bunch of questions to ask him about what happened on Fleet Day."

Braben hissed through his teeth. "We gotta tread carefully here. Look, if Zworykin is behind all this, he's going to be looking closely at what we do, make sure we don't get too close to the truth."

"I agree," said Avalon.

Kodiak nodded. "Yes," he said, "but remember, I'm just an analyst now. My job is just to help Mike, at least as far as the Admiral is concerned. So don't worry, I'll handle myself."

"Okay," said Braben, but he didn't look happy. Neither did the chief. And who would? thought Kodiak. Things were bad, he knew.

And he also knew that things were potentially going to get much worse.

13

Cait's head jerked back, and she coughed as the black bag was pulled off. She took in her surroundings as she sucked cold, dry air over her teeth.

She was sitting in a chair, her hands bound behind her, in the middle of a cavernous space, so large at first she thought she was still outside. She looked around, unable to see the walls or even the ceiling, but the floor beneath her boots was silvery gray and shiny—polished concrete—and there were a series of large metal cargo containers stacked nearby. She coughed again, noticing how the sound echoed metallically. She was in a warehouse. She had no idea where. Salt City presumably, but one warehouse was the same as another, whether it was in the slum or in New Orem proper. The last thing she remembered was the bag and the sting in her neck. They could have taken her anywhere. She could have been out for minutes, hours, days.

There were four men in the warehouse with her—three in black uniforms and masks, and the man in the pale coat. Two of the men in black were armed with small, compact plasma weapons; the taller man on Cait's left had his pointed at her, while the other let his hang from his loose hand. The third had his arms folded tightly across his chest. Cait tried to focus, to assess her situation, to gather, observe, anything that might be useful. It helped keep her head cool too. She remembered her Academy training: Survival, Evasion, Resistance, Escape.

I guess this bit comes under resistance, she thought.

The man in the pale coat leaned against one of the cargo containers. Next to him, on a stack of smaller packing crates, Cait saw her backpack and the components of the sniper rifle, lined up in a row. The weapon's display was on, the blue glow bright. They'd checked the log, then.

The man with the folded arms—the leader of the group, Cait thought, based on his body language, and, unlike his black-uniformed companions, his holstered weapon—moved toward her. Cait shrank back in the chair as much as she could, scraping the legs across the hard floor. She managed to rock it backwards a little, but then she hit something behind her. Cait pulled at the bindings holding her wrists, ignoring the fact that it was pointless.

And then her hands flew free. Surprised, Cait toppled forward from the chair, her knees hitting the ground, her hands splaying out to stop herself from falling flat on her face. From behind her stepped another uniformed guard, folding a small black blade in one hand.

"Fucking *ow,*" she said, and she looked up. The leader of the group laughed—the voice was muffled by the flat mask, but it was female. Then she pulled the mask off and stepped forward, holding a hand out to Cait.

Cait stared at her. The woman was older than she was, perhaps late thirties, long dark hair pulled back into a tight ponytail. She wasn't smiling, not quite, but one eyebrow was arched, the corner of her mouth doing the same.

Cait didn't take the offered hand. Instead, she pushed herself back up onto her haunches and rubbed her wrists.

The woman withdrew her hand and stood back, folding her arms. She looked down at Cait, head cocked like Cait was something small but interesting.

"So who the hell are you?" asked Cait, still rubbing life back into her wrists. Her throat was dry as anything, and she coughed.

"We're sorry about the cloak and dagger treatment," said the man in the pale coat. "But it was important to get you to safety. You can call me Glass." He pointed to the others in turn. "Curran, Schwab, Segura."

The woman standing over Cait tilted her head, but still didn't speak. Glass nodded at her. "And that is Samantha Flood."

Cait pulled herself back up onto the chair. She leaned forward on her forearms and rolled her neck. It was sore from where they had needled her.

And that wasn't all. A small ball of panic rose in her chest. She splayed out her fingers, curled them, turned her hands over as she rested on her knees.

There was no tingle, no buzz. Nothing. She had no control over her talent, not consciously anyway. But it manifested in times of stress, times of fear.

She was afraid now. No matter how hard she tried to keep her mind clear of such thoughts, she'd been captured, she was in enemy territory. She was afraid.

And she was alone. No voice in her head. No power under her skin.

"What the hell have you done to me?" she asked. "And who the fuck are you people?"

This time Flood spoke. "There's been a slight change of plan," she said, ignoring the questions. "We have some more work for you to do."

Cait blinked, her heart rate kicking up a gear. So, this was the group? Her mysterious employers? Her secret contacts? She glanced around them. The uniforms, the weapons. They looked new, or at least well maintained. Only Glass was different, wearing a gray suit under his pale coat. Their undercover man, clearly. The others, they were . . . organized. They looked like soldiers, were equipped like soldiers.

Cait made it to her feet. She wobbled slightly. She clenched her fists by her side, willing herself to stay calm. "I've done exactly what you wanted," she said, nodding over to where her rifle was in pieces. "So, where is he?"

Flood and Glass exchanged a look that lasted more than a few seconds. Cait took a step toward Flood, gritting her teeth, staring the woman down. The two men with guns—Curran and Schwab—lifted their weapons, but Cait saw Glass gesturing at the pair to lower them.

"*Where's my brother?*" Cait yelled. "You promised me you'd take me to him!"

Flood didn't react to Cait's outburst except to raise a single eyebrow. It was all Cait could do to stop herself from taking a swing at the smug bitch.

And why the hell couldn't she talk to him now? Her power had been dampened by drugs, she assumed—was that it? No, she hadn't heard from her brother since . . . well, since waking up in the high-rise, however long ago that was. She had no way of telling.

No, there was something else, some other reason for his silence.

Flood tilted her head to the other side. "We will," she said. "We will."

"So where is he? Why isn't he here?"

"All in good time, Ms. Smith," said Glass.

Cait shook her head. She glanced around the group again. The guns. The uniforms. Something wasn't adding up. She rubbed her forehead. "For all I know you're a bunch of secret Fleet agents running some kind of black op, with me in the middle, ready to take the fall. The perfect set-up—"

Flood struck Cait across the face with enough force to knock her back onto the floor. Cait gasped as her tailbone connected with the hard ground, the pain from that drowning out the searing heat that spread from one side of her face to another.

"When you speak to a High Priestess you will show *respect,*" said Flood. Her expression was dark. Very, very dark.

Cait felt the side of her face with her fingers. The skin was unbroken, but it hurt like hell. But . . .

"Priestess?"

Careful.

Cait started, looked around. A voice in her head. Her brother? No, it was different, it sounded like . . .

Cait glanced at Glass. He nodded, almost imperceptibly.

Flood stepped forward, towering over Cait.

"You follow the Morning Star now," she said. She turned and waved at the others. "This is taking too long. Get her ready."

Cait stood up again. "Ready for what?" she asked Flood's back.

The black-clad men moved forward. Cait backed away until her legs hit the chair. One of the men was holding a thin silver wand, like a pen. Or like a hypodermic.

Cait met Glass's gaze. "Ready for *what?*" she screamed at him. Then she tripped over the chair behind her, just as she was grabbed by Flood's men.

She struggled and cried out, and there was a sharp, hot sensation in her neck, and then there was nothing.

14

"I trust this investigation will be run with the utmost expediency, Agents." Admiral Zworykin paced back and forth in front of Avalon, Kodiak, and Braben, who stood side by side in the Fleet Admiral's private office. Kodiak felt Avalon bristle beside him as her rank and authority were figuratively reduced to nothing in front of her two staffers by the arrogant bluster of the Fleet's new CIC.

Kodiak frowned as he watched the Fleet Admiral. He was an impressive figure, exuding authority and power, his back ramrod straight, his chest filling out the black uniform of the Psi-Marine Corps, but Kodiak didn't like him. Less than ten minutes into their audience, the first time he'd ever met the man, and Kodiak had already decided. The only way to describe the Admiral was "intense," with his dark hair, dark eyes, and a scowl perpetually on his face. Avalon had told both him and Braben about what had gone down at the Fleet Command Council meeting, when Zworykin had removed his predecessor, Sebela, from power. Zworykin's behavior then had been arrogant, even conceited. Kodiak thought he could see shades of that in the Fleet Admiral today, but there was also a burning impatience and annoyance.

True enough, he had been thrust into an unusual, stressful

situation, suddenly having to deal with a crisis of historic proportions on literally his first day on the job, his assumption of command announced in a public address just a few hours earlier. Kodiak could only imagine the kind of bureaucratic nightmare the Admiral had become mired in.

Kodiak shifted his weight. Behind his back, he squeezed his interlocked fingers until they hurt.

Unless, he thought, Zworykin was responsible. In which case, the bluster, the annoyance, was a bluff for their benefit. Kodiak found himself wondering what Zworykin had meant, just now. A fast investigation . . . just standard military efficiency, or was he looking to have this all swept under the carpet?

And, if he *was* behind it all, then he would have a contingency. A plan to counter the Bureau's investigation. The wheels would be turning already.

Kodiak wondered how much time they really had to get to the bottom of the mystery. Then again, they were at an advantage—Kodiak's status kept him off the records. Anything he looked into, he wouldn't leave a trace. It was logical to assume Zworykin would be tracking the investigation himself, making sure he kept ahead. But with Kodiak—now Avalon's anonymous consultant analyst—the Bureau had a significant advantage.

If the Fleet Admiral was responsible.

Kodiak glanced to his left. The office had a huge window wall, overlooking the Fleet Capitol Complex and the central quarter of New Orem. Brilliant morning light poured in, casting a bright, wide oblong across the floor between the three of them, and the Admiral. Kodiak glanced down at it, considering how accurately it represented the barrier between the investigation and the head of the Fleet. Kodiak glanced at Avalon, standing next to him. The sunlight caught her long red hair, her whole outline glowing.

"Of course, sir," said the chief. "The Bureau will use every resource we have available. Special Agent Braben has full authority under my special powers provision. Analyst Amell is a specialist we have brought in to assist."

Kodiak felt his throat tighten. Amell was his new cover identity—the Bureau had hundreds of these prepared, each with a long, entirely fake, history seeded through Fleet records. The Fleet Command Council knew about this, of course, and Kodiak was sure the military arm had a similar program in place. But there was no reason for Zworykin to be suspicious. No reason for him not to take Commander Avalon's word.

Zworykin stopped pacing. He looked Kodiak up and down, gave a *hmmm,* then moved to stand by the window wall. He gazed out at the city for a moment, squinting into the light.

Then, without turning, he said, "Your supposition is understandable, but your theory spurious."

Kodiak exchanged a look with Avalon, with Braben. He had to keep quiet, falling into his role as the consultant, but the Admiral's comment caught him by surprise. They hadn't voiced any particular theory yet, but it appeared that Zworykin was already suspicious.

So what was this? A double bluff? The guilty deliberately protesting? Or was Zworykin innocent and simply stating the truth?

Braben, as official head of the investigation, took a deep breath. "So it wasn't you eliminating the opposition?"

Kodiak winced. He might have put it in slightly different terms. He glanced at Avalon. She looked back at him, her eyebrow raised.

Zworykin turned from the window, a thin smile on his face as he faced Braben. "I had already eliminated the opposition, as you put it, when I relieved Admiral Sebela of his duty. He had failed the Fleet, Agent. Remember that. What I did, I did for *all* of us. We can afford no more failures, no more rash experiments like the Shadow Protocol. Change was needed, and not a moment too soon." He took a step forward, hands clasped behind his back, head held high. "But I was not involved with Sebela's death."

Kodiak scratched his cheek. He glanced at Braben, who nodded, giving "Consultant Analyst Amell" permission to speak.

"But, sir," said Kodiak, "having Admiral Sebela killed was, at the very least, convenient, right? I mean, there's no risk he could gather his supporters, push you out again, right? His faction is thrown into chaos, which only serves to strengthen your own loyalists."

Kodiak held his breath. Had he gone too far? Maybe. But now wasn't the time to pussyfoot around. Zworykin had brought it up himself. So why not confront the issue head-on?

Zworykin laughed and turned back to the window. He gestured to the expanse of New Orem beyond. "As I said, Agent, your supposition is understandable. Logical, even. The impact of Sebela's assassination is beneficial to my own position. That is a fact I cannot deny. But, as I have already said, I have no connection to the murder. The assassin, whether acting alone or in concert with some other groups, is out *there* somewhere." Zworykin pointed to the window.

That was when it shattered, the entire wall exploding inwards.

Kodiak recoiled, turning instinctively from the shower of glass that seemed to fill the office. As he turned, he saw Commander Avalon dive for Braben, but as Braben was pulled around, a shard of glass sliced through the arm of his suit, leaving a bright red trail. Kodiak ducked his head and curled his back to the explosion as hundreds of the shards pummeled his armored vest. He crabbed sideways toward the other two, thinking he could shield them . . . but then it was over. Braben and Avalon were crouched on the floor, Kodiak standing over them as a stiff wind whipped smoke, glass dust, and thin plastiform files from the Admiral's desk into the air around him. Already he could hear Avalon yelling into the comm on the collar of her uniform as the doors to the office burst open, the two marines on guard rushing in, weapons raised. An alarm screamed, but was nearly drowned out by the sound of the wind.

"This is Commander Avalon, L, one-triple-nine-double-zero. Initiate full security lockdown on the Capitol Complex itself. Nobody gets in or out. Confirm please."

Kodiak spun around, fearing the worst. And he was right.

Zworykin lay on his back in front of his desk. His eyes were open, staring at the ceiling, and there was a long seeping line of red down the side of his face. In the center of his forehead was a black circle. As Kodiak watched, the pool of blood under Zworykin's head grew.

The marines pushed Kodiak aside as they checked Zworykin's body. Kodiak felt Braben's hand on his shoulder.

"Are you okay?" asked the agent, raising his voice in Kodiak's ear so he could be heard.

Kodiak just shook his head. He turned to Avalon. The chief had her staser pistol out and was by the wall, peering out, her other arm shielding her face.

Kodiak jogged over to her.

"I guess that proves it wasn't him, then," she said. She gestured with her gun. "The shooter must have been positioned somewhere over there."

Kodiak followed Avalon's line. The Capitol Complex was a complicated collection of buildings, some low, some the tallest skyscrapers in New Orem, occupying a sizeable chunk of city real estate. The Fleet Admiral's office faced west, looking out toward the Fleet Memorial, a vast patch of green visible between the city buildings, stretching to the horizon. Other structures in the Capitol Complex were clustered around either side of the office block they were in, curving around to form a plaza at street level below. Directly across from the office was a large, wide building with a flat roof.

Kodiak looked back toward Zworykin's body. The direction he had been thrown, the angle of the shattered glass covering the office. Avalon's estimate seemed pretty good.

More marines ran in, along with medical staff. Within moments, the large office was crowded as Avalon began issuing orders.

Kodiak pulled Braben over to one side, their feet crunching on glass.

"What are you thinking, Von?"

"I'm thinking that it might not have been Zworykin, but this is still an inside job, has to be," said Kodiak. He pointed to the building opposite their own.

Braben nodded. "There's no way anyone would be able to access that rooftop without Fleet authorization."

Kodiak rolled his neck. He felt his strength begin to ebb, the aftereffects of the massive jolt of adrenaline. Because . . . holy *shit,* what the hell was going on? Now it was two Fleet Admirals down.

Kodiak turned back to where Zworykin lay, his body now surrounded by marines and medical staff. Kodiak almost felt light-headed . . . the surprise, the shock. Jesus, it was . . .

Two Fleet Admirals dead?

Two Fleet Admirals dead.

My God.

Who would be next? Because this sure as hell was the start of something big. As if the first assassination hadn't thrown them into chaos, this was . . . unprecedented.

The Fleet was under attack.

And it was up to him, and Braben, and the chief, to figure it all out. But not only that, they had to *protect* the Fleet. Whoever was next in line from Zworykin was now, presumably, a prime target as well.

And . . . what about them? If it *was* an inside job—if Zworykin had been *watched*—did that mean they, the investigative team, were targets too?

Too many thoughts. Too many possibilities. Jesus, what was the *motive* for all this?

Kodiak turned on his heel, looking around the room, running his hands through his hair. On the other side of the room, Commander Avalon was talking to two others in uniform, clearly some of Zworykin's staff. She still had her staser out, a sight that made Kodiak twitch his hand over his own gun on his belt. He looked down at his chest, which was covered in glass dust. But his vest had protected him. Then he remembered what he had seen—Braben was watching the crowd around Zworykin's body, the Admiral himself hidden in the middle of the crush of marines and medical personnel.

"Hey," said Kodiak. Braben turned; Kodiak pointed to his arm. "You need to get that looked at."

Braben lifted his arm, his eyes going wide as if he hadn't noticed he'd been injured. "Oh, shit. *Dammit.*"

Kodiak nodded toward the door. "Go get fixed up. We'll stay here—meet back in the bullpen."

"Roger that," said Braben, already heading out of the office. He gave a nod to the chief as he passed her; she acknowledged, but was still deep in her conference. As Kodiak watched Braben go, the chief caught his eye. She shook her head.

Kodiak sighed. Dammit, he'd been right. Things were getting much, *much* worse.

15

Wake up, sis.

Cait took a breath and blinked, but saw nothing but infinite, formless black.

Come on, you can do this. Wake up!

Maybe she was asleep. Maybe she was dead. Maybe she was dead and dreaming and the reason she could hear her brother's voice in her head was because she was dead like he was.

You're not dead.

Well, okay then. She blinked, and stared, and opened her eyes wide to the dark, but it didn't change. There was a funny taste in her mouth. Sour. Rotten.

I'm not dead either.

I know. I know. IknowIknowIknowIknowIknow.

So wake the hell up, Caitlin Smith. You have to move. Now!

Caitlin Smith. He said it in that certain, cheeky way, mocking the tone their parents used when they were in trouble when they were young, just like every parent in the world did. Back then, that world was full of life and color and light. Now there was nothing but a void. An absence of everything.

They drugged you. It's heavy stuff but you'll feel better soon. You need to move.

She wondered where he had been. Wondered why he hadn't been answering her calls, her cries for help.

I know. I'm sorry. But sometimes . . . it's like there's a barrier between us. Like they isolate me, cut me off. I'm sorry. But it's time to move. Now.

Cait sighed. It was a deep breath, somehow too deep, making her lungs ache. It was loud too. Loud enough to attract the attention of whoever it was who was standing near. The soft darkness around her was filled with the sound of hard boots on a hard floor; then the darkness was replaced by a bright white light as the black bag was pulled off her head.

Glass peered down at Cait's face, scrunching the bag in his hands. Then he moved away, and Cait was blinded by the bright light hanging directly above her.

"I'm sorry," said Glass, somewhere to Cait's left. He even sounded like he meant it. There were more footsteps, and then someone else leaning over her. It took a moment for Cait's eyes to adjust as the new person blocked out the light, her silhouette resolving into the hard features of the High Priestess, Flood.

Inside Cait's mind, the voice of her brother told her that she could *do it,* and then it was quiet, and all Cait could hear was her own ragged breathing, wet and heavy.

Drugged. Drugged and black-bagged, again. Cait rolled her head away from the light and she found this helped clear her mind. She had a fair idea now of how things were going down. She knew that she wasn't *working* for Flood's group, not how they had said, back at the beginning, when they had first got in touch that night at the Fleet Academy. Cait, alone in her dorm, the message appearing on her personal comm with, impossibly, no sender. And each night after that for one week, for two weeks. Impossible to ignore. They *knew* things. Things about her. About her brother.

About what had happened to him. What had *really* happened to him. And about what the Fleet was doing. What the war was about.

Who they were really fighting.

And what she could do about it. If only she joined them.

But it wasn't like that, was it? No. They were *using* her, plain and simple. And like a fool she hadn't realized that until it was too late. Like a fool she thought she was going to be part of the group, one of them. She had abandoned her family, her training, her old life—*everything*—because she thought she was going to make a difference, because the secrets the Fleet was keeping were too big and that people had to *know.* Because millions of people were being killed for no reason, and that had to stop.

And together, they had promised they would do just that.

And now she was lying in a dark hole somewhere in the wreckage of Salt City. Because they had lied. Because they were the Morning Star.

And nothing the Morning Star said was true. *Nothing.*

Cait wanted to cry, but her vocal cords just clicked and she sighed breathlessly. There was a tapping sound, metal on metal, from her other side. Cait turned her head in that direction, and a small metal table resolved in her vision. Flood was fussing with something on it. Metal instruments. Lots of them. They looked medical. *Surgical.*

Cait took a desperate breath and tried to lift her head up, straining as hard as she could. She couldn't move it, and she realized there was a restraint across her forehead, loose enough that she could turn her head to the left and right, but that was it. She pulled on her wrists, tried to raise her legs, but they were held in place too. She was strapped to the table.

She lay back and closed her eyes. Her head continued to clear as the drugs wore off. Her breathing settled. Maybe her talent would come back. Maybe it would help her.

She held her breath, willing with all her energy to feel that buzz, the electric prickle on her skin.

There was nothing.

Cait let out her breath and licked her dry lips and, turning once more to watch Flood at the other table, tried to speak again.

"Where is my brother?" she spat between clenched teeth, the effort making her head thump and black stars flutter around the edge of her vision.

"You'll see him soon," said Glass from somewhere out of sight. Cait turned her head back to the left, but all she could see was the edge of his long pale coat as he stood somewhere just behind her. Flood still hadn't spoken. Cait couldn't work out who was in charge of the group—it had seemed to be Flood, and she had called herself a High Priestess, but Glass seemed pretty chatty, and much more relaxed. He seemed out of place, the opposite of the tightly wound, fervent Flood. Maybe it was just a good cop, bad cop routine.

And maybe they were behind it, behind her brother's voice. Glass was psi-abled, apparently. So maybe it was them, faking it, using his dead voice to string her along.

No, it's okay. It's really me, sis.

Cait felt herself tense up.

Don't answer. They can't hear me, but they'll probably be able to hear you. I'm getting a little boost, is all. All part of the plan, don't worry.

Cait focused on her breathing. In, and out. In, and out.

Remember that time when I climbed that tree in the front yard, and you told me not to but I wouldn't listen? And you were right, because I slipped on the high branch and fell and cracked my arm on the ground. And then we both ended up in the hospital, because when Mom found us we were both laid out at the bottom of the tree, both of us with broken arms? We had to tell them we had both climbed the tree and fallen out, because there was no other explanation for why we had both got hurt.

Tyler's voice filled Cait's head like warm morning light. It was him, had to be. His voice wasn't faked. He really was alive. Which meant her captors were telling the truth.

Cait screwed her eyes tight. A thousand thoughts crowded her mind. The members of the Morning Star were delusional. She knew that much. Everything they said about the Fleet, about the war, was a lie. Their worldview was skewed far, far into the realms of fantasy.

But they were telling the truth about her brother. And if what they said had happened to him was true, what did that mean for everything else they said was going on?

Were they actually *right?*

Cait opened her eyes and pulled on the straps holding her wrists, enough to rattle the table. Flood's face reappeared, floating over her own.

"Time for your next task," she said, "and the glorious future that awaits you." Flood pursed her lips and turned her face as she looked down on Cait, like she was waiting for an answer.

There it was. The crazy. The Morning Star disciples were psycho zealots. Samantha Flood a prime example.

"Glorious future?" Cait whispered. "You really are one screwed-up bitch, aren't you?"

Cait flinched, waiting for the sting of the blow she was sure was coming as the High Priestess lost her very short temper again. But all Flood did was laugh.

"You'll understand soon enough," she said. Then she stood up and vanished from Cait's vision.

The table jerked suddenly, and the room began to move, rotating slowly from right to left as the table to which Cait was strapped was turned over with the grinding hum of an electric motor. Cait pulled against the restraints on animal instinct, fight or flight, as she saw Glass standing nearby, and then Flood's guard dogs, watching. She saw another table and then cables, thick and thin, trailing away from equipment.

And then the table stopped with a shudder, and she was looking at floor. It was shiny, plasticky, covered in more of the cables.

She felt the strap across her forehead tighten, removing her ability to turn her head. Her senses now cleared of the lingering effects of the drug by a fresh surge of adrenaline, she realized that there was nothing behind the back of her head and neck—there was an opening in the table, running from her occipital bone down to the middle of her shoulder blades.

Now she knew what she was on—it was an operating table, the same kind used by the Fleet, when direct access to a psi-marine's central nervous system was required. But she was not in a Fleet medical center. The equipment had to have been stolen, or someone had built a pretty good version of their own.

Cait struggled against the restraints, but hanging upside down was disorienting, and the more she strained, the dizzier she felt.

"Let's get it over with," she heard Glass say. Cait cried out in protest, screaming as many curse words as she knew at the bastards who were doing this to her. Then she felt something cold and wet applied to the back of her neck.

And then she felt something exquisitely sharp, pain like nothing in the world, and the room and its contents were once more, thankfully, replaced by the infinite and pillow-soft blackness.

16

The Bureau bullpen was even fuller than before, if that was possible, thought Kodiak as he stood back to survey his work. On one side of the room, close to his desk—bathrobe from the safe house still on the back of his chair—he had wheeled in a new operations board, a sheet of translucent material four meters wide, two meters tall. With it, he could call up any data a holodisplay could, but with a real board, he could do something you couldn't do with a hologram—stick things to it. Kodiak felt a little old-fashioned, but screw it, this was how he liked to work.

The Fleet was in trouble. Big trouble. It had been from the moment their leader, Sebela, had fallen in front of millions of viewers at the Fleet Memorial. But now, with his replacement taken out the same way, the buzz of everyone working at the Bureau felt like it could tip over into full-blown panic. The work helped—for Kodiak too, burying himself in it, not allowing dangerous, fearful thoughts to cloud his judgment.

But as he turned, arms folded, to look out across the bullpen, he began to feel better. The room was full of anxiety and stress as dozens of agents worked furiously, coordinating the city-wide lockdown and collating reports that came in from the marines and agents out there enforcing it, analyzing data from the crime scenes, examining forensic data.

But that anxiety was good. That stress.

If you weren't afraid of failure, then something was wrong.

Kodiak walked back to his desk, the holodisplay floating above it showing a stack of unread messages. Kodiak sat and began sifting through the most urgent ones.

They were mostly reports on the lockdown. New Orem had been flooded with marines, who were conducting a building-to-building, door-to-door sweep. The city itself was, for all intents and purposes, closed and sealed: no one in or out, all road traffic stopped, bridges and tunnels sealed, air traffic likewise grounded and the public spaceport shut down. The Fleet's own space facilities continued to run as required, more marines arriving and only vital supplies being sent on automatic, the cargo loaders checked and scanned manually before they headed to orbit and Earth's quickspace jump point.

The lockdown itself had actually been easy to implement, the process following a standard set of procedures and orders established in the wake of the Spider attack on Earth forty years before. That was the only time the war had struck at the heart of the Fleet, the surprise attack destroying the moon and most of the Southern Hemisphere. It had happened before Kodiak, Braben, and Avalon had been born, but there were agents in the bullpen who remembered that day well. The jagged shards of the moon had remained in the sky for a year afterward—a horrific memorial to the millions of dead and a reminder that humanity was fighting for its very existence—before they'd been mined, cleaned up by the Hollywood Mining Conglomerate. To save Earth from the devastating tidal effects of losing its only natural satellite, the Fleet had constructed a series of gravitational platforms, orbiting at a quarter of a million klicks.

And now they had a new kind of conflict to deal with. Out there, on the Warworlds and in deep space, the Fleet engaged the Spiders. Here, on Earth, the very heart of the Fleet had been ripped out in a crisis unheard of in Fleet history.

Kodiak felt that ever-present anxiety bloom in his chest. Not just one Admiral dead, *two*. This had to be the beginning of something much larger, a conspiracy designed to unravel the Fleet in its entirety. And then the Spiders really would win, and it wouldn't just be the Southern Hemisphere burned away next time.

Kodiak closed the last report and stood, moving back to the ops board. He tapped the surface, bringing up an image of Zworykin's body, sprawling in the Fleet Admiral's office. Face up. Eyes open. Black circle in the forehead, blood draining out underneath him. The sniper's plasma bolt had been right on target, shattering the wall window as it passed through it and taking out the target with surgical precision. It had been the same with Sebela, at the Fleet Memorial. Ballistics evidence was scant at both scenes—the shooter had been an expert and had used a weapon appropriate to his level of skill—but even though the weapons report had been brief, the two men had been killed by the same gun, that much was clear.

Kodiak frowned, tapped the board again. Next to Zworykin's image appeared his predecessor, Sebela. In contrast to the crime scene photograph, Sebela's picture was an official Fleet portrait, the Fleet Admiral looking out into the bullpen in a three-quarter turn, a faint smile on his lips. There were plenty of images taken at the Fleet Memorial. Kodiak had reviewed them all, but right now he didn't feel the need to repeat the process.

Kodiak dragged the two images over to one side, dragged their corners until they were roughly the same size, then reached for the pen sitting on the small sill that ran along the base of the board. Underneath the pair of pictures, he wrote SHADOW PROTOCOL in fluorescent green capitals and underlined it.

"You think that's important somehow?"

Kodiak turned as Braben approached, holding two steaming cups of coffee. He held one out to Kodiak, then shifted his cup to the other hand and flexed his injured arm.

"How you feeling?"

Braben winked as he sipped his drink. "On the mend, my friend."

He pointed at the board with an index finger extended from the rim of his cup. "So . . ."

Kodiak shrugged. "Is it important? Yes. No. Maybe. Whatever the Shadow Protocol is, it was bad enough to freak out some very important people."

Braben took another draw on his mug. "Enough for them to start knocking off Fleet Admirals?"

Kodiak tapped the board with the pen. "We can't discount it. Sebela announces the failure of a major project, one that's a big old secret. Zworykin uses that moment of weakness to move his people into position and take over command. Then they're both killed, one after the other. Could be a coincidence—"

"Or could be connected."

"Right."

Braben lowered himself onto the edge of the nearest desk. Kodiak watched his partner as he stared at the pictures on the ops board.

"At least this means it wasn't Zworykin."

Kodiak frowned. "Unless something went wrong, the people he was working with deciding he was a liability as well." He shrugged. "Maybe, I don't know."

Braben reached forward to tap at the board, bringing up commands and scrolling menus. Soon, next to the pictures of the two victims, were displayed a dozen different items: a schematic map of the Fleet Memorial; photographs of the podium and tiered seating behind it from five different angles and distances; a schematic map of the Capitol Complex, and photographs of the exterior, including some taken from the rooftop opposite the Fleet Admiral's office, the shooter's likely position; a map of New Orem, a grid so tightly packed at this scale it looked more like a piece of abstract art than a map; lists of high-ranking Fleet officers and their photographs, some outlined in red—loyal to Zworykin—and some in blue—members of Sebela's inner circle.

Kodiak drained his coffee, wincing at the heat as he looked over the data. Everything they knew about the case was there in front of him. If only they could see the connections, start building a picture.

Then he tapped the schematic of the building opposite the Fleet Admiral's private office. "There's no way the shooter could gain access to the roof if they didn't have clearance."

Braben nodded. "We're running through the security lists now, interviewing everybody who has access to that building, right down to the cleaning crews and maintenance. But we really need to look at the manifest, pronto. That'll be a big help."

Kodiak glanced over Braben's shoulder. "Speaking of which," he said, as Commander Avalon walked over. Her expression was dark. Kodiak braced himself, wondering what fresh batch of bad news she was bringing from the emergency meeting of the Fleet Command Council.

"Gentlemen," she said.

"So, how did it go?" asked Kodiak.

Avalon pursed her lips. "As well as expected. With Zworykin and Sebela both dead, they've instituted emergency powers. Commander Hammerstein has been promoted to Admiral—he, Admiral Laverick, and Commandant Vaughn have formed a triumvirate to command the Fleet until the situation is resolved. It's out on the lightspeed link, but a public statement will be issued in an hour."

Kodiak nodded. That was good, at least. The public needed reassurance, and fast—they needed to see the Fleet was handling the situation, that everything was, on the surface anyway, under some kind of control.

"That makes three new targets for the shooter," said Braben, looking at Avalon. He gestured to the ops board. "We don't know who's behind this—their motives, even their means. We don't know what's coming next. This could be just the beginning."

"That's true," said the chief. "And for the moment, the triumvirate is being taken to more secure facilities under the Capitol Complex. Access is going to be very tight."

"Okay," said Kodiak. "Let's start looking at the Fleet manifest then."

But Avalon shook her head. Kodiak looked at her, his eyes wide.

"What?"

"We don't have clearance yet."

Kodiak's jaw flapped. He looked at Braben, who rolled his neck and turned to their commander.

"What do you mean, we don't have clearance?" he asked. "Manifest access is SOP. So why don't we have it now?"

"Because someone doesn't want us to have it," said Kodiak.

The pair looked at him.

That clinched it. Something was going on, something in the Fleet Capitol Complex itself. Two Admirals removed. Maybe the start of something more.

Avalon sighed and folded her arms. "Dammit," she said. "There's someone in authority, watching us."

"Right," said Braben. "They would have known the Bureau would investigate, so now they're running interference."

The three of them stood in silence for a moment, the chaos of the bullpen swirling around them as Kodiak let that information sink in. How far did it go? Who was involved? Was it the Fleet, or did the tendrils of the conspiracy's network reach into the Bureau itself?

Now there was a comforting thought. Then again, that was part of the reason for bringing him back from Helprin's Gambit. Officially dead, with a clean new cover ID, anything he did would go under the radar.

Which gave Kodiak another idea.

He lowered his voice and pulled close to the other two, making sure his words were covered by the hubbub in the bullpen. "I have an idea." He moved to the ops board and picked up the pen, then nodded at his colleagues to join him.

Avalon raised her eyebrows. "I'm listening."

Kodiak smiled. "I'm not going to tell you."

The chief blinked, and looked at Braben. Braben shrugged, his brow creased in confusion.

Kodiak waggled the pen at the chief. "Why did you bring me back from deep cover?"

"Because this is a red ball situation, Von," said the chief. "You're a good agent. We need all hands on deck."

"Right," said Kodiak. "And, as a consequence of my current legal status, I can stay off the radar."

Avalon nodded. "Yes. Mike has clearance to get you anywhere, but your cover ID is a blank slate. If anyone is looking for you, they won't find a thing."

"Which is exactly what we need right now."

A small grin started to creep up the chief's face. "Do what you need to do," she said.

Kodiak matched her smile. He glanced at Braben. "You ready?"

Braben raised an eyebrow. "Me?"

"Yup. You heard the chief. You're my clearance. And I'm going to need that where we're going."

Braben sighed. "Are you going to tell *me* what your grand idea is?"

Kodiak considered. He should tell him, at least. But . . . no, he was going to take a risk. He might be off the radar with his cover ID, but Braben wasn't. And if someone *was* watching the investigation, the closer he kept things to his chest, the better. At least for now.

"Sorry Mike, I can't. You just need to trust me."

Braben's response was quick. "With my life, Von. You know that."

Kodiak looked at the chief, who nodded. "Do what you need to do. Just report back when you have something, okay?"

"Yes, ma'am," Kodiak said. He turned to Braben. "Ready?"

Braben sighed and gestured ahead of him.

"Lead the way, man."

17

As he and Braben made their way through the Capitol Complex, Kodiak considered that this was exactly the kind of thing his cover identity had been designed for. Special Agent Von Kodiak was officially dead. He was now Consultant Analyst Nico Amell. Operating on a temporary security clearance granted by Commander Avalon, he was, to anyone outside the Bureau, just an anonymous agent accompanying Braben, the real lead investigator. If anyone was watching, they wouldn't pay him much heed.

That was the theory, anyway.

With security on maximum alert, nearly every door in the Capitol between the Bureau and their destination required security clearance. For the purposes of the investigation, to ensure there were no delays, Braben had been granted level ten clearance—as high as Commander Avalon's herself. Kodiak—as Amell—was classed as Braben's assistant, meaning he could go wherever Braben went without requiring his own authorization. It was that very fact that had inspired Kodiak's plan.

As they walked, Braben had kept up a barrage of questions, but Kodiak had kept tight-lipped, much to the obvious frustration of his partner. Eventually Braben had given up, content apparently to walk in silence, fuming perhaps at Kodiak's lack of transparency.

But it was a deliberate decision. Cover ID or not, Kodiak didn't want any of the potential consequences of his plan piling back onto Braben. He'd take full responsibility—which meant the less Braben knew, the better.

And besides, he had Avalon's backing. Okay, so *she* didn't know what he was doing either. But she had given him carte blanche. He could do what he needed to do to keep the investigation moving, to get results.

Kodiak glanced at the map on his wrist computer as he led Braben on through the labyrinthine cluster of buildings that made up the Fleet Complex. The slight glitch in his plan was that he wasn't entirely sure where exactly they were going . . . but he had a fair idea of where to start looking.

The Complex was filled with marines. It was unsettling, a constant reminder of the dangerous situation the Fleet had been plunged into. Most times the marines just kept on marching, teams of three or four going to wherever they were going, or, as they stood guard at various key positions, ignoring the two agents as they went about their business. But sometimes those guards would watch, their elliptical, opaque helmets tracking Kodiak and Braben. It was an odd feeling, one Kodiak didn't like. He could see Braben was feeling it too, their journey in silence accompanied by a frisson of tension. Kodiak felt for him, but he stuck to his resolve. He would tell Braben what the plan was when he needed to, and not before.

After a half hour of walking corridors, taking elevators, passing through checkpoints, stopping and checking the map, changing direction, walking some more, Kodiak finally pulled up to a large double door at the end of a wide corridor. They were on the fourth level of this particular building, and aside from the marines on duty at the last checkpoint farther back down the passage, they were, for perhaps the first time, now alone.

If he'd read the map correctly, they were close, thought Kodiak.

He glanced at the security panel next to the door and stood back, gesturing to it.

Braben nodded and pressed his palm to the chrome scanner. The red light next to the panel changed to green as it accepted his clearance.

Braben sighed. "You ready to tell me what we're doing yet?"

"Not yet," said Kodiak. He stepped up to the door, which hissed open. He stepped through, Braben on his tail.

The corridor beyond the door was dark and narrow, and ended in just a few short meters in a high gallery that ran around the circumference of a huge, nearly spherical room. Below them were rows of consoles, manned by hundreds of uniformed staff, each wearing the peculiar, insect-like headsets that gave them their FlyEye nickname. The consoles gently curved from one side of the vast room to the other, all facing the giant display that occupied the wall to Kodiak and Braben's right. The display was holographic, but flat, two-dimensional, at least fifty meters tall and double that across. In the center was a projection map of the Earth, a great jagged red line demarcating the destroyed Southern Hemisphere, most of which was featureless. Around this map were others, showing the continents and topographies of a half dozen other worlds. There were star system schematics, quickspace network plots, and other diagrams Kodiak didn't recognize. The vast display was crawling with a mind-boggling amount of data, icons moving and text scrolling as the business of galactic war was managed.

"Holy *shit,*" whispered Braben, his hands on the gallery railing as he took in the scene before him.

Kodiak nodded. The vast chamber was an impressive sight, that was for sure. "Welcome to mission control." He leaned over the rail on his elbows. From the floor of the Fleet's master command center the hum of the hundreds of staff below at work drifted up.

"I've never actually seen it before," said Braben, his voice low, like they were standing in some kind of holy place. Perhaps they were, thought Kodiak. This was a cathedral of war.

"Neither have I," he said, looking around. "Big, isn't it?"

Braben turned away from the rail. "And we are here because?"

Kodiak shook his head and pointed farther down the curving gallery, toward another door. "Call this a shortcut," he said. "What we're looking for is underneath this. Come on. We need to find some stairs."

The two agents stood outside a nondescript door in an empty gray corridor. The corridor was narrow and dim, somehow fitting given they were in the bowels of the Capitol Complex.

The door had a standard Fleet barcode on it and a string of numbers, nothing that indicated what was behind it. Kodiak checked his wrist computer, the icon indicating his location flashing in the middle of a gray nothingness. According to his best guess, this was it. And it made sense too, if he'd guessed the layout and organization of the Capitol Complex correctly. As an agent of twenty years standing, he'd worked both on Earth and off-world, including U-Stars and other platforms. Nearly everything the Fleet built, whether it moved or not, whether it was a temporary command post or a permanent structure like the Capitol Complex itself, followed the same design.

Braben tapped his foot impatiently as he looked up and down the corridor.

"Keep it cool, Agent," said Kodiak.

"You really need to tell me what we're looking for, Von."

Kodiak pointed at the barcode on the door. He was right. It was time to talk. "This is an auxiliary control room," he said. "The Capitol Complex is built like a U-Star, which means that below the bridge—which is mission control, upstairs—there is a secondary center of operations."

"I'm going to regret coming with you, aren't I?" said Braben. "Because we really shouldn't be here."

Kodiak sighed, but he couldn't blame Braben for his cautious approach. He knew he would be the same if he were in his partner's shoes. "But that's the whole point, Mike. Someone doesn't want us to have access to the Fleet manifest. Which means they're hiding something. Which means we need to get access ourselves."

Braben closed his eyes and put his hands on his hips, body language Kodiak recognized all too well. The agent was annoyed . . . and again, Kodiak couldn't blame him. But this was important. Surely his partner realized that? They had two assassinations to solve. The Fleet was in serious trouble.

And someone was withholding vital data from them.

Braben opened his eyes and sighed again. He nodded at the door. "Someone upstairs is going to notice me keying this door. We're not going to have much time before we're caught. How long do you think it will take to look through the manifest?"

"We'll be gone before they know it," said Kodiak. "We're going to take the manifest with us."

Braben shook his head, but he reached forward and activated the door panel with his palm. The lock indicator went from red to green, and the door opened. Braben waved at it. "After you, buddy."

As Kodiak stepped through, he felt a deep sense of relief. As he had predicted, behind the door was a computer room—smaller by an order of magnitude than the vast control center above them, more the size of the Bureau bullpen. But like the main mission control, it housed rows of curved consoles, each with their own holographic displays, all arranged to face the large display that occupied the far wall. The main display was dark, but the holographic monitors above each station were on, a faint blue three-dimensional Fleet logo lazily rotating above each. The control room was inactive, but the stations were asleep, not powered down. That would help speed things up at least, Kodiak thought.

He pulled out the nearest chair and tapped the terminal in front of him to life. The Fleet logo disappeared, replaced with a terminal window. Kodiak flexed his fingers and began typing. He logged in as Nico Amell without any difficulty, then began to navigate through the system until he found what he was looking for.

They were still locked out of the manifest application itself—that required special clearance even for the Bureau Chief, Commander Avalon, clearance that was mysteriously *not* forthcoming, despite the gravity of the situation—but from the auxiliary control room Kodiak had access to the same data feeds as mission control above. Data feeds that included the manifest streams themselves, even though there was no way to view the information.

"Got it," he said. He pulled a data stick out of a pocket and laid it on the console, the device glowing blue as it paired with the computer. Braben moved in beside him and leaned over the console to watch.

"I hope this is a good idea."

"We need this data, Mike," said Kodiak. That was true. What was also true was that accessing the data stream without clearance was a serious offence, if not treasonous.

But it was the right thing to do. Carte blanche. The cover ID. *This* was exactly the kind of thing all that was for. What they were afraid they might *have* to do, if their theory that the assassinations were part of an internal Fleet conspiracy proved true.

Kodiak watched as the manifest data from the time period around the two shootings was copied off onto the data stick, his eyes fixed on the progress bar. There was something buried in there that someone didn't want them to see. He really hoped it was the information they needed to blow this case wide open.

Beside him, Braben checked his wrist computer. "We need to get out of here. How much longer?"

Beep-beep. Beep-beep.

Kodiak spun his chair around. Next to him, Braben already had his staser in his hand.

A machine had entered the room. It was humanoid, bipedal, but clunky and awkward. It had no face, just a blank metal curve with two small but bright lights, one green, one blue, on the left-hand side. It had two arms and two legs, but they were bare metalwork, a series of frames that seemed to fold into each other as the machine took another step forward.

Kodiak's heart raced. It was a servitor, clearly, but he'd never seen one like it in the Fleet. "What the hell is that?" he asked.

"Systems servitor," said Braben. "The Fleet is running a trial program on more human-like systems. A co-op with private enterprise."

Kodiak caught his breath. The machine hadn't moved again. He thought back to his stint on Helprin's Gambit. "What, for maintenance or something?"

"No," said Braben. "Combat."

The machine stood still near the door. It beeped again, the blue and green lights flashing in time with alternating tones.

A combat servitor? That was new, thought Kodiak. The Fleet had kept as much AI tech off the battlefield as possible, unsure if the Spiders would have some way of taking them over at close proximity.

But more pressing was the fact that a *combat servitor* was in the control room with them. With the city lockdown stretching resources, Kodiak guessed they'd unboxed some of the units for back-up.

Before Kodiak could ask his partner another question, Braben lifted his gun and shot the servitor. The machine was enveloped in crackling white arcs of energy; then it toppled forward onto the floor.

Kodiak looked at his partner, his eyes wide.

Braben holstered his gun. "Stasers on stun are great for scrambling electronics," he said. "With any luck they'll just think it was an internal failure."

Kodiak turned back to the console and swept up the data stick. Then he stood and approached the fallen servitor. It was an impressive piece of machinery—clearly designed for function over aesthetics, but there was a certain beauty in that, he thought. "Here's hoping it wasn't reporting to base."

Braben joined him. "Your plan works and we ID the shooter, none of this will matter. In fact, they'll give us the goddamn Fleet medal for this."

Kodiak frowned. "Maybe they will," he said. He went to the open door and ducked his head out. The corridor was still empty. "Let's go before we get more company."

18

Cait screamed. She couldn't move, couldn't see. There was nothing but darkness and pain. She screamed again, and the world resolved around her.

Glass was there. He held a damp cloth in one hand, and he mopped her brow. Cait stared at him, wide-eyed in terror.

She couldn't feel the cloth against her skin. Couldn't feel the water as Glass gently squeezed it out of the cloth, the look on his face one of kind, gentle concern. The signal-to-noise ratio of her senses was too low. Everything—her, the world, the universe, *everything*—was pure pain, an infinite cycle of hot and cold, electric sharpness, and a dull wooden ache.

And she couldn't move. She screamed again.

"She's alive, then." A voice from somewhere in the room. Flood. Cait clenched her teeth and ground them. Yes, she was alive. Despite the pain, the horror of it, she was one up.

She was still alive.

"I don't like her reaction," said Glass. "I've reduced the dose of suppressant to see if that helps. It's a risk, though. It might be . . . dangerous." He glanced sideways as Flood moved into view.

The High Priestess of the Morning Star, still clad in her black combat uniform like she was a front-line soldier in the very war she wanted to derail, just sniffed and whipped a stray line of hair behind one ear.

"She survived the procedure," she said. "That's all that matters." Then came her smile, cold and cruel. "Well done, Glass. You have proved your usefulness admirably." And then her face was gone.

Damn, she's cold.

Cait laughed weakly as her brother whispered his thoughts to her. Her laugh turned into a choke, her choke into a cough. Glass pulled the damp cloth away as Cait wrenched her head to the side, letting a mouth full of sour bile spill to the floor. She turned her head back and blinked away the tears. The pain was fading already. Glass nodded at her.

"Side effect of the anesthesia, I'm afraid," he said.

Cait closed her eyes. Flexed her toes, her fingers. The feeling was coming back, warmth spreading out across her body like she was being lowered into a blood-warm bath.

That's it, sis. Keep going.

Her brother's voice echoed in her mind. Maybe that was a side effect of the anesthesia too.

Nope.

Oh.

Or maybe it is, and you're dreaming all this.

Yeah.

Like you dreamed my dream. Dreamed about the war—my war. My death. That was all just a side effect too, right?

Cait smiled. Glass frowned and peered down at her, so Cait closed her eyes. She preferred the darkness to her current situation; at least while her head was clearing, the pain continued to subside. Without thinking she flexed an arm, lifted her hand—and realized there was no strap holding it down. She opened her eyes again, raising her head up to see.

She was in a bed, not on a table. There was black plastic padding underneath her, a silver survival blanket crinkling on top.

We need to leave soon.

"Okay," she said aloud. Then she glanced up at Glass. He was still frowning as he sat on a stool next to the bed.

"Try not to move too much," he said.

Flood reappeared at his side, her expression dark. She looked at Glass, and Glass sighed.

"She'll be fine. Stop worrying. I did my job—something nobody in your organization could do, remember."

Cait let her head drop back down. Your organization? So, that was interesting. She'd been right. Glass didn't look or act like the others, because he wasn't part of thc Morning Star.

Flood ignored him and walked around to the top of the bed to look down at Cait. Cait decided the High Priestess didn't look any better upside down.

"How long?" Flood asked.

"Three hours and we can get moving," Glass replied.

Flood said nothing more. She just walked off. Cait listened to her footsteps as they left the room and echoed dully until they were out of earshot.

Cait closed her eyes again, waiting for her brother's voice, but it didn't come again. She licked her lips.

"So where are we going?" she asked.

She heard Glass shift on the stool. "I'm sorry we had to do what we did, Ms. Smith, really I am. But I had no choice. It had to be done," he said.

Cait frowned. "What did you do to me?"

Glass appeared in her vision, leaning over her face. He smiled.

And then she winced. The feeling was returning to her body . . . and she became aware of a dull ache in the back of her neck. It seemed to pulse with her heartbeat, each crescendo becoming sharper and sharper.

Glass seemed to notice her increasing distress. He moved away from her eye line, and a moment later there was the familiar metal-on-metal clatter as he got something from a nearby surgical trolley.

Cait tried to shake her head as he reappeared, a hypodermic wand in his hand, but when she moved her head the back of her neck erupted in a blaze of exquisite fire. She cried out and remembered the way the operating table had been flipped over, allowing surgical access to her spinal column.

"What did you do to me?"

The pain was almost too much. The world began to dissolve again.

"It'll pass," said Glass. "I'm truly sorry."

He pressed the hypodermic to Cait's arm, and the pain faded. She closed her eyes, ready to accept the warm, soft embrace of oblivion once more.

Sorry, sis, not this time.

Cait's eyes flickered open. She was alone in the room, and it was darker, Glass having dimmed the lights as he left. How long she had been out, she had no idea.

She listened again, but there was nothing. Maybe she'd imagined Tyler's voice. Dreamed it. And all she wanted to do now was to sleep and to dream, luxuriating in the floating breathlessness of—

That's just the painkillers.

She opened her eyes properly now. The world became sharper as the effects of the last dose began to fade.

That's it. Fight it.

Cait sighed. She needed to sleep, to rest, to heal.

No time. Come on, focus. It's time to get out of here.

Cait raised her head. The dark room was lit only by the few instruments arranged near to her bed, displaying numbers, graphs, medical data to anybody who cared to look. Cait cast her eye over the equipment. There was a heart rate monitor alongside another machine that showed a series of moving lines racing across its display. Brain function? Cait couldn't have cared less.

All set.

She sat up and paused, just in case being upright made her puke or faint, or both.

Come on!

She closed her eyes. "Where are you? Where are they keeping you?"

First things first. We need to go before they come back.

"Okay, okay, okay." A deep breath. Upright seemed to be working.

Next step was to see if she could stand.

Look, we don't have time for this. But you are my only hope for getting out of here. We need to go. Now.

Cait opened her eyes. Her neck was stiff, almost immobile, the pain just a faint burn, like a sunburn. She reached behind her head and felt two things: a series of leads trailing from her skull, and a plastic bandage taped into place.

She felt around the leads blindly until she located the sensors. She gave one an experimental tug, and it came free easily. Relieved that they were not drilled into her skull, she pulled the rest off. Then she leaned forward and felt around the bandage. It ran from the base of her hairline down to the first big vertebra she could feel easily under her skin. She pressed the bandage and the room spun for just a moment, but then everything settled.

What the *hell* have they done?

Worry about that later, sis. You need to leave.

Cait swung her legs out from under the blanket. She was still dressed, even down to her boots, the only clothing they had removed being her gray T-shirt and the black hoodie. She looked around and saw them dumped out of the way against the wall, sitting on top of her backpack.

Cait stood, one hand braced behind her on the bed. It took a moment to adjust to being back on her feet, but she took that opportunity to get her bearings.

The room was small and plain—it wasn't a permanent medical facility, but a fairly well-fitted field hospital. Everything was portable, on wheels or in stacked cabinets that could be closed up and carried. Looking down, she could trace the various power cables from the monitors and lights across the floor to a large industrial board, the fat cable of which was laid out against the wall, snaking around half the room before connecting to a big wall outlet.

She was still in the warehouse, somewhere in Salt City, she thought, the temporary medical facilities set up for her benefit.

Whether it was that thought that made her feel nauseous, or the drugs Glass had pumped her with, or the abuse her body had withstood over the last few hours—days?—she didn't know, but the room spun a little.

Pushing off the bed, she made a beeline for her clothing and pack. Picking them up off the floor was a bigger challenge than she had expected, the dizziness coming upon her suddenly. She stood back up, balanced herself against the wall, and as the feeling passed, tried again.

Success.

She pulled the T-shirt and hoodie on. The pack, to her surprise, still had the disassembled gun in it. It was useless as a self-defensive weapon, but she didn't see any benefit in leaving it behind either. Zipping the pack shut, she flipped it onto her back and stood.

Footsteps, approaching from behind the closed door.

Someone's coming.

"No shit," Cait muttered. There was nowhere to hide, and she knew in her addled state she was too slow to get back into the bed. Instead, she flattened herself against the wall behind the door and hoped she could summon the strength to fight her way out with her bare hands if she needed to.

The door opened, and the light rose up to full brightness. Cait squinted, the sudden light painful. She held her breath, fighting down the nausea creeping up from her stomach. A light-headedness came over her, along with a pins-and-needles pricking on her skin, like all her hairs were standing on end.

It was Glass. He walked to the bed quickly, pulling the survival blanket aside as he realized it was empty. He spun around, and—

Cait launched herself forward, almost without thinking. She threw her hand forward, like she was going to shove him in the back. But before she made contact, Glass buckled, his back arched like he'd been struck, sending him crashing into the side of the bed. Then he spun sideways, banging his head on the hard edge of the instrument table on his way to the floor, where he lay on his back, his neck at a peculiar angle, his eyes open and staring.

Cait toppled forward onto the bed, cradling her hand in her arm like she'd been hurt herself. She pushed her forehead into the bed, gasping for breath. Then she forced herself upright, clenching her jaw as she fought to control the dizziness. She gasped again as her movements pulled the bandage on the back of her neck painfully tight.

The lights were on, and the door was open. There was no sound except a steady tick from the monitors next to the bed. Glass's lifeless eyes stared up at her.

She lifted her hand, flexing the fingers. She hadn't touched him, but she knew exactly what had happened. Glass himself had said it. He'd cut the suppressant, and now her talent was back. Cait was relieved and scared at the same time. She'd killed Glass, unintentionally.

But she had to escape. She was fighting for her life now. She had to get out, get somewhere safe, figure this mess out.

"Shit. Shit shit shit shit *shit.*"

What are you waiting for?

"Jesus, wait a second, will you?" Cait said. Shaking her head clear, she moved to the door and stepped out into the corridor.

There was no sign of anyone. The corridor was lit by ceiling tiles, but they were set into an unfinished grid of pipework, tendrils of translucent plastic hanging at regular intervals—packing material of some sort, the tattered streamers slowly unraveling from the abandoned construction work over her head. Looking around, she saw the walls were likewise unfinished, wiring still visible, running alongside a steel framework.

She slowly headed down the corridor. As she closed in on a corner, she heard sounds and pulled back. Footsteps and male voices.

Back, around the corner.

Cait nodded, managing to stop herself from speaking aloud this time. She crept back along the wall, down the passageway she had just come, passed the door to the makeshift medical unit, and found herself in a large open space, perhaps intended to be the building's lobby, or a vehicle garage. There were boxes all over the place, and big stacks of long-forgotten, decaying building materials.

There was an entranceway ahead, a low, wide arch, with orange-yellow light pouring in.

Cait ran across the open space, then slammed her back into the archway, gasping in pain and pausing to check that the way was clear.

On the other side of the arch was a street, lit in the dim flickering streetlights she knew so well.

Salt City, industrial quarter, looking pretty much the way it had when she'd walked down on her way to the rendezvous.

No, not rendezvous. *Ambush.*

The ground was wet, and it was still night, although Cait had no idea how much time had passed since she'd been grabbed by Flood's cell. Glancing up, she saw the sky was bruised indigo. Dawn was approaching.

Cait took a breath and ran for her life.

19

Kodiak and Braben slipped back into the Bureau control center. The place was still rammed with agents coordinating the security lockdown and sifting through the data being fed back from the hundreds of marines sweeping the city. The task was monumental, but had so far come back with no results—or at least nothing that required his, Braben's, or Avalon's personal attention. The trio had status reports to review, but as far as Kodiak was concerned, they could wait. Anything important would come directly to them.

The two agents orbited the bullpen on the raised walkway that ran the perimeter, Kodiak picking the planning room on the opposite side, close to where the main ops board was. He gestured for Braben to enter first, then he followed, closed the door, and activated the privacy screen. Immediately the glass walls faded to a flat steel gray.

Braben paced in a tight circle, shaking his head. Kodiak could understand his partner's edginess. What they'd just done was well beyond their authority, even with Avalon's personal authorization. But needs must. The delay in getting access to the Fleet manifest was a deliberate tactic from whomever they were up against, further proof, Kodiak thought, that the whole business was an inside job. There were people in the Fleet who didn't want them to have the information.

Kodiak sat at the table. Braben came to a halt, hands on his hips. He stared at the floor, like he really wanted to say something.

"Take a seat, Mike," said Kodiak. "We need to start sifting data."

Braben sighed and with one hand still on his hip, lifted his other, waggling a finger at Kodiak like he was an angry parent. "Someone is going to find that servitor."

"And when they do they'll send it down to maintenance."

Braben threw his hands up in the air. "They'll know what happened to it, Von. We are going to be in some deep trouble."

Kodiak frowned. Braben was right but, honestly, did that matter? They had the data from the manifest. They'd foiled whoever had been trying to stop them from looking at it. True enough, they'd find the servitor and figure out what had happened to it, but Kodiak thought that hardly mattered at the moment. They could deal with that when this was all over. When they found the shooter. When they figured out *why* the Fleet manifest had been kept from them for so long.

And then nobody would care about how they had got hold of the data, or what they had done to get it. If this let them ID and even locate the shooter, that was all that mattered. The ends most certainly would justify the means.

Kodiak would let nothing stand in the way of the investigation. Nothing.

Kodiak gestured for his partner to sit. "We can worry about that later. Come on, let's get to work."

Braben complied, but he was still agitated, not meeting Kodiak's eye. Kodiak sighed. He really needed his partner's head in the game. But all he could do was get on with it. Braben would be okay, eventually.

Kodiak took the data stick from his pocket and laid it on the table, which lit up, drawing a blue outline around it. A progress bar appeared in front of Kodiak as the table's computer began transferring data. After a few seconds, the copy was complete; then the table display was lit end to end with scrolling text, code from the Fleet manifest taken from the auxiliary control room. Kodiak had to stand up from his chair to see it all. Braben joined him. He whistled.

"This is the raw data from the manifest feed. How the hell do we process this ourselves?"

Kodiak watched the scrolling text. Dammit, Braben had a point there too. The Fleet manifest was a large application, a live-fed database of everything the Fleet owned. He'd used it before—most likely everyone in the Bureau had at some point during the course of their duties and cases, whether to find stolen or missing equipment, or to locate people . . . or their bodies. If it was tagged by the Fleet, it was in the manifest.

But this wasn't the manifest *application*—as Braben had pointed out, this was the raw data feed, millions of lines of meaningless machine code that the manifest application itself would read and process. While the Bureau had access to that application itself on the Fleet's shared servers, as far as Kodiak knew, there was no way to load up a raw data file.

He pulled on his bottom lip, thinking it over. He thought back to his little hack on Helprin's Gambit—that had worked rather well to throw the casino games. Six months on that station and he'd learned quite a lot about computer systems—aided, of course, by the AI maintenance glasses. They did the heavy lifting.

Kodiak turned to Braben. "Did anything get brought back with me from Helprin's Gambit?"

Braben blinked, then shook his head at the change in subject. "Ah . . . yeah, there's a box of evidence. Just what you had on you. Unfortunately we had to leave the casino chips behind."

"Is there a pair of glasses in there? Big, black things. Heavy."

Braben frowned. "Yeah, I think so. Why?"

"Call up the evidence locker and get them brought up." He pointed to the table and the endless screeds of text flowing across its entire surface. "I think I have a way of reading this."

The planning room, even with the privacy shields down, was a perfectly controlled environment. Air temperature, oxygen content, humidity. Sealed off from the Bureau office, it was much like being inside a U-Star in deep space. With even lighting and a stable environment, you could spend *days* in the room and not know it.

Kodiak rubbed his face. Despite the environmental control it felt hot and stuffy. It was his imagination, of course, just the blank gray walls making him feel a little claustrophobic, the pressure of the investigation—of his idea of how to read the manifest data—playing at the back of his mind. Kodiak rolled his neck and began to roll his sleeves up, and then Braben did the same, taking his jacket off and making a big show of folding it nicely over the back of the empty chair next to him. Then he carefully detached his cufflinks and folded the sleeves of his shirt up until both arms were perfectly even. Kodiak couldn't help smiling. Braben noticed and paused, mid-adjustment.

"What?"

Kodiak laughed. "Nothing."

The table chimed, and the data display altered. Kodiak refocused on his task, leaning over the table for a closer look.

At Braben's request, an agent had brought in Kodiak's AI glasses from Helprin's Gambit. They were standard issue for the maintenance crews aboard the platform, using a short-range psi-fi field to pair with the wearer's mind, assisting with any kind of technical repair. On a platform as big as the Gambit, with systems as advanced as they were, the AI glasses were a good way of forgoing hundreds of hours of training for the tech crew, a population of workers with a high turnover.

Now the glasses were being put to a new use. They sat on the table next to Kodiak's arm, pairing immediately with the table computer and, consequently, the Bureau's main systems, as well as Kodiak's mind. Using a standard interface on the table in front of him, with the help of his little AI friend, Kodiak had spent the last couple of hours programming a filter for the manifest data, using the master application itself to read the code they had taken from the auxiliary control room without actually loading it up. Access to the master app was no problem—it was the actual data loading that was blocked until they had the requisite security clearance. Something they *still* didn't have.

Kodiak was pleased with the results—Braben, less so, although he had admitted he was impressed. The processed data, now displayed in the manifest application, was still too much to handle manually, but once his system was working, Kodiak had set up a series of filters, using a simple process of elimination to disregard the bulk of the irrelevant matches and ditch them right from the start, allowing them to drill down to the salient leads.

The table now showed a big map of the Capitol Complex, zoomed in on an area that included the Fleet Admiral's private office on one side and the flat-topped building opposite, the shooter's supposed vantage point. The map was swarming with tags, each representing somebody carrying a Fleet manifest tracker embedded in their brainstem. But as the manifest ran Kodiak's script, systematically parsing data, individual markers began to be distinguishable.

But there was a problem. Even with the filter running, there were still too many tags. It wasn't so much like looking for a needle in a haystack, it was like looking for a needle in a stack of *needles*.

Braben sighed and slumped back in his chair. Then he pushed it away from the table, put his hands behind his head, and spun around a few rotations.

Kodiak frowned at the table display, then he rubbed his face. Okay, what else could he run? They had the data. Thanks to the glasses, they had a way of reading it. That was what they had wanted all along, right? So . . . now what?

Kodiak licked his lips, considering the different ways to cut the data. Then Braben pulled himself back to the table and tapped it with an index finger.

"Von, there are IDs all *over* the place." He pointed at the rooftop schematic. Even at the time of the shooting, there were several tags in the area. "Any one of these could be the shooter, or part of his team, or his handler, or whatever."

Kodiak nodded. "That's right."

"And that's if they are tagged in the first place. Even if this *is* an inside job, they could have used contractors—personnel from outside the Fleet who aren't in the manifest."

"Right again." Kodiak felt his stomach sink. Had this all been a colossal waste of time? Surely not . . . the assassinations *had* to be an inside job. But even so, as Braben had just said, that didn't mean they had used tagged Fleet personnel to carry out the shootings.

So why had their access to the manifest been delayed and delayed? Somebody didn't want them to see it. And there had to be a reason for that.

But Kodiak wasn't done yet. He squinted at the table display in concentration, then reached and swiped the Capitol Complex map to one side; then he tapped a sequence, bringing up the schematic of the Fleet Memorial. As on the other map, the place was covered in tags.

Braben nodded as he got the idea. "Comparative search."

"Yep," said Kodiak, typing up the code for a new set of filters. By his arm, a small blue light winked on the inside of his AI glasses as they assisted with feeding his commands directly into the manifest application. "We run another script, matching manifest tags at the time of the two shootings at both the Capitol Complex and the Memorial."

"And see what sticks out. Nice work, Agent."

Kodiak allowed himself a smile. Work complete, he sat back as the manifest data was re-processed. "Might take a few minutes." He yawned. "You wanna go get us some coffee while we wait?"

"Now *there's* a plan." Braben lifted himself from his chair and stretched, then headed to the door.

Kodiak turned in his chair. "Maybe get me a—"

The tabled chimed. Kodiak and Braben exchanged a look; then Kodiak turned back around, Braben returning to stand over the table.

There was a manifest tag highlighted in red on the Fleet Memorial map. Another on the schematic of the Capitol Complex.

Braben let out a breath. "Well I'll be. It worked."

Kodiak nodded. "Damn right it did."

He began typing, calling up the manifest ID data. The two maps slid out of the way, and the agents were presented with the image of a marine, an official portrait, the young man in full uniform, facing the camera in the customary three-quarter turn, his expression firm. His records came up next to him.

One line caught Kodiak's eye. It was a piece of boxed text, in bold red.

Kodiak had that sinking feeling again.

Braben leaned down, reading the text off the display aloud.

"Sergeant Smith, Tyler. Seven-five-three-five-three-eight-zero. Psi-Marine Corps." He paused. "Oh *shit*."

Kodiak nodded as he read off the rest. "Killed in action, Warworld 4114. Twenty-ninth February, twenty-nine seventy."

"They're good, I'll give them that."

Avalon sat at the table in the planning room, Kodiak and Braben standing on either side of her. The two schematic maps were displayed on the table, the two red manifest tags blinking. Below the maps, right in front of the chief, was the official record of Sergeant Tyler Smith, Psi-Marine Corps.

Sergeant Tyler Smith, *deceased*.

Kodiak rubbed his chin. "They *are* good. That's just what worries me."

"Okay," said the chief, "so what does this tell us?"

Braben smoothed down the front of his shirt, lining his tie up with the buttons, as he spoke. "We have a couple theories."

"Go ahead."

"The first is that this isn't a real ID—the *tag* is genuine and belongs to Tyler Smith. But they're using the ID of a dead marine to cover someone else, the real shooter. It's impossible to remove a manifest tag without killing the subject—that means they might somehow have got Tyler's tag from his body and used the data on it to spoof another tag to show his ID."

"Which means," said Kodiak, "that the shooter *is* Fleet. They're tagged. Only it's broadcasting Tyler's ID."

The chief nodded. "Like yours is broadcasting a cover identity."

"Right," said Braben. "Option two, the more likely one, is that Tyler Smith is *not* dead—according to his records he aced elective marksmanship at the Academy. Which points to him as the shooter, and the manifest ID really is his. Only that presents its own problems."

Avalon turned to her agent. "Starting with how a psi-marine listed as killed in action three months ago is actually alive and walking around New Orem?"

Kodiak clicked his tongue. "Not only that." He sat next to the chief and touched the table, bringing up some simple controls under his fingertips. As he rotated his hand, the timestamp on the manifest moved backward in time a few minutes.

The red tags on both maps vanished. Kodiak then moved forward to a few minutes after each shooting had taken place. The red tags blipped into view, then vanished.

Avalon frowned. She turned to face Kodiak. "How the hell is that possible?"

Kodiak shrugged. It was a big problem, a glitch in the manifest data that was hard to account for. Tyler Smith's tag showed up at the time of each shooting, but only for a short while—a couple of minutes at each location. Before and after, there was no sign of it.

He sighed. "Neither of our first two options explain how they got in and out of each location without the tag showing up in the manifest. Whether it's Tyler, or someone spoofing their tag to be Tyler."

"And," said Braben, "if you could somehow magically turn the manifest tag on and off, like this seems to indicate, then why let it show up on the manifest at all? They could go anywhere, do anything, and not show up. Doesn't make sense."

Kodiak cast his eye over the manifest data again. They'd gone to a lot of trouble to get it—Avalon hadn't said much when they'd told her what had happened—in fact, all she had done was nodded, telling him she would handle it. The fact was they had the manifest data and now it showed *something.* It was just a matter of figuring out what that was.

"Has the Bureau been granted manifest access yet?" he asked.

Avalon shook her head. "No. Still in process, every time I ask."

Braben folded his arms. "They really don't want us to see this, do they?"

Avalon leaned back over the table, slowly shaking her head. As Kodiak watched, her eyes moved over the data, taking it all in. Without looking up, she asked, "What's your next step then, Von?"

Wasn't that the question?

"We have two hits," he said, pointing to the data on display. "And we've had two events. We don't know if that's it, or if they plan to strike again. If we can get access to the live manifest, we can monitor it, and when Tyler's ID pops, we can try and grab him."

Avalon nodded and pushed her chair from the table. "I'll go down to the Fleet Command Center myself and get the feed piped up to us."

"Good," said Kodiak. "In the meantime, we pull up everything we can on Tyler Smith. Full Fleet record, personality profile, Academy records, family, the works. Either he's still alive, or they're using his ID. Either way, they will have chosen him for a reason."

Avalon nodded and looked at Braben. Braben adjusted his tie. "On it," he said. Then he headed out of the planning room.

Kodiak looked at the chief. Her expression was firm, determined. Kodiak could see the muscles at the back of her jaw work as she gritted her teeth.

"We're onto something," said Kodiak.

The chief nodded. "Time to get that manifest access," she said, then she left.

Alone in the planning room, Kodiak turned back to the table. The face of Tyler Smith stared back at him.

Tyler Smith. Psi-marine. Killed in action.

Kodiak pulled on his bottom lip again in thought.

So, what makes you so special?

Kodiak was fixing himself another coffee when Braben marched back into the bullpen. He trotted down the stairs onto the busy main floor, nodding at his partner to join him once again in the planning room. Kodiak acknowledged and followed.

Braben flicked the privacy shield on as Kodiak entered the room after him, and once again they were ensconced.

Kodiak nodded at his partner and took a sip of his drink. "What have you got?"

Braben held up a data stick between his finger and thumb. "Check it out," he said, moving to the table and placing the stick on it.

A new military record appeared—it was a young woman, dressed not in full, dark marine uniform, but in the light fawn tunic of a Fleet Academy cadet. Kodiak blinked at the image, not sure if he was seeing what he was seeing. There was a distinct resemblance to the dead marine, Tyler Smith . . .

Braben leaned on the table, nodding at the record on display.

"Exactly," he said, answering Kodiak's unaired question. "Psi-Sergeant Tyler Smith has a sister—a *twin* sister, Caitlin. She didn't follow her brother into the Academy until six months after he enrolled. More important, she never completed her training."

Braben slid data around the table. More records, more personnel files. Finding the page he wanted, he tapped at it to emphasize his point.

"But she didn't just drop out of the Academy. Three months ago she *disappeared.*"

Kodiak frowned. "Disappeared? She would have been tagged when she entered the Academy. . . ."

Kodiak's words trailed off. Yes, she would have been tagged, like everyone and everything else in the Fleet.

Like her brother.

Braben stood from the table and looked at Kodiak. Kodiak felt his mouth form a small "O."

Braben nodded. "She's listed as missing, presumed dead—with no tag showing on the manifest, it's assumed she was killed, the tag itself destroyed."

"So she's officially dead," said Kodiak. "Just like her brother."

"And," said Braben, "Caitlin's absence from the Academy was noted March eighth. About a week after her brother was apparently killed in a Spider skirmish on Warworld 4114."

Kodiak said nothing, but he raised his eyebrows. The two agents locked eyes for a while, Kodiak's mind racing, no doubt Braben's as well. Two psi-abled siblings, one a marine sent into battle, one still at the Academy. One killed in action. The other missing, presumed dead.

Yeah, right, thought Kodiak. His gut told him something different. So did the Fleet manifest—Caitlin's tag was lost. And yet Tyler's had shown up briefly at the shootings before vanishing again.

It was time to throw out everything they knew about how the tags worked. They were clearly hackable, controllable.

Which meant Tyler Smith was alive. And, chances were, his sister as well. It was too much of a coincidence otherwise, especially given the timings.

Kodiak sipped his coffee as he looked over the table display. "Says she was inducted into the Psi-Marine Corps accelerated program. Class of Alpha One."

Braben nodded. "Just like her brother. Apparently his psi score was so high they leap-frogged him to sergeant and sent him into combat as soon as they could."

"Where he was killed," said Kodiak. "Officially."

Braben cocked his head. "Except now he's back, apparently."

"If that is him and not someone using his ID." Kodiak drained his drink, the hot, bitter liquid and the buzz of caffeine helping him clear his thought processes. "And where did his sister go?"

"That's assuming she's alive too."

Kodiak shrugged. "It's looking more likely, isn't it? There's a conspiracy going on, and these two might be at the heart of it." He looked at Braben again. "I think we have two targets to find."

There was a chime from the planning room's door. The two agents turned at the sound, Braben moving over the control panel on the wall to unlock the door. Commander Avalon nodded a greeting and stepped in. As she walked over to the table, she pulled the silver square Bureau badge from her lapel, then, looking down at the data display, pressed the badge to the tabletop.

"Finally got a security override," she said. "We have official access to the live manifest."

Kodiak shook his head. Hands on hips, he moved to stand next to the chief, looking down at the table as her Bureau badge was read by the computer and the display changed to show current feed from the manifest, showing the Fleet Capitol Complex and environs.

"About time," he said. "What the hell was going on?"

"I don't know," said the chief, lifting her badge and reattaching it to her uniform. "Nobody down at the command center could trace where the security block had come from."

Braben gave a low whistle. "Gotta be someone high up, right?"

Avalon glanced up. She just nodded.

"Okay then, let's see what we can see," said Kodiak, leaning over the table. He began tapping at a keyboard at the bottom of the main manifest display. The schematic of the Fleet Capitol Complex and the crawl of tags all over it zoomed out until they were looking down at a map of New Orem itself. While he worked, Braben explained to the chief about Tyler's sister, Caitlin.

"Okay," she said, when Braben was done. She moved closer to Kodiak, leaning over the table as well, her eyes scanning the display. Kodiak finished keying the tag data, then stood back, his arms folded.

He sighed.

Nothing had happened. The map of New Orem was barely recognizable, an undulating square of tiny moving icons—the tags of every member of the Fleet in the city. He'd set the manifest to pick out the IDs of Tyler and Caitlin Smith. There were no results.

But, what had he expected? Tyler's ID came and went—hidden, somehow—and Caitlin's had been inactive for three months. So the plan was not to find them immediately, but to watch and wait. In the meantime, they could direct the ground search a little better. At least they had two specific targets to look for.

If they were still in New Orem in the first place.

"They could have taken them off world," said Braben. "They might not be in the city anymore."

Kodiak shrugged. "That's possible. But we have the live manifest now, we can track them across all of Fleetspace."

"That's going to take a lot of time, and—"

There was an alert from the table. Kodiak winced at the sound, too loud in the confines of the planning room.

"Look!" said Avalon. She pulled at the map display with her hands, moving the city schematic around, focusing in on a green icon floating among the infinite sea of red.

Kodiak's heart kicked into gear. Tyler Smith, making his third appearance. He was going to kill again. They needed to get to that location, fast. They also needed to get any high-ranking Fleet personnel out of there. He reached for the comm on his collar, ready to make the order.

"It's not him," said Avalon. She brought up a text panel and began scrolling through the readout. Then she looked up at Kodiak. "It's Caitlin Smith. Her tag is active."

Kodiak's eyes widened. He looked at the chief, looked at his partner. Braben gave a nod. "I'll get a drop team ready. Let's roll."

"Go," said Avalon. "I'll call ahead. You need to pick her up, *now.*"

Kodiak nodded and headed to the door, Braben on his heels, as the chief began relaying orders into her comm.

20

They flew in over the slums of Salt City, two thousand meters high, following the path of the two surveillance drones that had been sent out ahead. Kodiak was strapped in the transport compartment next to Braben and ten other agents, the simple box plugged onto the back of the one-man hot seat where the pilot sat. The transport, like every vehicle in the Fleet, whether designed for space travel or atmospheric flight, was modular. The hot seat was the basic structure, a wedge-shaped block that was essentially a one-man flying machine, little more than a cockpit and basic propulsive unit. Anything and everything could be attached to it from the Fleet's catalogue of parts, creating anything from a small, agile fighter to a heavy assault vehicle, to this, a transport craft.

Kodiak hadn't needed to change from his borrowed combat uniform, just adding a light helmet and gauntlets to the outfit. Braben had swapped his suit for gear identical to Kodiak's, except his armored jacket had sleeves. The eight other agents were more heavily protected, as they were the ones going in first, all dressed in combat fatigues and helmets that made them look more like Fleet marines, each with a short plasma rifle clipped to the front of his flak jacket.

Both Kodiak and Braben had the same weapon, but were wearing them on their backs. For maximum mobility, they would instead rely mostly on their stasers, stowed within easy reach on a thigh holster.

The object of the mission was to find and capture Caitlin Smith. Nothing more, nothing less. A precise, surgical operation. As soon as her ID had reappeared on the Fleet manifest, unmoving in a warehouse on the outskirts of Salt City, Kodiak had ordered surveillance drones in first to get a real-time picture of the area, and it looked quiet. The target hadn't moved for hours. So either she was alive, with no idea they were coming, or somehow the dead manifest tag had been reactivated. It was more than possible they were going in to recover her corpse.

The transport banked sharply. Through the open side of their compartment, Kodiak watched the lights of New Orem sweep around below them as they changed course. The Fleet capital was blazing white, with the Fleet Capitol Complex itself a cluster of the tallest, the sleekest, the brightest buildings in the heart. The aerial view was a familiar site to many, Kodiak included, but he still felt awed at the size of both the Fleet's headquarters and New Orem itself. This was the largest city in Fleetspace, the heart of the empire.

Kodiak frowned behind his visor. From above, the city and the Capitol Complex looked just the same as they always did, but he knew that was deceptive. Down there in the Complex itself, and across the streets of the city, Fleet personnel swarmed to control the situation.

Kodiak glanced at the others packed into the transport compartment. The comm in his ear was silent, the raiding party still aside from the buffeting of the carrier as they were airlifted to the drop zone. Even Braben, strapped in next to Kodiak, so close Kodiak could feel the hard plates of their armored jackets rubbing together, was quiet, focusing his gaze somewhere on the floor of the compartment.

Caitlin Smith. How the hell had her manifest tag suddenly come back online? She was missing, presumed dead, the only possible reason she couldn't be located by the Fleet's systems. And yet, her tag had shown up, appearing on the manifest almost in front of Kodiak's eyes. The fact that she was showing up and Tyler *wasn't* was a mystery, but it was too much of a coincidence. There had to be a connection, which made Caitlin Smith—the prime suspect's only surviving family—their first solid lead.

Kodiak's comm chimed as the pilot updated them on their position. As Kodiak acknowledged, Braben tapped him on the arm and pointed to the view outside.

The bright lights of New Orem stopped suddenly, cutting a long, jagged border against what appeared to be impenetrable darkness. As the edge of the city moved out of view underneath the carrier, Kodiak's eyes adjusted, and he could now see they were still over a built-up area, but one populated by low buildings, crosshatched with narrow streets lit with a dim, flickering orange-yellow.

Salt City. They were getting close.

"You'd never find anyone down there," said Braben, his voice loud and clear over Kodiak's comm. "It's the perfect hiding place."

Kodiak nodded. "Only if you aren't tagged by the Fleet."

"Amen to that."

His partner was right. Salt City was not only a huge, sprawling conurbation of buildings both makeshift and permanent, a mix of a thousand architectures and building techniques brought with the influx of refugees from the Southern Hemisphere, but it was largely ignored by the Fleet. That wasn't to say it wasn't well-known—the slum was mapped, the skies patrolled by surveillance drones sent over from New Orem proper—but whatever went on in its crooked streets, whatever crimes and vices and villainy, so long as it stayed within the bounds of Salt City, the Fleet simply didn't care.

"We're five minutes away," said Braben. In the HUD inside Kodiak's short visor, a small red indicator appeared, hovering over a location in the middle distance. A line drew itself from the edge of the visor to the point indicated, and a counter began to wind down the closing distance between them and their target.

"Roger that," said Kodiak. Then with just a thought he flicked the comms to the public channel, allowing not only the members of the raiding team seated around him but Avalon and the other agents back in the Bureau bullpen to listen in.

"Okay," said Kodiak. "Listen up. We're going in a few minutes. The drones have been over the area, so you've all seen the layout, and you know what to expect. You also know what we're looking for. This is an extraction. Nothing more. We are running on the assumption that the target is *alive*. Which means, if they've somehow been hiding, they won't be too happy to see us. But we do not engage unless they engage us first. As far as we know, the target is on their own down there, but it's possible they have company. We need this to be smooth, and we need this to be quick—in and out before they even know it. That's the whole plan. Understood?"

The agents each indicated their acknowledgment.

Kodiak nodded. Then, for the benefit of those back at the bullpen, he ordered the team to link comms. Inside Kodiak's HUD, a new indicator appeared on the left of his vision: ten green icons. The raiding team. *His* raiding team.

The transport's engine thrummed, and the view outside changed again as the vehicle came to a stop and spun about its axis, then descended gracefully to a height of two hundred meters. There was a double chime in Kodiak's ear, indicating they had arrived, the pilot ready and waiting for orders. The carrier was stealthy, with baffled engines and no external lights—at this altitude they were not invisible, but unless someone looked directly up, they were hard to see. The secrecy of their arrival would be gone as soon as the agents rappelled from the side of the carrier and hit the ground, but they were right on top of the target location, and the team was primed, ready for a lightning strike.

Another tone in Kodiak's ear and in his HUD—and everyone else's—a green icon flashed as the destination counter hit zero.

Showtime.

Kodiak and Braben looked at each other; Kodiak gave a thumbs up, and at once the team slid out of their harnesses and, in a well-drilled routine, lined up along the open side of the compartment, the first four reaching up and clipping the end of their rappel cables to the frame that ran along the edge of the opening as, behind them, the remaining agents held their cable clips at the ready.

"Tac One and Two going in," said Kodiak. At this, the first four agents dropped over the edge of the carrier and vanished from view; then the next batch clipped their cables to the rail and followed. Last to leave were Kodiak and Braben. In perfect synchronization, the pair reached over their shoulders and yanked their own cables out from the reel secreted in their packs. Clipping them to the rail, they paused on the threshold, Kodiak's booted foot hanging over the edge. With one hand on the cable, he drew his staser with the other and turned to his partner. The upper half of Braben's face was hidden by the visor of his light helmet, but his teeth were brilliant white against his dark skin as he grinned at Kodiak.

Braben lifted his staser pistol. "Let's go!"

Braben jumped first, Kodiak close behind. The ground approached at a surprisingly fast rate, but aside from the whirr of the cable reel, it was quiet outside of the carrier. Looking down, Kodiak saw the eight armored agents on the ground scoot forward, guns raised. Then he hit the ground with a bump and the cable pack detached automatically from his back and began reeling itself back up to the carrier.

Kodiak looked around. Beside him, Braben nodded and, holding his staser in both hands, moved forward.

They'd touched down on a wide, dusty street in one of Salt City's industrial thoroughfares. The place was quiet and washed out in a sickly orange-yellow by the weak streetlights. Directly in front of them a large warehouse squatted, the front a gaping maw of blackness. According to Kodiak's HUD, the target—Caitlin—still hadn't moved. They'd made it in, so far, without detection.

The comms in his helmet clicked as the assault squad checked in, gathering themselves around the warehouse. No sign of anything yet.

"Split up," said Kodiak. "Tac One, take the main entrance. Tac Two, secure the rear."

The lead agents acknowledged, and the main assault party split into two pre-arranged teams of four. Kodiak and Braben held back by the warehouse entrance. As Kodiak watched his team move in, he had the feeling that eight agents didn't really seem like that many. The building was huge—although they had Caitlin's tag pinpointed, who knew what else, who else, was hiding inside the warehouse.

Within moments the two teams were gone, the first melting into the blackness of the warehouse entrance, the other splitting into pairs, each vanishing around opposite perimeters.

Kodiak glanced at Braben. "Rear?"

"Sure thing."

They split up, Kodiak following the first team, Braben jogging around the edge of the building.

Inside, Kodiak's visor switched to night vision, lighting the warehouse up in a blue monochrome. He could just see the backs of two agents on the other side of the large, empty space, heading toward a doorway that led farther into the building. Kodiak jogged toward them, keeping close to the cargo containers that lay scattered around the warehouse.

Then there was a sharp popping in his ear, and he skidded to a halt as his comms sprang to life, the two teams coordinating with calm, rehearsed ease.

"Shots fired, two-ten, northeast corner."

"Confirmed."

"Tac One, report."

"Negative. Heading in."

"Tac Two?"

"One target sighted, four shots fired. Think we got the jump—target opened fire then ran deeper into the building. They weren't expecting company. Tac Two in pursuit."

"Copy," Braben's voice came over the comms. "Rear exits secured."

Kodiak adjusted his grip on his gun. He ground his teeth, gaze darting around the empty warehouse in front of him. There was no sign of any movement, and so far, no further shots.

Despite the action, Caitlin Smith's manifest tag hadn't moved. They'd disturbed someone else, and Caitlin was either still hiding, or maybe she *was* dead and they would find her body. As Kodiak scanned the warehouse, he began to think that was the most likely option. Still, the recovery of her body might provide them some clues as to her brother's whereabouts. It was still too big a coincidence to ignore.

Kodiak swore under his breath and ran toward the doorway. As he crossed the threshold, entering a wide but featureless corridor, there were more pops, more gunfire. In his HUD, one of the green icons indicating the status of his team changed to red as the biosystems of the agent's combat suit sent out a high-priority alert.

Kodiak, heart pumping, stalked forward, gun raised. That meant just one thing.

One agent was down.

"Tac One, report," he said. "Tell me what's going on."

Instead of the Tac One leader, Braben answered. "Celestin is down. Shooter still running, heading toward the northeast corner."

Shit. That wasn't as planned. Whether the shooter was connected to Caitlin or not, it was impossible to tell.

Shit, shit, shit.

"Cut them off, but take them alive if possible."

Kodiak moved forward, his HUD picking up the team's trail on the dirty floor and highlighting a path for him to follow.

Shit *shit.* Celestin? One agent down already. *Fuck.*

More pops of plasma gunfire. Kodiak took a left and a right and a left again, heading toward the sounds, letting his HUD lead the way. He saw movement ahead, someone vanishing around a corner, the hard interlocking plates of the armor on his back catching the dim light and flaring in Kodiak's night vision—an agent in pursuit.

The comms crackled as one of the team leaders handed out orders.

"Tac Two, take the stairs, south corner. Tac One, with me. We can cut off their escape."

Kodiak burst into a room, gun at the ready. Braben was there, kneeling on the ground over the fallen body of Agent Dan Celestin. Braben looked up as Kodiak entered, then shook his head.

"Negative," he said.

Kodiak bit his tongue. One man down was one man too many, but he couldn't afford to be distracted now. With the remaining agents fanning out across the building to get a squeeze on the runner, they needed to focus on finding Caitlin. Without a capture the mission was a bust.

Kodiak took in the room. It looked like a storeroom, no doubt one of dozens in the warehouse. It was roughly square and nondescript save for the equipment in it: a stretcher bed with foil blanket shining brightly in his night vision; electronics—some kind of medical monitors—on wheeled trolleys, thick power cables running to an outlet on the other side of the room. It looked like a field hospital, not dissimilar to the temporary set-ups used by both the Bureau and the Fleet. The bed was pulled out at an angle from the wall, and the equipment cabinets were partially turned around. The room had been disturbed, presumably during whatever skirmish had led to the death of Agent Celestin.

The equipment was strange. It looked new. Expensive. Not at all the kind of gear commonly found in Salt City, let alone in the back of an old, empty warehouse.

Another coincidence, too good to be true. Kodiak bit his lip, thinking, thinking. They'd stumbled into something. There had to be a connection with Caitlin, with Tyler. Had to be.

They had to stop the runner, whoever he was. He'd killed one agent already, but Kodiak's gut told him the runner was involved with the bigger picture.

Braben raised himself from his crouch. He still had his staser in one hand. He looked down at the body on the floor.

"I was right behind," he said. "Celestin came in and surprised whoever was here. I managed to get a shot off but the target ran out the back." He gestured to the other side of the room, where another door led out to a dark corridor.

"Did you hit him?"

"Yeah," said Braben. "Think so, but it just clipped him. Hopefully it'll slow him—the rest of Tac Two were behind me, and they went after him. Sounds like they have a bead on the runner."

"I heard," said Kodiak. He walked around Celestin's body to the doorway opposite and poked his head through. The corridor was empty. His HUD chimed, reminding him they still hadn't found the primary target. He looked around as the HUD indicator pointed him in the right direction. Then he waved at Braben. "The target still hasn't moved. Come on."

Leaving Celestin's body, the pair crept out of the storeroom and into the next corridor. Kodiak's HUD chimed again, and the target indicator began to move. He turned to Braben, knowing he was looking at the same thing. Braben nodded, and without saying a word, the two sprinted down the corridor.

The comms sprang to life.

"Tac One, target found. In pursuit."

"Tac One, do you have eyes?" asked Kodiak. "Primary target is on the move too. Unless you can take out the runner now, you need to break off and acquire Caitlin Smith."

"We have eyes," came the response. "Computer confirms primary target and runner are the same signal, sir."

Kodiak and Braben stopped together and looked at each other.

What the hell?

"Confirm, Tac One."

"Confirmed, sir. Closing in."

"Advise caution," said Kodiak. "Target may be injured. Do not engage. We're on our way."

The Tac leader confirmed; then Kodiak turned to Braben. Braben nodded and raised his gun to indicate readiness.

And then the comms sprang to life as members of both teams started screaming at someone to get the fuck down and don't fucking move and get on the ground now get on the ground now get on the ground now.

Kodiak sprinted toward the fray, Braben on his heels.

The corridors led back to where they had started—the main warehouse floor. Kodiak and Braben emerged from a side door and skidded to a halt on the dusty floor. So, eight agents—*seven*, Kodiak reminded himself—had been enough, and their tactics had worked, one team in pursuit, the other doubling around and coming in from the other side of the building. The runner—the *target*, according to the blinking indicator in Kodiak's HUD—was caught right in the middle.

Yes, the plan had worked. But the result was nothing like what they'd expected.

The man was wearing a long pale trench coat, the edges of which flapped in the breeze as he stood with his hands raised as the seven agents tightened the circle around him, seven blue target dots painted into his body by Kodiak's HUD. The inside of his visor was filled with data—line of fire, distance to target, probability of success, mission statistics. It was too much. Kodiak clenched his jaw as he concentrated, the weak psi-fi field in his helmet picking up his thoughts and clearing the HUD almost completely so he could see what the hell was going on.

The agents continued to bark orders at the target—who definitely *wasn't* Caitlin Smith—but aside from remaining stationary, he was doing little else to obey their instructions. As the agents stepped closer, he turned on an axis until he was facing Kodiak. He was middle aged, thick brown hair on his head and thick-rimmed glasses on his face. Under the coat, he was wearing a smart, if nondescript, civilian suit with matching shirt and tie. He looked ordinary, a regular guy, citizen of New Orem—a man with absolutely no business standing in the middle of a deserted warehouse in Salt City, surrounded by a Bureau tactical assault team.

Was this Caitlin Smith's handler? Kodiak focused on his HUD, on the manifest tag indicator which was the only thing left on display. The indicator that said the man in the pale coat was, somehow, Caitlin Smith herself.

The man was holding something in one hand. Kodiak glanced sideways at Braben, but Braben was in a firing stance and had the mystery man lined up along the top of his staser.

Kodiak stepped forward to the line of agents, staser ready but feeling safe enough with eight other weapons pointed at the target. As he approached, Tacs One and Two ceased their barrage of orders, and the warehouse suddenly felt very, very quiet.

"I'd get down on the floor if I were you," said Kodiak, his voice echoing metallically in the huge warehouse space.

The man met his eye, but didn't speak. He looked calm, one corner of his mouth upturned by a tiny degree. There was amusement in his expression that Kodiak didn't like one little bit.

Who the hell is this guy? He's calm. He's professional.

This isn't right.

"A staser hurts like hell, even on stun," said Kodiak, aloud. "Believe me, I've had firsthand experience. If you don't get acquainted with the floor in three seconds, we're going to have to put you down there ourselves."

The man didn't move.

"One."

Out of the corner of his eye, Kodiak saw his agents, ready and waiting for his command.

"Two."

Kodiak raised his gun. If anyone was going to shoot this guy, it was going to be him.

"Three."

The man reached for something in his coat pocket. A warning flashed onto Kodiak's HUD, large red text along the top of his vision.

POSSIBILITY OF AGGRESSIVE ACTION 87.5%

It happened quickly. Kodiak clenched his back teeth, lifted his gun just a little to get better aim, when there was a blue flash and the man careened backwards, a staser bolt slamming him square in his chest. The shot lifted him off his feet, and he hit the deck on his back and didn't move.

"Shit."

Kodiak ran over, Tacs One and Two quickly closing in, keeping their weapons trained on the body. As Kodiak reached toward the man's neck to feel for a pulse, his HUD flashed another warning.

LIFE SIGNS NEGATIVE. TARGET DECEASED.

Kodiak's hand stopped before he touched the body. The man's eyes were open and staring behind his glasses. Kodiak rocked back on his haunches and waved at the agents behind him. He sighed.

"Stand down," he said. "Target is deceased." He stood up. "Well, shit." He turned to Braben, standing at the back of the group, his pistol still drawn and aimed.

Kodiak marched over. "Weapons were supposed to be on *stun,* Agent."

Braben shook his head and lowered his gun. "It *is* on stun, Von. He must have been injured from where I clipped him with the first shot."

Kodiak sighed and turned back to the body. The Tac teams were standing around, awaiting orders.

"Tac Two, go and get Celestin and signal the carrier for pick-up."

The three remaining members of the downed agent's team moved away. The Tac One leader gestured with his plasma rifle to the body on the ground. "Sir?"

Kodiak licked his lips and nodded. The target indicator in his HUD—in all their HUDs—said the dead man *was* Caitlin Smith.

Kodiak stepped over to the body. The dead man still had his hands raised, the fingers of the left curled around the mystery object. Kodiak knelt down and lifted the man's hand. The fingers were cold and, surprisingly, very stiff. Whatever he was holding, he was holding onto it tight.

"So who is this guy, do you think?" asked Braben, kneeling beside his partner. "Some kind of Fleet agent? Blacker than black ops?"

"Her handler, you mean?" Kodiak nodded. "Let's run facial recog and see what comes back. We can confirm his ID once we get the body back to the Bureau. Aha!"

Braben leaned forward. "What you got?"

Kodiak stood, Braben joining him. Pried from the dead man's hand was a small silver square, the size of a thumbnail, no more.

"Is that . . ."

Kodiak nodded.

"It is. They dug it out of her brainstem."

Inside Kodiak's HUD, the manifest tag shone a bright green in his hand, the floating label identifying it loud and clear.

Caitlin Smith.

Kodiak stared at the tag in his hand. Well, that answered that question.

Braben sighed loudly. "Which means she's dead."

Kodiak nodded. Braben was right. The tag couldn't be removed without killing the owner. That the tag itself had been unreadable ever since Caitlin had left the Academy then had sprung back to life just a few hours ago was still a mystery, but one that Kodiak had no doubt would be answered once they got it back to the Bureau labs.

"Which means," Braben continued, "we're back to fucking square one."

Kodiak held the manifest tag delicately between finger and thumb. It took all his will not to toss it to the hard warehouse floor and crush it under his heel.

21

She tripped. She fell. The street was wet from a rain shower she didn't remember, and when she pushed herself up from the hard surface on skinned hands, she found herself staring at her own rippling face in a large puddle. Water dripped from her face, and the world around her was black and orange, lit by the sickly glow of the underpowered streetlights of Salt City.

She wasn't sure where she was, or how far she had come, or how long it had been since she had escaped from the horrors of the warehouse and the insanity of the Morning Star. All she was sure about was that the back of her neck felt like it was on fire, and that she felt ill, and that if she didn't make it, she was going to die, here, in a gutter in a slum.

But make it . . . where? She pushed herself back onto her haunches, wiped her hands on her top, then pressed her fingers into her eyes. She'd escaped. That was good. She was in bad shape, she had no idea what had been done to her, but she was alive. Alive and moving . . . for the moment. How long she could keep going, she wasn't sure. She needed to rest, recover, at least a little. Then she could think of . . . something. A plan. What she had to do next.

She dropped her arms and looked down at her reflection in the puddle. She started, her breath caught in her throat, her heart thudding in her chest.

There was someone behind her. A man wearing glasses, wearing a pale coat.

Glass.

Cait spun around on her toes, but she was alone in the street. Besides which, Glass was dead. She'd killed him herself in her escape.

She turned back to the puddle, slowly, afraid of what she might see. But the only thing reflected was herself.

Cait let out a breath. A hallucination, a side effect of whatever the hell they'd dosed her with. Time was what she needed. Time to rest, to let her body clear the toxins so she could focus on her situation and what to do about it. She was afraid, on the verge of panic, and she knew it. She also knew this was exactly the wrong time to be making important decisions. She had no idea what to do next, but it was not something to be thinking about now, she told herself. No, she had to rest, to wait it out. Then she could come up with a new plan.

She looked down at the puddle again. It was deep, the surface oily. But survival was key. She knelt down, leaned over the water, scooped her hand into it and had a sharp, bitter mouthful.

I can assure you, Ms. Smith, that I am as real as you are.

Cait's hands fell from her face, and she stood, quickly. She looked at the rippling reflection in the water. There was nobody behind her. She was still alone. Alone and hallucinating, hearing Glass's voice in her head. Like it had been before, like her brother's had been. Her brother was supposed to be dead, but he wasn't. Glass was dead too. And yet here he was, talking to her in her mind. Just like her brother.

You need to keep moving, Ms. Smith. We might be alone now, but we won't be come sunrise. You might be dead by the time someone finds you, but you might be alive, which is most definitely the worst-case scenario.

Cait stared at her reflection. Glass was right. Maybe it wasn't him, wasn't his voice. Maybe it was her own mind telling her what to do, the drugs and the stress and her injuries combining, causing her own thoughts to manifest as the hallucination. She needed to rest. She needed to hide for a while.

"Okay," she said aloud. "Okay, okay, okay." She rolled her neck and then hissed in pain as the thick plastic bandage taped to the back of it was pulled. She took a deep breath of cool night air.

Then she leaned to one side and puked like a superhero. It was hot, dark liquid, splashing into the puddles around her, steaming in the night air. She spent the next minute spitting furiously, trying to clear her mouth, wiping it with the back of her good hand.

And, actually, she felt a lot better.

She looked around, getting her bearings. She had to get under cover, somewhere she could hide. On each side of the street, the flat sides of prefabricated buildings rose up, their walls a patchwork of graffiti so dense it almost looked like camouflage patterning in the murky orange light. She squinted ahead, wondering whether she remembered this part of Salt City's industrial quarter or not. Was that building the same one she had passed on her way to the rendezvous—to the *ambush,* she corrected herself—or was it near to . . .

She looked over her other shoulder. Behind her, the wide street vanished into a dark area where the pathetic street lighting had given up entirely, leaving the rest of the block cloaked in the deep shadow cast by the tall, jagged spire of a half-built skyscraper right at the end of the street. The structure was silhouetted by the bright glow of New Orem behind it, nothing but a broken black framework—part solid, part abandoned, skeletal superstructure.

The incomplete office block that she had called home for the past few weeks. It was right there. She'd burnt out her hide, but she knew the building well. She'd be able to find another spot to lay low.

Summoning all her strength, Cait pushed herself forward. But with each step it felt like she'd walked a mile, and as she looked up, trying to judge distance, direction, the broken spire of her old building seemed suddenly to be a distant point on the horizon.

She needed to rest. She needed to be safe. That building was suddenly her only hope, her entire reason for being, and reaching it her only goal.

She stumbled, slowly, onward.

22

The Bureau bullpen was as busy at four in the morning as it was during the day, staff pulling multiple shifts to handle the situation. New Orem was still on full lockdown, the citizens uneasy and restless, which just gave the Bureau more to do.

But Kodiak didn't blame them. He glanced around the bullpen, noting the marines in full combat kit positioned at the exits. The whole complex was on alert, and the marines were there to protect the agents . . . but with their opaque helmet visors, Kodiak couldn't help but feel he and the other Bureau agents were being watched.

He stifled a yawn. No, simple paranoia, brought on by a chronic lack of sleep. Time for another caffeine boost.

As he stood and moved to the machine in a corner of the bullpen, dialing up a mug, he realized there was more to it than just tiredness. He was a Special Agent, used to dealing with pressure, but this investigation was unique. Not only that, what he'd thought was going to be a huge breakthrough had turned into something else entirely. The case was complex, its path winding. And now perhaps that pressure Kodiak felt was starting to bear down on him. Everyone wanted results, wanted him and Braben and the chief to get to the bottom of it.

Kodiak sipped his drink. It tasted terrible, but it was hot and strong. He walked back to his desk and continued taking small, searing sips as his gaze fixed on the small plastic bag sitting in the middle of his desk.

Caitlin Smith's manifest tracker.

Now, wasn't *that* a mystery?

The Bureau techs had examined it closely. The tag was genuine, Fleet issue. The serial number microetched onto the device matched the ID that the device was still broadcasting. Kodiak glanced at the holographic display floating on the left side of his desk. It showed the Academy record and photograph of Caitlin Smith, and a live feed of her manifest record.

Caitlin Smith who was, according to the tracker, sitting on Special Agent Von Kodiak's desk.

Kodiak sniffed and rolled his neck as he regarded the tracker. He frowned as he considered the situation—it felt like it *almost* made sense, that they were *almost* on the right path. If they could just fill in the blanks, find the last pieces of the puzzle, then it would all make sense.

Their prime suspect was Psi-Marine Tyler Smith, officially killed in action but with his manifest ID showing up at both assassinations—time *and* place—but somehow not before or after. Shielding IDs was, as far as Kodiak knew, impossible.

Tyler Smith's twin sister Caitlin had vanished from the Academy—*her* tracker had been untraceable since her disappearance, with the assumption that she was dead, her tracker destroyed by whatever had happened to her.

And then her tag had shown up in the manifest. The tag was in perfect condition and functioning normally, according to the lab techs, which meant it hadn't failed or malfunctioned, it had been *shielded*, somehow.

Which was . . . not possible.

Neither was removing the tag from a living person. The lab examination of Caitlin's tag had found plenty of biological material on it. However the tag itself had been shielded, Caitlin had been alive and well, at least up until a few hours ago when the tag had been dug out from her brainstem. But if she'd been alive *then*, the fact that the tag was now on Kodiak's desk was proof enough that she was now dead.

Kodiak took another sip. That, he suspected, was another fallacy. The field medical unit found in the warehouse was advanced and set up for complex surgery. They had attempted, at least, to take the tag out, leaving both it and the subject intact.

Whether they had been successful or not, it was impossible to tell. But Kodiak figured there was more than a fair chance that Caitlin was alive.

But if they could take the tag out, why not do that with Tyler, assuming both he and his sister were in it together? His ID showing up at the crime scenes seemed like a gigantic oversight. Unless it was a deliberate attempt to throw them off? They—whoever *they* were—would have known the first thing the Bureau would check was the Fleet manifest. How much easier, cleaner would it have been for them to just have taken Tyler's tag out? Then the Bureau would still be completely in the dark.

Kodiak finished his coffee and turned his attention to Caitlin Smith's Academy picture. She looked young, bright-eyed, her chin held high. There was pride in that picture.

What the hell had the kid gotten herself into?

"Von!"

Kodiak blinked, the chief's call snapping him out of his thoughts. He turned and watched as Avalon marched across the bullpen, glancing sideways at him and nodding toward one of the planning rooms before disappearing into it.

Kodiak rushed to follow her into the room.

"Holy shit."

Kodiak looked up from the table display to Avalon, back to the table, back to the chief. He licked his lips as he considered what to say next.

"Holy *shit,*" he said again.

Avalon nodded, her lips pursed, her arms folded as she stood by the wall. She hadn't bothered setting the planning room to private; behind her, through the wall, Kodiak's eyes moved over the buzzing crowd of agents working at their stations, the impassive, unmoving forms of the marines looking over them by their positions near the doors.

On the table display were images from the necropsy of the mystery man in the pale coat Braben had shot at the Salt City warehouse. Braben himself was now down at the labs, where the body had been moved from the morgue. Because what had started as a medical procedure had turned into something else, quickly.

The images showed the man's naked body lying on a wide laboratory bench. His head had been removed and sat at the top of the table. From the torso's neck sprouted tubes and wires and a silver, articulated piece of metal.

"He's artificial? A servitor?" Kodiak felt like he was stating the obvious, but he had to be sure this meeting with Avalon was real, not just some dream or nightmare, his body twitching restlessly as he slumped over his desk out in the bullpen, finally succumbing to the lack of sleep and adrenaline hangover.

The chief nodded. "A machine, yes. Biomechanical, well in advance of what the Fleet has developed. Certainly good enough to pass for human—alive *or* dead. It was only when the morgue technician went in with a laser scalpel that he realized it wasn't . . . well, human."

Kodiak stroked his chin as he brought the events of the warehouse raid back in his mind's eye. The man in the coat had shown no fear, and had been apparently killed by a *stun* shot from Braben's staser. Kodiak's HUD—which, on the way back to the Bureau, had come back negative on facial recognition—had reported no life signs, and the man's skin had been cold, the pulse absent. He'd had to force the fingers open to retrieve the manifest tag—fingers stiff and cold because, Kodiak now realized, they were mechanical, not biological.

Avalon raised an eyebrow. "What are you thinking?"

Kodiak exhaled a long, slow breath. "Not much at the moment except holy. Shit."

And it was remarkable, to say the least. That the man in the pale coat was a servitor—a *robot*—that looked like a human, down to the last detail . . . the Fleet had never gotten that far with robotics technology. With the Spider war getting progressively more difficult, there had seemed to be little need for such development.

Obviously, such advancement was not impossible—the partially dismantled servitor lying on a lab bench proof positive—but Kodiak thought back to the two other surprises the investigation had brought up.

That a manifest tag's signal could be shielded. That the tag itself could be removed without killing the subject.

Kodiak rubbed his face, wishing for another coffee to materialize on the table next to the images from the lab.

"The Fleet doesn't have anything like this," he said, another obvious statement but one that allowed his mind to process the information.

Avalon folded her arms. "We don't. The Fleet has robots and artificial intelligence, but not 'androids.' We've only just entered into a contract for combat servitors in the last year."

Kodiak nodded. She was right—of course, the Fleet used robots all the time, everything from surveillance and maintenance drones, to service robots like the cleaning machines on Helprin's Gambit. When there was heavy lifting required, you used a robot. U-Stars were constructed by them. So was most of New Orem. The combat servitors *were* new—but even those were experimental. But while the Fleet ran as much automation as possible, AI itself centuries-old tech, its use was deliberately limited—it was enough to give battle computers and management systems an edge, assisting the Fleet with real-time pre-emptive data and decision making, but it had its limitations. A self-aware, fully autonomous artificial intelligence was considered far, far too dangerous to use when the entirety of humanity was battling for its very existence against an enemy that was itself an artificial intelligence: the Spiders.

Avalon pushed herself away from the glass wall and took a seat next to Kodiak. She slid some of the report images around. "The Fleet doesn't have anything like *this* either."

The new picture showed a gun. It was tiny, little more than a molded grip and small barrel no bigger than Kodiak's little finger. The agent leaned over the table, rotating and enlarging the image to get a better look.

"What's that?" he asked. "Not sure I've seen a design like that before."

"It's a PJH four-ninety-three," said the chief. "But most people call it a Yuri-G." She swiped the table and a few more images slid into view, showing the weapon in various stages of disassembly.

Kodiak frowned and glanced sideways at the chief. "Looks kinda small." The Yuri-G seemed barely big enough to fit into an average-sized hand.

"Small but powerful," said Avalon. "It got its nickname because people say it'll put you into orbit. They were Fleet issue once, but were actually banned a long time ago. Too dangerous."

Kodiak whistled. "So our mystery man is not only an advanced servitor, something beyond Fleet tech, but he's packing heat that the Fleet doesn't even use." He rolled his fingers along the edge of the table, deep in thought. "I wonder," he said.

The information he had learned was undeniably bad. Whatever was going on, they were up against a well-prepared, well-equipped enemy with serious resources and technology.

Avalon stared at the images on the table. "This all suggests it *can't* be an inside job. Not if the Fleet doesn't even have this stuff itself."

Kodiak nodded. "And who knows what other tricks they might have—if they can do all this, then they could probably circumvent Fleet security. That's how they got the shooter into and out of their positions without being caught."

"What about black ops?" asked Avalon, clearly going through a list of alternatives in her mind, as Kodiak was himself.

"Could be," he said. It was a distinct possibility—who the hell knew what kind of tech the dark side of the Fleet had, what secret plans they were following. But it was almost a pointless line of inquiry—if this was part of some official, but secret operation, one not even the Command Council knew about, then they would never get to the bottom of it. Kodiak voiced that opinion to Avalon and the chief agreed.

The two sat in silence for a while. Outside, work went on in the bullpen, the place a hive of activity that was, to the two agents sitting in the planning room, totally silent. Kodiak watched them for a while, letting his mind wander. They needed to come up with a new plan, but he was aware he was tired. He needed some rest, and soon, even if it was just for a few hours.

Kodiak sighed. He could survive on coffee for a while longer. There was a bigger, more important thing he needed than sleep.

He turned in his seat. Avalon was leaning over the table, examining the lab report, her forehead in her hands. Her long red hair framed her face, hiding it from Kodiak.

"We need to find Tyler and Caitlin Smith, *now*," he said.

Avalon looked up. "And how do we do that? Caitlin Smith doesn't have her tag anymore, and Tyler's is shielded and doesn't show up on the Fleet manifest."

Kodiak rolled his neck. "And the door-to-door hasn't picked up anything yet." Reports from the city lockdown were flooding the Bureau—with so many agents and marines enforcing the lockdown out in the city, it was all the bullpen could do to keep up with the flow of information. Kodiak curled his hand into a fist and bumped it against the table in frustration. "The two prime suspects are psi-abled. You'd think that would be some kind of help at least." He gave a sigh and slumped back into his seat, wracking his brains for options. Damn, he was tired.

Then Avalon sat up in her chair. She turned to her agent. He sat up too, recognizing a fire in her eyes.

"What?"

"Moustafa," she said. Kodiak frowned and Avalon tapped a fingernail on the table. "*Commander* Moustafa," she explained. "He's a lead psi-trainer at the Fleet Academy."

Kodiak pursed his lips. "Okay . . . one of the Smiths' teachers, I assume?"

The chief nodded. "Yes. He's a good friend. I remember

something he once briefed the Command Council on, maybe six months ago. They were working with the Alpha One class on something—they could take the psychospore of an individual and follow it back to them."

"Psychospore?" Kodiak's eyes went wide.

"The psychospore is the psychic echo everyone leaves—it's what our psi-fi equipment uses when it pairs with our minds."

Kodiak rubbed his eyes as his Fleet training came back to him—specific information on psionics that he hadn't needed to call on in . . . well, in years.

"I remember," he said, nodding. "That's how the psi-marines link up to form their gestalts—they kinda listen out for the psychospore of the other members in their fireteam, using it to lock their consciousnesses together to form the hive mind."

"Exactly," said Avalon. "And while their minds are linked, the gestalt is essentially one single entity. Like the Spiders themselves."

"So what was the Academy working on?"

"I don't remember the details," said the chief, "but I think the idea is that if the gestalt is a single mind, in theory each of the psi-marines will know where the other members of their team are. Their physical location."

Kodiak's jaw worked as he processed the concept. It sounded logical, although he knew he was very much a layman when it came to the Psi-Marine Corps. But, if this "technique" was viable, then maybe they had a new option available, one that would allow them to find both Tyler and Caitlin, even without the manifest tags.

Then he frowned as he thought again. "But doesn't that mean Tyler and Caitlin need to be part of a team's gestalt?"

Avalon shrugged. "Like I said, I don't remember the specifics."

"I think you need to talk to Commander Moustafa. If there's a chance this might work, we need to take it."

"Agreed," said the chief. She pushed her chair out and headed for the door, but she stopped, one hand on the handle as she turned back to her agent. "You need to get some rest. I'll talk to Moustafa. I'm not sure how long it would take to organize, if we can do this at all, but

I'll call you. You'll have a couple of hours at least. You look like you could use that."

Kodiak nodded. "Thanks," he said.

As Avalon left, the sound of the busy bullpen came through the open door for a few seconds, then cut out again as the door clicked closed.

Kodiak allowed himself a yawn, then stood and stretched. He could rest, just for a little bit. And yes, he certainly needed it.

But as he walked to the door, he felt excitement grow.

Maybe they had another option open.

Maybe they could find the Smith twins.

Maybe they could get some damn answers.

23

"I don't know about you, but this is giving me the creeps. Seriously, man. The *creeps.*"

Braben sipped his coffee as he stood next to Kodiak and Commander Avalon. They were in a large and perfectly circular room, the walls Fleet-standard silvery gray but angled outward from the floor, so the chamber was considerably wider at the ceiling than ground level. In the ceiling of the strange chamber was a white circular light panel, spotlighting the center of the room and the eight reclining couches arranged like petals around the hub. The couches were thickly padded and articulated, like the medical equipment they were. Arranged around them were three separate consoles, curved like the walls of the room. The entire set-up was minimal, symmetrical. It was, Kodiak thought, like standing inside a giant metal flower. It was beautiful too, but Braben was right. The strange space was also a little creepy, the weird design making the chamber feel very . . . *unfamiliar.* He swallowed a ball of tension.

"Yeah, I know the feeling," said Kodiak, exchanging a look not just with Braben but with the chief too. Avalon was silent, but her expression was firm. They were venturing into unknown territory with this, but if this was successful, it would mean a lot to the Bureau—not just in terms of the current investigation, but as a new technique for them to use.

If it was successful.

But, at least he was feeling better after a couple of hours of sleep. Now it was Braben's turn to look ragged. He'd been up all night in the lab apparently, in case the techs had discovered anything as they dismantled the servitor from the warehouse. Then the pair had spent the best part of the last few hours going over the data down at the bullpen while Avalon flexed her authority and made contact with her friend, Commander Moustafa at the Fleet Academy. The technique they were about to employ was experimental. New territory. But Moustafa had been cooperative, and for that Kodiak was grateful.

It sounded so simple too. The search would be conducted by a psi-team, who lay on the couches, closed their eyes, and . . .

What, exactly? Kodiak wasn't sure. He had zero psi-ability himself, aside from the general low-level aura every human being possessed that allowed various bits of equipment—the helmet computers Fleet personnel wore out on the field, for example—to function by thought alone. So whatever the psi-team was about to do, whatever they saw, or felt, or heard, or whatever the hell it was, he really had no idea. All he could do was sit and watch and hope they succeeded in finding their two targets: Tyler Smith and Caitlin Smith. Tyler was the priority, but ideally they wanted both of them in custody.

The main doors slid open behind them. The trio turned as a dozen personnel filed in: at the front, a tall officer with a closely cropped black beard, the rank insignia on his chest set onto the black inverted triangle of the Psi-Marine Corps. The officer was followed by two women and a man dressed in the white uniforms and garrison caps of technical operators—FlyEyes without their multifaceted headsets—and eight younger personnel in tan uniforms marking them as students from the Academy.

As Kodiak watched the team arrive, Braben turned to the chief, his eyes wide in surprise. "These the best for the job? Cadets?"

Avalon ignored the comment, instead snapping a command.

"Attention, Agents!"

Braben and Kodiak automatically obeyed, Braben ducking down to place his coffee on the floor before joining Kodiak in a salute while Bureau Chief and Commander Moustafa saluted each other, then shook hands.

"Thanks for this, Ibrahim," said the chief.

"Of course," said the Psi-Marine Commander. "We have to throw everything at this. The Academy is honored to be of assistance."

Avalon introduced Kodiak and Braben to her colleague. After they made their greetings, Moustafa insisted the two agents stand at ease. Then he gestured to the three ops he had brought with him. "This is First Sergeant Epstein and Corporals Sigler and Holt, three of our best technical trainers."

The technicians saluted, which Kodiak, Braben, and Avalon acknowledged. Standing next to him, Kodiak thought he could physically feel Braben's anxiety, radiating off him like heat. Moustafa had clearly heard Braben's earlier comment. He nodded at the agent, then turned to the group of eight cadets assembled just behind him.

"I know what you are thinking," he said. "Yes, they are young. Yes, they are cadets. But I can assure you, they are the best." He turned to regard his students and held out his hand, palm open. "This is Alpha One, the elite class of Sixty-Nine from the Psi-Marine Academy. They may not have served the Fleet yet, but believe me, they are ready." He turned back to the Bureau agents. "More than that, Alpha One-Sixty-Nine, along with their ops trainers, were actually the ones to help develop the technique we're about to test for you."

At the edge of his vision, Kodiak saw Braben narrow his eyes as he looked at the group of cadets. There were five men and three women, and Kodiak had to agree that they did all look barely out of their teens. Braben retrieved his coffee from the floor, but didn't say any more.

But he knew Avalon trusted the Academy commander, and *he* trusted the chief. Alpha One *were* the best of the best. Both Caitlin and Tyler Smith had been part of that class, after all.

Avalon cocked her head. "Are you able to give us an estimate on the probability of success?"

Moustafa pursed his lips. "That's a difficult question, Commander. I am certain we *will* obtain a result, but what I cannot estimate is how long it will take. There are risks involved with this new technique, so we will need to proceed cautiously.

Kodiak lifted his head. "Risks, sir?"

Moustafa nodded, bouncing on his heels a little as he folded his arms. "To locate the two missing persons, the cadets will form their own gestalt. While this is a standard skill for any psi-marine, directing the gestalt to find other minds is not. To achieve this, the gestalt will essentially act like a magnet, drawing other psi-abled people into it. If the targets are still in New Orem, they'll be able to sense them both." Moustafa glanced at the chief. "And therein lies the problem."

The chief raised an eyebrow as Moustafa gestured to the circular chamber in which they stood.

"This training room is psychically shielded," he said, "so it will mitigate the effects somewhat, but the ops will be monitoring the gestalt field constantly. In a city the size of New Orem, there is a very high probability of there being psi-abled citizens out there who don't even know it."

Avalon frowned. "I'm sensing that's a problem."

Moustafa nodded. "As part of a gestalt, you sacrifice your sense of self, deliberately. Psi-marines are trained to deal with this and control it, but it is dangerous for those without that skill. An untrained mind caught in the gestalt may not be able to escape it."

Kodiak sighed. Okay, that *was* a problem. He knew the technique was experimental, still very much in its infancy, but that seemed to be an almost insurmountable drawback. He drew his finger under his bottom lip as he considered the implications. He felt his confidence in the plan begin to sink.

"So," he said slowly, "how do we do this without killing a certain percentage of the city's general population?"

Commander Moustafa walked over to the couches at the center of the training room. "Carefully is the answer, Agent. Everything is monitored from here"—he pointed to one of the freestanding consoles—"along with control of the training room's shielding field.

The ops will let the gestalt out into the city a bit at a time. Any sign of trouble, we can pull it back and try again."

"Trouble like people dropping dead in the street?" asked Braben. He turned to Avalon and flapped his arms against his sides. "Chief, please tell me you don't agree with this? We can sweep the city again, get more teams out. Put agents on everything going in and out of the starport. Maybe we can find the targets without frying the minds of every unsuspecting psi-abled person in a fifty-kilometer radius."

Avalon sighed, then folded her arms. She looked first at Braben, then at Kodiak. Kodiak wondered what was going through her mind—the same as his, most likely: fear, uncertainty, doubt. But desperate times called for desperate measures.

And . . . if this *worked* . . .

Finally, perhaps after giving the matter one last moment of consideration, the chief spoke.

"It's a calculated risk," she said. She turned to face the psi-marine officer. "You may proceed when ready, Commander."

Kodiak exhaled the breath he'd been holding. This was it. Avalon had made the right decision.

Beside him, Braben sighed and folded his arms, but he stayed quiet.

Moustafa gave the chief a short bow, then he stepped up to the group of cadets.

"Alpha One, *ten-shun,*" he said, his voice suddenly loud in the circular room. Immediately the class snapped to attention, then shuffled their feet as their trainer gave the command to stand at ease. Eight fresh faces looked at the mentor. They weren't smiling, but Kodiak could see an eagerness there, and a pride also. Alpha One. The best of the best.

"As you are aware, this is a live mission," said Moustafa. "You have all been briefed. The psychospore of the two targets have been isolated from Academy records, so we have a good chance of tracking that back to them. Remember, the targets were psi-marines as well, like you will be. More than that, they were Alpha One as well. Whatever trouble they are in, whatever they have gotten themselves into, it's our duty to bring them back to the fold."

He paused and looked up and down the rank of cadets.

"I won't lie to you," he said. "This is beyond the normal parameters of your Academy training. But you are all aware of the recent events that have brought about these extraordinary circumstances. Extraordinary circumstances that demand extraordinary service. You have helped develop this technique, in cooperation with your ops trainers. You are more than capable of carrying out this mission to success. Is that understood?"

"Sir!" intoned the cadets.

Moustafa nodded, then gestured to the couches. "Alpha One, prepare."

The young recruits fanned out around the center of the room, and each climbed onto a couch. As far as Kodiak could see, the couches weren't connected to anything—no cables, no monitoring devices of any kind, save for the freestanding consoles, each of which now had a technician at station.

The eight cadets adjusted themselves, their heads all together at the center, their arms crossed over their chests. After a moment, First Sergeant Epstein nodded at the two other ops, who confirmed their readiness. She looked over at her commander.

"Alpha One, ready sir."

Moustafa acknowledged and turned to Avalon, his eyebrows raised.

Kodiak glanced at Braben. The agent was standing on his left, his arms folded, his expression dark.

Kodiak didn't blame him for his reluctance—this was dangerous, an experiment with so much riding on it. Alpha One were so young . . . but, Kodiak knew, so powerful. They could do this.

Then Kodiak glanced sideways at Avalon. She was watching the cadets, like he was, but her face was unreadable. She was the Bureau Chief, a position of considerable power within the Fleet hierarchy. But the results of this experiment were going to fall on her shoulders. She had accepted the risk, she trusted Moustafa and his team. But Kodiak thought he could understand what she was feeling, thinking—she was not just his commander, but his friend.

Moustafa's voice snapped Kodiak out of his reverie.

"Commence psi-link. Alpha One, over to you."

Kodiak blinked and took half a step back, his arms now folded as he watched.

The eight members of Alpha One acknowledged, and then they all closed their eyes. With arms drawn across their chests, Kodiak thought the scene looked a little creepy, the eight young cadets looking like war dead laid out for interment.

Minutes passed. Kodiak wasn't entirely sure what he expected to happen, but so far nothing had. The cadets lay still on their couches. Moustafa stood watching them. The three ops at their consoles studied readouts and occasionally tapped a control. But that was it. There was no sound. No change in the light. Nothing at all.

Kodiak cleared his throat, a nervous reflex that made Moustafa turn at the sound, but the commander merely gave Kodiak a curt nod then turned back to the cadets. Kodiak felt like they had to be quiet, like they were observing some kind of ceremony or delicate operation that could not be disturbed. Which, he guessed, was actually exactly right.

They waited. The technicians stared at their consoles. The cadets remained perfectly still, hardly even breathing. Kodiak moved his eyes from one to another, sometimes thinking they had stopped breathing until, as the seconds passed, he saw their chests rise and fall in a slow rhythm. He rolled his neck again. He was feeling very much more nervous than he thought he would.

And then the cadets started moving their lips, like they were whispering. Kodiak frowned and strained to hear, but he couldn't make anything out. Moustafa seemed to notice Kodiak's interest and leaned in to him.

"This is quite normal," he said quietly. "The psi-link requires immense concentration, and sometimes it helps them focus to speak the thoughts to one another."

Kodiak nodded. "Any idea when we'll find out if it's working?"

Moustafa pursed his lips. "We should know soon—"

One of the cadets convulsed and screamed. One of the technicians,

Corporal Holt, ducked around his console and moved to the cadet to hold him down. Kodiak started forward, but Moustafa grabbed his arm. The other seven cadets didn't move, apparently unaware of the seizure one of their number was having.

"Psi-feedback," said Moustafa. "Don't worry. It can happen." He called out to the technicians. "Epstein, report."

"Gestalt stable," said the First Sergeant. Then she leaned down over her console, peering at a readout. "There's something else, though."

Avalon and Kodiak exchanged a look. Braben moved over to the console and looked down over the technician's shoulder.

"What do you mean, something else?" Braben asked.

"I'm not sure," said Epstein. "Some kind of noise. Might just be the psychospore tracking off line a little. Trying to isolate now. . . ."

The cadets began to speak, the seven who remained still on their couches muttering in a monotone. The eighth cadet writhed on his couch, the technician holding him down, but his movements were slowing.

Kodiak watched, anxiety blooming in his chest. This was normal? He wondered whether they needed to call a medic, but Moustafa remained calm and collected. The commander moved to the couches, Avalon at his heel. Kodiak decided to follow, and together the three of them looked around at the cadets.

"What are they saying?" asked Avalon. Moustafa held up a hand, then closed his eyes and pinched the bridge of his nose with one hand. As Kodiak watched, the chief psi-trainer flinched.

The murmuring increased in volume. Then the cadets spoke clearly and loudly, one after another, going around in the circle.

"Eight."

"Seven."

"Nine."

"One."

"Two."

"Two."

"Juno."

"Juno," said Moustafa, and the cycle began again. When it came back to Moustafa again, he repeated the last word, and then it continued. Again, and again, and again.

Kodiak felt that anxiety blossom into full-on fear. He had no idea what was happening, but he knew he had to keep back, let Moustafa handle it.

Avalon moved to join Braben at the console. First Sergeant Epstein was busy at the controls, but Braben just shook his head. Avalon looked up at Kodiak.

"Eight-seven-nine-one-two-two-Juno-Juno?"

Kodiak held his hands up in confusion. "I have no idea. It sounds like coordinates of some kind. Juno Juno will be planetary."

Kodiak looked at Commander Moustafa. The pained expression had cleared, but his eyes were still closed. He was muttering the complete sequence to himself, now out of sync with the cadets around him.

Kodiak wanted to reach out and shake him out of it. "Commander?" he asked. Did Moustafa know what the sequence was?

Moustafa nodded. "Yes, it's coordinates, but I'm not sure what for." Then his face screwed up in pain. "There's . . . there's something else here with us." He cried out and doubled over. On the couches, the seven cadets suddenly convulsed and screamed in pain.

Moustafa collapsed on the floor. Now Kodiak moved to help. As he knelt by the collapsed commander, he looked up and waved at the technicians. Avalon turned to them.

"Pull them all out," she yelled. "Now!"

Moustafa groaned in Kodiak's arms, Avalon rushing back to help. His eyes flickered open and he looked around, clearly disoriented, but when he saw Kodiak looking at him, he licked his lips and scrambled to pull himself up with his and Avalon's help.

"Are you okay?" asked the chief. Moustafa seemed to have difficulty focusing on her, but eventually he nodded.

Kodiak pulled his arm. "What happened? Did it work? Is everything okay?"

Moustafa brushed Kodiak off and stood. He staggered to the nearest console and leaned against it. Corporal Sigler moved to help him, but he waved the technician away. Meanwhile, the cadets moaned as they lay on their couches, Holt now moving from one to the next, checking pulses and looking into their eyes. One of the cadets raised himself up on his elbows and rolled his neck. Moustafa went to his side.

"Augustine," he said. "How are you feeling?"

Cadet Augustine nodded at his superior and wet his lips. He rubbed his forehead with one hand. "I'm okay, I think, sir. We performed the psi-link and had a stable gestalt, at least until . . ." The cadet winced in pain, then grabbed the commander's arm and sat bolt upright, staring straight ahead, his eyes wide.

"Eight-seven-nine-one-two-two-Juno-Juno," he said, and said again, repeating the sequence as he began struggling against Moustafa. Holt pulled a small silver cylinder out of her tunic pocket and pressed it against the cadet's neck. Augustine immediately fell back onto the couch and didn't move again.

Kodiak swore and ran his hands through his hair. He began pacing around the circular room. This was wrong, wrong, wrong.

"Von, come here," called Braben. Kodiak went to the console where Braben and the technician were talking. Braben took his datapad out of the inside of his jacket and began tapping notes.

"It worked," he said, pointing at one of the readouts. "The gestalt made contact with one target anyway."

Kodiak peered at the screen. There were screeds of tiny text, but First Sergeant Epstein tapped the display at a single line of numbers. They were real coordinates, unlike the garbled sequence the cadets had spoken.

Braben finished copying the text down on his datapad, then held it next to the console display to double check it. He looked at Kodiak.

"You know where that is?" he asked, angling the datapad so Kodiak could see.

Kodiak shook his head. "We need to map it, but I recognize the first part: Salt City." He looked up at Epstein. "Which target did you locate?"

Epstein's fingers moved over the console display. "Psychospore trail is for . . . Smith, Caitlin."

Kodiak frowned. So, she *was* alive, having survived the removal of her manifest tag. But she was still the *second* priority.

"What about Tyler Smith?"

Epstein continued to work. She was silent for several moments; Kodiak looked down at the console but couldn't make any sense of the readout himself.

Then the op shook her head. "Negative."

Kodiak sighed. *Shit.* Well, okay, they had one, at least.

Braben waved the datapad in the air. "I'll get back to the bullpen, run the coordinates, get another Tac team together."

Avalon nodded her assent, and the agent strode over to the training room's door and left.

Kodiak frowned, then went over to where Avalon was helping Moustafa. The psi-commander still looked groggy and was leaning back against one of the consoles.

He smiled at Kodiak. "I'll be fine, don't worry. We'll get the cadets down to the medical center and have them checked out."

Kodiak nodded.

"What about those other coordinates?" asked Avalon, but Moustafa could only manage a shrug and a shake of the head in reply.

"Well, let's add that to the list of unanswered questions," said Kodiak. "But in the meantime we need to grab Caitlin Smith before she moves. We can figure the rest out later."

"Agreed," said Avalon.

With one last look at Moustafa, who held up his hand and nodded, Kodiak stood and headed for the door.

They were going to have to move quick if they didn't want to lose Caitlin again.

24

Cait's eyes flickered open. She jerked awake, then winced as pain shot across the back of her neck. Gingerly feeling for the bandage, she sat up and looked around.

She was behind a stairwell that stunk of dusty damp concrete and other things. It was morning, light pouring in through the huge open squares in the wall opposite.

She was in her old building, at the bottom of one of the stairwells on the north side.

She sat up, then stood, leaning on the wall for support. She felt better, having dragged herself under cover before passing out again. Whatever crap had been in her system felt like it was clearing. She took a deep breath, pleased at how her entire body didn't ache. Her neck was stiff, but that was to be expected. She needed to get someone to take a look at that, somehow. To find out what her captors had done to her in the warehouse.

There was movement nearby, someone or something shuffling on the rough concrete of the building's floor, heading in her direction. She needed to move, now, find a new position so she could consider her options.

Cait ducked out from under the stairs, heading toward the main entrance, but then quickly moved behind a pillar as a group of four large men, dressed in ragged, mismatched clothing, walked into the doorway and stopped. Cait watched them from her cover, willing them to move on. They were scavengers, lowlifes who went from building to building, pulling out people, looking for money, drugs, anything. This building had been hit before—the man Cait had sent tumbling from her twelfth floor window had been a scavenger—but it was impossible to tell whether it was the same group or not. And it didn't matter. They were dangerous. They were thieves and killers, and worse besides.

She couldn't stay here. She waited, listening with her mind, but Glass was quiet. Not for the first time, she wondered if he really had spoken to her, or whether it was just her own mind breaking down under the stress.

Her brother's voice was silent, as well.

The only way out of the building was past the scavengers. But she was near the stairs, which meant she could go up. Her old nest was burnt out, but she'd scouted the rest of the building. Plenty of places to hide out temporarily until the coast was clear. She knew the scavengers would scour the building, but they were unlikely to head too high up. That was what had made her old hideout ideal—apart from that single visitor, she had been undisturbed by scavengers, their attention spans fried by the crap they smoked or sniffed or injected, so they rarely made it past the first half dozen or so floors of what tall buildings Salt City had. She could pick a spot and wait until the group got bored and left.

She checked the doorway again. The gang of four were still there, talking, smoking something sweet and sickly, but they were all facing away from her.

Taking care to be silent, Cait slipped out from behind the column and headed up the stairwell.

* * *

It was a long haul up the stairs and soon enough Cait realized she wasn't in as good shape as she tried to tell herself she was when she'd been on the ground level. After the first floor, she'd been forced to pull herself up the stairwell with the rail one-handed, and when there wasn't a rail, she crawled up like an injured animal, her good hand pulling on the dusty concrete stairs ahead of her as she pushed herself up with her legs. But she could do it. The voices of the men down in the lobby faded the higher she climbed, and she managed to find a rhythm, one that was slow but regular. One that allowed her to keep going, no matter what. She was a marine, after all—well, not quite a marine, but being Alpha One had to count for something. Before she'd left, she'd completed all her training with flying colors. Including physical training. Out there on the Warworlds there were worse situations than having a bandaged neck and a head echoing with the aftereffects of the cocktail of painkillers and anesthetics and fuck knows what else they had pumped into her.

She didn't need the Academy to tell her she could do it. She could survive this. Because she knew she could. And not only would she survive this, she would rest, and heal, and then she would find her brother. She'd come up with a plan. And if that plan meant taking out that bitch Flood and the rest of her gang of crazies, then all the better.

She flopped chest-first onto the next landing of the stairwell and braced to push herself up to the standing position to turn and take the next section of stairs. Ten floors. Twelve was where she had lived before. Eleven was something of a warren, she remembered, and a good level to find a hiding spot. Just one more flight of stairs to go. And this one, thankfully, had a rail again.

"Hey there, my little chickadee."

Cait looked up as she was grabbed under both armpits by thick hands. She yelped in pain and surprise as the two men behind her pulled her roughly up. Then her attention was firmly on the man in front of her.

He was standing on the second stair, one hand on the railing, the other holding a long, thin blade, more like a razor than a knife. He wore a sleeveless tunic that exposed not just his arms but his bare chest, the skin of both covered in a hypnotic, concentric pattern of dark tattoos. He had hair shorn into a mullet, with a thick moustache on his face. He grinned, and his teeth shone as bright in the dim stairwell as the blade in his hand.

The men holding Cait up stank like nothing else—not just of sweat and muck, but something high, sweet, chemical. Whether they were anything to do with the scavengers down in the lobby, it was impossible to tell. Perhaps the whole building had been overrun, and Cait had just got lucky when she collapsed, out of sight, under the stairwell.

The leader of the group trotted down the last two stairs and stepped closer to Cait, so close she could feel his hot breath wafting over her face, the stink of it mixing with the other organic aromas of the gang. He grinned, his mouth moving wetly, as he touched his blade to her cheek. With his other hand he grabbed her right breast and squeezed hard.

Cait tried to turn her body away from him, but that only made the two men behind her tighten their grip. The leader licked his lips and said something to his friends in a language Cait didn't recognize. Whatever it was, they all laughed—hard enough for the hands on her to loosen, just a little. Just enough.

Cait's eyelids fluttered and her head was filled with a humming, electric and dangerous.

Cait screamed and rammed her knee up, catching the man in front of her square in his stomach. He huffed as the air left him, and as he curled down over her, Cait followed her knee with a jab from her good hand into his jaw. The man staggered backwards until his ass touched the wall by the stairs.

The other two were taken by surprise; one squeezed his hand harder on her arm, but Cait was already twisting free. She put a handful of steps between her and her captor, then, turning on her heel, she swung her hand up. The lowlife was out of range, but it didn't matter, not now. Cait gritted her teeth and the man staggered backwards, clutching his chest like he'd been hit. The other snarled and lunged forward. Now Cait's Academy training kicked in and she swiped one leg out, planting her boot in the man's stomach, sending him reeling backwards. Cait's world spun as her consciousness threatened to abandon her, but she sucked in a tight breath of air over her teeth and concentrated on survival above all else.

The three men rolled on the floor, blocking the stairwell leading down, their leader already recovering, pushing himself up against the wall. His eyes met Cait's. He snarled. Cait powered toward the stairs as he moved forward, heading up, the only option open to her. Running on adrenaline, she took the steps two at a time, bouncing off the wall on her shoulder as she weaved toward her former base on the twelfth level.

That was no good. As she rounded the top of the stairs at the next landing, she was confronted by blackened, sooty concrete and the acrid smell of fire.

She kept going up, her legs aching, her lungs burning. But she kept moving. Behind her, the three attackers were shouting—whether at her or each other, she didn't know.

Level thirteen. Empty, nothing but an open-sided platform lined with steel beams. Nobody lived on thirteen.

She swung herself onto the next stair section.

Level fourteen.

She ran from the stair block, then skidded to a halt. It was windy, enough for her to have to fight to keep her footing. As the wind whipped around, pulling her hair around her face, she turned, searching for—

There was nothing. Level fourteen was the roof. A flat platform. No walls. Nothing. On one side was a low-lying plain, glowing orange, stretching as far as she could see. Salt City.

On the other, the crystalline wonder of New Orem, the tall skyscrapers lit from within in brilliant white, while lower, toward street level, a multitude of moving light of every other color in the spectrum. The rooftop was wet and reflected the bright city lights in a million different ways.

"Oh, we're going to have some fun tonight, chickadee!"

Cait turned. The leader of the gang of three emerged from the stairwell. He was topless, having lost his open tunic somewhere during their struggle. Behind him came his two friends, one rolling his thick neck, the other still rubbing his stomach from where Cait had connected with her boot.

The leader wiped his mouth with a forearm as thick as Cait's leg and walked toward her. She backed away, toward the edge.

There was nowhere to go. Nowhere to go but *down*.

"Come here, my little chickadee. I'm gonna make you scream so loud you'll wake everybody in the city."

Cait fell onto one knee. She looked down, saw herself in the reflected pool of water, saw Glass standing behind her. Saw him saying something. Something she thought she'd heard before.

Her vision crowded with black stars and white static and her mind with the hum, the *hum* . . .

Kodiak looked out of the side of the carrier as ahead, two drones raced across the cityscape, completing another orbit of the target area. The HUD inside Kodiak's visor chimed and a green indicator appeared. The cadets had done well. The drones had confirmed the target's position. All they had to do now was go in and get her.

"We sure that's her?"

Kodiak tilted his head as Braben spoke from the Bureau bullpen, where he had elected to stay this time to monitor the pick-up. Kodiak frowned and, with a thought, brought up the surveillance feed from one of the drones as it made another pass over the target area. The playback showed a half-finished building with a flat roof. On top were four figures; three standing, one crouching.

"Affirmative," said Kodiak. "I have visual confirmation. The drones have been following her since the cadets picked up her location."

"She has company."

"Roger that." Kodiak turned to the team strapped into the carrier compartment with him. "Watch the drone feed. She's in the perfect place for pick-up. We go in, grab her."

"What about the other three?" asked the team leader. "Kill or capture?"

"Let's see what they do." Kodiak glanced up in his visor, focusing on the feed. The other three forms were indistinct, flaring badly in the enhanced night vision, their forms melting in a bright mess caused by city light reflecting off the wet roof. "Primary objective is to secure the target."

"Affirmative."

Kodiak zoomed in on the feed, then brought up audio. They were just minutes away. He wanted to know if they were saying anything.

There was nothing but the rush of the wind. Then the drone adjusted its directional microphones at the target and began processing the audio. It was hissy, barely understandable, but enough of what Cait was saying came through for Kodiak's stomach to do a flip.

"Eight-seven . . . un . . . oo-two-Juno-Ju . . ."

Kodiak clicked the feed off and pulled his staser from its holster.

Time to close the net.

Cait blinked, and Glass was gone. She looked up, saw the men loom over her, the leer on their faces, and then her hair was blown across her eyes as the wind suddenly picked up, swirling around the rooftop, strong enough to blow the water off the surface and fill the air with a fine, sharp mist.

The hum in her mind had turned into a roar like a jet engine. The prickle coursing across her body was so sharp she wanted to dig her fingernails into her arms and rip her skin off.

She stood.

The men staggered backward, squinting in the wind as they looked not *at* her, but *behind* her. Cait balanced herself as the wind buffeted her on the rooftop. She held her arms out, staggering slightly as the wind gusted, pushing her forward.

One of the thugs turned to run; Cait threw a hand forward and the man's feet left the ground. He flew forward through the air, then tumbled onto the roof and didn't move.

The remaining thug yelled something at his bare-chested boss; Cait's attention moved to him. She flicked her wrist, and he twisted, like something large had slammed into his shoulder, then his legs went out from under him, and he tumbled backwards.

The bare-chested leader roared something that was lost against the other sound, the sound of engines howling in the night, and went to grab Cait. He got two steps closer; Cait fell to her knees, head down, and pulled her hands together in front of him. The man doubled over and was flung back across the roof. He collided with the stair block, hard enough to crack the concrete.

Cait collapsed, falling sideways onto the roof. She squinted against the spray of water being blown from the object hovering between her and the lights of New Orem. It was long, rectangular, just a silhouette backlit by the city. It rocked slightly in the air, and there were other shapes, men jumping out from the side of it and running toward her.

And then she let herself surrender, finally, to the wonderful, glorious, warm, comforting bliss of nothingness, a world without fear and without pain and without thought.

25

Cait woke up and looked around. The room was steel gray, the walls made up of individual panels that slotted into each other. There were various small pieces of text and barcodes printed around the place in white, and here and there LEDs in multiple colors either shone or blinked.

She recognized it immediately. She knew exactly where she was.

She was back at the Fleet.

Cait raised herself up and leaned forward at an uncomfortable angle, but her wrists were held in place by manacles. She pulled against them, then cried out as electric hot pain surged down her neck. She slumped back onto the couch, panting. The pain faded quickly, replaced now with a dull thud across her temples.

"Yeah, you're going to want to take it easy awhile," said a voice nearby. She turned her head, wincing as her neck stretched again, and saw a black man in a suit the same color as the prefabricated walls standing next to the bed. His hands were in the pockets of his jacket, and clipped onto the lapel was a square of mirrored silver, an icon etched onto it in gold. Cait squinted, trying to recognize the insignia. Then she gave up and lay back on the bed, her head thundering. She was well and truly sick of being stuck in medical units, being restrained. She closed her eyes and waited for her headache to subside.

Footsteps. She opened her eyes and saw the black guy had been joined by another man. He was taller, white, with messy black hair that looked like it needed a wash and a stubble-covered chin. He was wearing a black uniform that included an armored vest over a black shirt, the words FLEET and BUREAU stenciled, one under the other, across his chest. Like the man in the suit, he sported a square chrome badge on one side.

Cait looked at the pair—one smart, manicured, in a tailored suit, the other the exact opposite. She glanced at the words on the second guy's vest again.

Fleet Bureau? The Fleet Bureau of Investigation? Cait's groggy mind raced. Of course. The Fleet's internal police force. Sure, she knew who they were. Everyone who worked in the Fleet did, even Academy dropouts like her.

Which meant they'd got her. Finally, they'd got her. And maybe that was good. Yes, it was good. She could tell them everything. Tell them about the Morning Star, about Samantha Flood.

About her brother? About the voices in her head? About Glass, the man she'd killed accidentally?

About the fact she'd nearly pulled the trigger on the Fleet Admiral?

She pulled at the manacles again. She was restrained because she was under arrest. They thought she'd done it. That she was the shooter. Public enemy number one.

Cait felt her pulse begin to race. She looked around, suddenly panicked. Where *was* she? The room didn't look like a medical unit. It was square and featureless. She craned her neck around and saw there was a stool at the head of the bed. Sitting on it was a woman in an olive and blue uniform, an inverted black triangle on her chest. She had short hair—shaved short—and she looked into Cait's eyes, her face expressionless, her mouth set into a straight line. Cait recoiled in surprise, but the woman didn't even flinch.

Cait's eyes dropped to the black triangle insignia on the woman's uniform. She thought she knew what it meant, but she couldn't remember.

Dammit, what the fuck was wrong with her? She couldn't think straight. Couldn't remember.

Where was she again?

"Caitlin Smith?" asked the tall man. Cait blinked and turned her head to look at him. He frowned, glanced at his colleague, then turned back to her, hands on hips, his whiskered chin creasing as he frowned. "I'm Special Agent Von Kodiak from the Fleet Bureau of Investigation. This is my partner, Special Agent Mike Braben. Do you know where you are now?"

Cait nodded, just a little. Her head still hurt, and the light in the room was too bright. All she wanted to do was sleep and sleep and sleep.

"I'm in the Fleet complex," she said. Her voice was stronger than she expected. The man called Kodiak nodded. And then she said: "I didn't do it."

Kodiak exchanged another look at Braben. Braben seemed to shrug. Kodiak turned back to her.

"Do what?"

Cait shook her head. "I didn't kill him. It wasn't me."

"Okay, well, that's what we're about to find out," said Kodiak. "Under Fleet Bureau of Investigation primary directive one-zero, I have to inform you you are currently being held in connection with an ongoing investigation. Under Fleet Bureau of Investigation primary directive one-one, you are now the physical property of the Fleet—"

"It wasn't me," said Cait, her eyes wide.

Kodiak ignored her. "And as per Fleet Bureau of Investigation primary directive four-six-one pertaining to desertion of duty, you will now be subject to psi-interrogation to ascertain your level of guilt and culpability."

"Okay," said Cait. "Okay, okay, okay." She gritted her teeth, preparing for what was to come. Psi-interrogation? Good. Psi-interrogation would reveal the truth, everything. They'd know it wasn't her. They'd know everything she did about her employers, who had turned out to be the Morning Star. She presumed they already knew what they'd done to her physically—perhaps now they'd be able to figure out why.

Cait closed her eyes. "I'm ready."

She heard Kodiak shift on his feet, and then he said, "Authority to proceed granted."

Cait tried to relax. Psi-interrogation wasn't a cakewalk. It wasn't standard procedure either, an extreme technique usually only used on the most uncooperative suspects, or those otherwise unable to provide voluntary statements. She guessed that as prime suspect in the assassination of the Fleet Admiral—the head of state himself—psi-interrogation was considered the first option.

Good, good. She didn't know what to expect, but she thought that if she relaxed, opened her mind, tried to squash the fear she felt welling inside her, that it would be easier. Both for her, and for her interrogator.

Okay. Okay, okay, okay . . .

She felt the interrogator seated behind her place hands on Cait's shoulders, and Cait suddenly felt her strength ebb away like melting ice. She lay back on the couch, watching the shapes crawl behind her eyelids as she recalled her training, trying to remember how psi-interrogations worked. She'd seen some recordings of real ones as part of her basic psi-training. She knew the principles, but it was a specialized skill, not something taught as standard. But the numbness, the feeling of warmth—like drifting to sleep but staying awake, aware at the same time—that seemed to make sense. The interrogator sitting behind her had just blocked Cait's motor centers with a single thought. Next she would begin peeling away the layers of consciousness, extracting thoughts, ideas, memories that would be used against the suspect.

Okay. Okay, okay, okay. That was good. Because she was innocent. She hadn't shot the Fleet Admiral. She hadn't shot anyone.

Her eyelids fluttered, and she could just see the two agents heading toward the door to leave the interrogation room. They were talking to each other, but she couldn't hear what they were saying, only the roar of the blood in her ears, the sound of an ocean far away.

"My brother," she said . . . or she *thought* she said—she wasn't sure because she couldn't feel her mouth or her lips or her tongue anymore. She could just see the two agents stop and turn around. "My brother . . . where is my brother?" Had she said that aloud, or was that just in her head?

The agents looked at each other, then turned back to the door.

Cait felt her eyes close and the darkness move around her like it was a thing alive, like warm water. Blood warm.

She felt like she was falling. There was a moment of fear, that sudden panic that something was wrong. Instinctively she reached out, not with her hands but with her mind, searching for something—*anything*—to indicate that she wasn't alone and that Tyler was there, somewhere, somewhere where he could see her and hear her and tell her that everything would be all right and okay.

There was someone there. She could sense it. Tyler? No. The interrogator. Or was it . . . ?

"Glass?"

She wasn't sure if she'd spoken his name aloud. She stared into the swirling blackness, shadows chasing shadows.

But there was nothing but silence. Her brother was gone. Whether she'd ever heard or seen Glass at all or whether it had been her addled mind playing tricks, she didn't know.

Inside her mind she screamed, and she thought she might have screamed in the room too, but she didn't know, she wasn't sure. She tried to open her eyes but there was nothing but blackness, nothing but darkness, nothing but a void, and *absence.*

This room is shielded.

Cait started at the voice, a movement that was involuntary, bypassing the psychic spell cast by the interrogator to block her motor pathways. Cait's neck ached as she jerked against the couch. She thought maybe she was straining against the manacles too, trying to pull herself upright while her mind sank in a world of infinite nothing. But she wasn't sure what was real, what was a figment of her imagination.

Like the image of Glass, the man in the long pale coat with the enigmatic smile. She looked at him, and the more she looked, the more she wasn't sure she was seeing anything at all. He flitted away, at the edges of consciousness, just the echo of afterimage lingering.

Don't answer back. They'll hear us.

Okay. Okay, okay, okay.

The interrogator is good, I'll give her that. But don't worry. I'm well hidden. She won't find me in this corner of your mind, so long as you keep quiet and don't show her the way.

Cait tried to think of nothing, but her head was filled with a thousand thoughts, a million questions. Most of which were about how she needed to get away from Glass, the monster who did . . . did *something* to her. What, she still didn't know. She wasn't afraid of him, not now. This was anger. This was rage.

Glass laughed.

Yes, that's good. That'll confuse them for a while. Just long enough for us to talk.

Listen.

She did, and then she felt it. It was almost like a physical sensation, a rush of nothingness, like a door had suddenly been opened and beyond was a space so vast it was infinite, black and endless. A sensation of presence so strong, so real it felt like she was being lifted up by a multitude of arms. Like sleep paralysis, that split second when the mind awakes but the body doesn't, the weight of a demon crushing the chest, staring into your soul with eyes that spin like blue stars falling.

Cait's lips twitched, and her eyelids flickered. That she felt too.

Oh, the interrogator is getting close. She's heard something. Very well. Just listen.

And then the room spun and Cait saw orange and red clouds and heard a howling wind.

Listen very carefully . . .

Braben left Kodiak in the observation gallery. Kodiak, alone in the dark, flicked the wall panel to "view" and stared into the psi-interrogation room, rubbing his eyes at the brightness that flooded in. He knew he needed sleep, but now was not the time. There was no telling how long the interrogation would last. Could be minutes. Could be hours. Could even be days, Kodiak recalled with a sigh. And he needed to be here when the results came in. Braben had offered to take it in shifts, but Kodiak had told him to get some rest. Braben had left, muttering something about how Kodiak was such a hero. The observation gallery at least had its own coffee machine. Kodiak made a cup and leaned with one arm against the wall as he turned back to the observation window.

It looked like absolutely nothing was happening in the other room—the psi-interrogator leaning over Caitlin Smith's head, Caitlin herself still on the angled couch. In reality, the psi-interrogator was extracting information by the gigabyte. But there was nothing Kodiak could do until the procedure was over and the psychic data feed had been analyzed and interpreted in a way he could read, or hear, or see.

As a Bureau agent, Kodiak was trained in standard interrogation techniques, but he didn't enjoy it. Some agents were better at it than others—some even seemed to have a natural talent, a knack that made watching interrogations a fascinating and highly educational experience. Kodiak knew he was not one of these agents. Back in the day, before Helprin's Gambit, he'd preferred to let his partner do the hard questioning. Kodiak's main problem—as Braben had often said—was that he was impatient. This he knew. Interrogations were frustrating, an open-ended game in which one partner steadfastly refused to play for as long as possible, if at all. And when they did—and most did, eventually—Kodiak drew no particular satisfaction. If they'd just told the truth from the beginning, nobody's time would have been wasted. Crimes would be solved, resources saved, and in some cases, lives saved.

Psi-interrogation was altogether different, and Kodiak had to admit he liked the technique, whatever moral qualms churned somewhere at the back of his mind. The special kind of cases psi-interrogation was reserved for were rare on Earth, and for most reluctant suspects, just the threat of psi-interrogation was enough to make them talk. But out on the Warworlds, things were different—

out there, there *were* secrets to be sold, missions to be sabotaged, escapes from the madness of a never-ending war against a nameless, unrelenting machine race to be made. Out on the Warworlds, psi-interrogators were kept very busy indeed.

Kodiak sipped his coffee. It was terrible but strong. He'd been awake for . . . he'd forgotten how long. But he was close now. Answers were coming. He could feel it.

And then, as Kodiak watched, the interrogator tilted her head. After an age of nothing, the slight movement sent Kodiak's heart thundering in his chest.

Caitlin Smith was saying something. Kodiak could see her lips moving, but only just. It reminded him of the cadets earlier, just before things went batshit crazy.

With that good old sinking feeling, he reached for the controls on the wall next to the observation window and pumped the sound up.

"Eight-seven-nine-one-two-two-Juno-Juno."

"Eight-seven-nine-one-two-two-Juno-Juno."

"Eight-seven-nine-one-two-two-Juno-Juno."

Oh, *shit*.

The interrogator tilted her head to the other side, then began looking left and right, like she was following something in the room. On the bed, Cait's body was still, her lips moving as she intoned the secret, mysterious, meaningless code.

The interrogator stood from her stool, still turning her head, left and right and left, then looking over her shoulder, spinning around in a complete circle, knocking her stool over.

Something was wrong. Very, very wrong. Kodiak's hand found the comm on his collar and he thumbed the call button.

"Control? This is Special Agent Kodiak down at the interrogation center. Can you get me—"

The comm barked in his ear. Kodiak yelled in surprise and jerked away from the window, sending his half-dead cup of coffee flying across the gallery to splash against the wall.

He looked around. He had the feeling something else was in the room with him. He turned back to the observation window and saw the interrogator was still on her feet, looking around her room like Kodiak was in his.

Kodiak gingerly reached for his comm again, but his hand paused as he watched the scene unfold in front of him. The interrogator had stopped moving and now looked at the window—at *him,* he thought, even though from the other side the window was just another gray wall panel. She held her hands to the side of her head and appeared to be squeezing the sides of her skull. She sidestepped Caitlin's supine form.

And ran at the window.

Kodiak watched, eyes wide in surprise, as the interrogator smacked head-first into the window with a loud thud. She bounced back and, tripping over her own feet, fell onto the floor of the interrogation room. Without pause, she pushed herself up and ran again. This time the impact didn't throw her off her feet. Instead, hands braced against the panel, she began smashing her forehead into the window, again and again, right in front of Kodiak. The skin on the interrogator's forehead split, blood splashing across the window.

Kodiak jolted back and thumbed his comm again, but was rewarded with another burst of ear-splitting static. His back hit the opposite wall and, unable to tear his eyes from the horror in the other room, he dragged himself sideways until he could reach the gallery's in-built comm panel next to the door. He pressed the button.

"Emergency in interrogation room A!" he yelled. "Get someone down here *now!*"

He let go of the button and someone responded to the affirmative, but their voice was lost under a wash of white noise and something else . . . a rapid, mechanical staccato, the sharp rattle of a radiation meter running at full tilt.

The psi-interrogator's face was a mess of torn skin and blood, each crash against the window spreading more and more gore. As she pulled back, it looked like she was looking right at Kodiak. He pushed himself against the back wall of the gallery, afraid that the interrogator was somehow going to smash the wall panel and climb into the gallery with him.

Reaching for the staser on his hip, he made for the door. He could get in and stun the interrogator and call for a medical team.

Kodiak left the room but was immediately pushed back by three armed agents as they ran past, heeding his request for help. He followed them down the short corridor and into the interrogation room. Immediately the agents fell into a firing stance, their weapons raised, but Kodiak yelled at them to keep back. He raised his staser and, as the interrogator turned to face him, to *charge* at him, he felled her with a single stun bolt.

Kodiak fought to control his breathing. His heart was racing, and his ears were filled with the blind roar of adrenaline. The three agents ran to the interrogator's body, one of them calling for medical assistance.

Kodiak turned away, not wanting to look at the crushed remains of the interrogator's face, his mind reeling with what had happened. He steadied himself on the edge of Caitlin's bed. She was still out for the count, but her lips moved silently.

Kodiak held his breath and leaned closer, lowering his ear to her lips. Behind him, two medics arrived and rushed to the aid of the interrogator.

He squeezed the grip of his staser as he listened to Caitlin's whispers.

"Eight-seven-nine-one-two-two-Juno-Juno."

The coordinates.

"Eight-seven-nine-one-two-two-Juno-Juno."

Whatever they were. *Wherever* they were.

"Eight-seven-nine-one-two-two-Juno-Juno."

It was important.

"Eight-seven-nine-one-two-two-Juno-Juno."

He had to know what was at the other end of them.

26

Less than a cycle later—just enough time to get at least something to eat and grab a couple of fitful hours of sleep—Kodiak found himself staring at the ops board in the Bureau bullpen. On display were the results of Caitlin Smith's psi-interrogation. Whether he could call it a success or failure, he wasn't sure, because now they had a psi-interrogator lying in the medical center with a smashed-up face and zero brain activity, the suspect she had interrogated sleeping peacefully in the unit next door.

The data extraction itself had gone well though, before everything had gone to shit. Specialized analysts had worked through the night to decode the raw feed, piecing together Caitlin's story out of her own memories—memories of how she had decided to follow her brother into the Academy after learning he had been deployed early, fearful perhaps of being separated from her twin, with whom she shared a psychic connection, by such a gulf of space; how, eager to follow in his footsteps, she entered the Psi-Division and made it straight into Alpha One.

How, as soon as news arrived that Tyler Smith had been killed in battle, she knew, *knew,* that it was a lie. Despite the distance between them the brother and sister had maintained their connection—until his final battle, in which the Fleet lost Warworld 4114 to the Spiders. Their connection had been severed, suddenly, without warning.

But . . . he was alive. She knew it. Felt it. He may not have been able to talk to her anymore, but his mind was still out there.

Tyler Smith was alive. She just had to find him. The Fleet was covering up his fate—he was dead, they said, but she knew that was a lie. Enough to sow doubt. So much of what the Fleet did out there, as it struggled against impossible odds, was classified.

And that made her think. Think about what else they might be covering up.

Then came the contact. Mysterious and anonymous, an untraceable communiqué left on her personal computer. A contact that had said yes, Tyler was still alive. A contact that promised to not only reunite them, but to show her what the Fleet was *really* doing. A contact that demanded one task of her, to show her loyalty but also, said the nameless sender, to initiate a chain of events that would reveal the Fleet's secrets to *everyone.*

She hadn't known who "they" were. But over several nights of discussion, she began to think of them as her employers. She accepted the task she was given—she was a *warrior,* something she kept telling herself, one that was following new orders, fighting on a new front, not just to save her brother, or herself, but to save everyone.

Save them all from the *real* enemy: the Fleet itself.

So she left, abandoning her training, abandoning the Academy. She was so afraid, so desperate to escape. They would find her, she knew that—her Fleet manifest tag had been implanted on day one of her training—but . . . they didn't. Either they weren't looking, or they couldn't track her tag. Somehow, they couldn't find her.

And then, cycles later . . . she heard Tyler speak.

At first she'd thought it was her imagination, her experiences finally catching up with her, producing phantoms in her mind. But they talked, and she knew it was real, and she knew she'd been right. From the very beginning, she'd been right. Tyler was alive, somewhere, somehow.

Her employers left more instructions. They suggested hiding places. They left her packages.

They outlined the plan.

Kodiak frowned, and folded his arms. His eyes moved across the ops board.

Then he sighed. Caitlin Smith was young, naïve, foolish. Gullible, clearly. Her mind pushed by the shared trauma of her brother's "death" on Warworld 4114, she had accepted her employers' instructions without much question. All she wanted to do was get her brother back. She was single-minded to the point of pathology, unheeding of consequences.

All she wanted to do was get her brother back, and if that meant taking down the Fleet itself, then so be it.

Because the Fleet was lying to everyone, weren't they? Tyler Smith was proof of that. Caitlin's employers knew what was going on, and they were going to change things. No, they were going to *fix* things.

And all Caitlin Smith had to do was carry out one single task. Shoot the Fleet Admiral, save the world.

Caitlin had no idea who she was working for, who her employers were. According to the psi-interrogation report, when she found out she was working for a cell of the Morning Star, she began to have doubts. They were terrorists. Fanatics. A violent, chaotic organization that couldn't be trusted, not now, not ever.

Except they knew where her brother was. They promised they would bring them back together and bring down the Fleet while they did it.

And then they operated on her.

Kodiak frowned. An Academy dropout gone rogue. A terrorist cell operating in New Orem. It was a workable theory, but there were two problems.

One, the Morning Star was, as far as Bureau intel went, little more than an extremist group—officially categorized as a banned terrorist organization, but one that hadn't been seen for . . . well, years. Their interests didn't lie with the Fleet—or so it was believed. They claimed to be pilgrims searching for their missing god, a mission that took them way out to the very peripheries of Fleetspace.

They weren't supposed to be a threat. And yet, here they were, operating a cell on Earth. A cell that had funding, equipment, weaponry. And more important, *training*.

None of that was in the Bureau's intel. Either the intel was hopelessly out of date, or the Morning Star had got help from somewhere else. And that was a *whole* new kettle of fish; Kodiak felt a small, cold ball of anxiety grow in his stomach even as he considered the point.

Kodiak scratched his cheek as he considered the second problem: Caitlin Smith hadn't carried out her assigned task. She hadn't shot the Fleet Admiral—either of them. She had fled the first assassination without firing a single shot, and as far as *she* knew, the Morning Star seemed to think that she had pulled the trigger. Mission accomplished. The Bureau had her weapon, the sniper rifle with the hacked, pirated operating system. The weapon had been fired—she'd done that herself, according to the psi-interrogation report. A bluff to make the Morning Star think she *had* carried out her mission successfully.

The assassination of Zworykin, the Fleet Admiral's self-declared successor, posed a real problem. The ousting of Sebela just a cycle before his death and the elevation of Zworykin to Fleet Admiral was unknown to the public. And according to Caitlin's own memories, she didn't have anything to do with his death—she didn't even know about it.

Kodiak sighed and took a step back. Finding Caitlin and extracting the information from her mind had been vital to the investigation, if for just one piece of information it confirmed: that their original suspect, Tyler Smith, *was* alive. His tag had shown up at both crime scenes. That it had not appeared on the manifest before and after was still a mystery—but Caitlin's own tag had also been inactive, only broadcasting again once it had been removed from her brainstem.

Something that was supposed to be impossible.

And of course, that wasn't the only impossible thing Kodiak had experienced lately. Servitors that were perfect facsimiles were also supposed to be impossible, a thing straight out of science fiction.

And yet one lay in parts down in a Bureau laboratory.

Nearby, Braben sat at his desk. Out of the corner of his eye, Kodiak could see the agent swiping his fingers across his datapad, faster and faster, until he sighed and let the pad fall to his desk with a clatter. Braben caught Kodiak's eye, and Kodiak turned around from the board. It was early morning, but the bullpen was packed with agents and analysts, all deep in their work. The longer the situation went on, the worse it would get too, Kodiak knew that. The Fleet was teetering on the brink. The city was on lockdown. It was still red ball, everyone on duty.

And despite the activity, the chaos, Kodiak still felt like they were on the back foot. Caitlin's data was useful, but it was a lot to process, and as Kodiak sighed, he tried to figure out the next step.

Braben leaned back in his chair and put his hands behind his head. "So she was telling the truth. She didn't do it."

Kodiak nodded, then pursed his lips, a new thought coming to the forefront of his mind. "That's what she believes, anyway," he said.

"You think she might be wrong? Like her memories were tampered with or something?"

"I don't know," said Kodiak. "She's been through a lot, including surgery to have her tag removed. There's a lot of tech involved that seems beyond what we have. Brainwashing, memory implantation . . . it seems like it could be possible."

"I sense a 'but' coming."

Kodiak nodded. "But it seems unlikely. Why bother going to all that trouble? Caitlin Smith's knowledge that her brother is alive tallies with his manifest ID showing at the crime scenes."

"A manifest ID that magically appeared and disappeared from the tracker."

"Right. But if Tyler Smith *is* alive, and the tech exists to remove the tags surgically, without killing the subject, then why leave his in at all?"

Braben gave a sort of noncommittal shrug. Kodiak frowned. Not helpful.

He turned back to the ops board. The official Fleet photographs of the Smith twins were on display, next to the portraits of the two deceased Admirals. He moved close to Tyler Smith's image.

He was the key.

"I get the feeling we're still looking in the wrong place," said Kodiak.

"Still think there's a Fleet connection? An insider helping the terrorists?"

"Oh, there's a Fleet connection all right." He tapped Tyler Smith's image, enlarging it. He turned to Braben. "Psi-Marine Tyler Smith is alive and well, despite the Fleet saying he was killed in action. That in itself doesn't add up."

Braben stroked his chinstrap beard. "Some kind of cover-up, then. A conspiracy."

"Damn right," said Kodiak, his expression dark. He began rearranging data on the ops board, then paused as he brought up an image. He tapped to enlarge it—it was grainy, distorted, a processed piece of data pulled from Caitlin's visual cortex and reassembled in the computer. It showed a man, apparently wearing glasses. His body was indistinct, but he looked like he was wearing a long, pale coat.

The servitor, the one they'd cornered in the warehouse.

Braben stood from his desk and moved over to the ops board. He nodded at the image. "The mysterious Glass."

"A servitor that looks like a real person," said Kodiak. He could hardly believe he was saying it.

"According to her own memories, Caitlin Smith killed him. Or she thought she had. A little push with her mind and, *pow,* down he goes."

Kodiak folded his arms. "You can see why she was fast-tracked through the Academy." Kodiak replayed the moment the carrier had come up onto the roof of the building in Salt City. He'd watched with the other agents as Caitlin had sent her attackers flying without laying a finger on them.

Kodiak tapped the board and brought up a panel of text. He tapped again, and text began to scroll. It would have been too fast to read, except for the fact that the lines of text were an infinitely repeated sequence. Six numbers and two words.

Eight-seven-nine-one-two-two-Juno-Juno.

Braben shook his head. "And *that,*" he said, jabbing a finger at the board, "gives me the creeps, man."

Kodiak nodded. He agreed with Braben's comment—just seeing the sequence stirred a certain nervousness inside him. "It's a message, not broadcast over the comms, or lightspeed link, but broadcast over the same psychic wavelengths used by the psi-marines. A broadcast powerful enough to overwhelm the gestalt the cadets created when we were looking for our suspects. Powerful enough that when the psi-interrogator heard it she was driven out of her mind."

Braben put his hands in the pockets of his jacket and pushed them out, away from his body while he turtled his neck. "We haven't been able to decode the coordinates yet—they're proprietary, somewhere in the Jovian system. Jupiter and everything in orbit around it is private enterprise, owned by the Jovian Mining Corporation. The chief has put a request for an assist through to them. We should hear back soon."

Kodiak frowned. Private enterprise. Well, great. Even with a war on—even with the Fleet's command structure in danger of toppling altogether, dealing with private enterprise would be difficult. The independence of corporations was even enshrined in the Fleet's constitution. Topping it off, the JMC was the largest corporation of them all, a political power bloc all its own. Getting their assistance was paramount—and they *would* get it, considering the circumstances, but that didn't mean it was going to be easy.

"Good," said Kodiak. "Because as soon as we know where those coordinates point, I'm going to take a look myself."

Braben's eyes widened, and he shook his head. "You're not serious?"

"I am," said Kodiak. "And I'm going to take Caitlin Smith with me."

27

"I told you, I don't know what that means."

Cait sat on the other side of the table from the Bureau agents. Her wrists were manacled. She still ached all over, her neck stiff and encased in a thin plastiform medical collar to accelerate the healing of her surgical wound. She felt rested, physically at least—although she knew that was because she'd lain, sedated, in a medical unit rather than any kind of natural sleep.

She was torn inside. On the one hand, being in Fleet custody was actually a good thing. Her ordeal at the hands of the Morning Star was in the past, and the results of the psi-interrogation would show she hadn't killed anybody. All she wanted was to get her brother back. They would know that he was alive. And if he was alive, then maybe there were others officially listed as killed in action who were still alive too.

But maybe they knew that. There was the problem: the Morning Star had promised to expose the secrets of the Fleet, secrets so dark and terrible it would cause the military-industrial complex to collapse.

The fact that Tyler was alive—and presumably others too—was likely one facet of that terrible truth.

A truth the Fleet wanted to keep very well hidden indeed. Which meant being in Fleet custody was perhaps worse than being used by the Morning Star. Which meant, Cait thought, there was a good chance she wasn't making it out of this building alive.

The agent called Michael Braben narrowed his eyes at her as he sipped his coffee. The other guy, Kodiak, looked like he hadn't slept in days. He was sucking in his bottom lip, his eyes wide. Clearly he was expecting her to give a different answer.

Cait sighed. She moved her hands, rattling the manacles against the tabletop. "Look, I'm telling the truth. Didn't your interrogator suck it out of my brain already?"

The two agents glanced sideways at each other. Not for the first time in her life, Cait wished her wild talent enabled her to listen in to their thoughts, but that kind of direct telepathy was impossible, even for someone special like her. The best she could do, with a little concentration, was to reach out and get a very general sense of what someone else was feeling, thanks to the low-level psi-field every living mind broadcast. But even that didn't tell her anything she couldn't pick up with her normal senses. Kodiak was tired and annoyed. Braben's emotions ran a little hotter . . . underneath his own quiet anger was something else. Fear, perhaps. It was hard to read.

Agent Kodiak licked his lips. He glanced down at the table, tapped the translucent red datasheet in front of him. Cait's eyes flicked down, then back up. She'd been staring at the sequence for what felt like hours.

Eight-seven-nine-one-two-two-Juno-Juno.

She sighed, shook her head. "How many times do we have to go through this?"

Kodiak frowned. "Okay, fine. They're coordinates. *Proprietary* coordinates. They belong to the Jovian Mining Corporation, IDing something within Jupiter's system. We don't know what yet, but the JMC is looking into it for us." He tapped the datasheet with an index finger. "So what I want to know is, where did you get the coordinates from? Did the Morning Star cell tell you? How did they get them? Do they know what they point to?"

Cait blinked. She looked back at the code. "Jupiter?" She'd heard of the JMC, but Flood had never mentioned anything about them, or the Jovian system. She also knew that the whole planetary system, moons, rings, and all, was owned by the corporation, a giant slice of private company real estate right in the middle of the solar system.

Cait pulled the sheet closer, staring at it. She didn't know why they were asking her these questions—wouldn't they have the information extracted from her own mind? They knew that she *didn't* know anything about it. She'd never heard or seen the coordinates before the agents had shown her the datasheet.

And then it clicked. She looked up at the two agents.

"That's where my brother is, isn't it? He's there. Jupiter. That's where they were going to take me."

Braben and Kodiak exchanged a look. Cait shook her head. "Have you caught them?"

Kodiak sucked on his lip again, like he was considering whether to answer her question. They would know she wasn't part of their group, so there wouldn't be any harm in telling her, would there?

After another beat Kodiak shook his head. "No. We cleared out the warehouse—they left a lot of gear behind. All brand-new, expensive, but untraceable. They were good at covering their tracks. The city is on lockdown and we have multiple sweeps in progress. No sign of them yet."

Cait nodded, then winced as her neck ached. She reached up to feel the collar, but was brought short by the manacles. "Why did they take out my tag?"

Kodiak spread his hands. "We don't know that either."

She shook her head. She looked at the datasheet again.

Jupiter. That was where Tyler was. She had to get there, somehow. But it seemed impossible. She was a prisoner, on Earth. The only place she was going was a holding cell prior to her trial. She was in it, and in it deep, that she knew. Even if the results of her psi-interrogation showed she wasn't the assassin . . .

Cait looked down at the datasheet, looked up at Kodiak.

"We have to go to Jupiter. We have to find my brother."

Braben leaned forward across the table. He tilted his head and fixed Cait with a hard glare, almost as though he'd been able to read her own thoughts, as he outlined her situation.

"We've got you on conspiracy and collusion with a known terrorist organization, conspiracy to commit acts of treason, felony evasion, and about a dozen other serious charges. You're not even looking at life imprisonment—we're talking the death penalty here. Under martial law we could even carry out your sentence here and now."

Okay. Okay, okay, okay. Cait closed her eyes as the room spun a little. There was a faint prickle across her skin, but her power seemed to be exhausted after her ordeal.

And what was she going to do with it, anyway? Break free of her manacles and kill the two agents? Smash her way out of the interview room, smash her way out of the Bureau offices, out of the Capitol Complex?

Yeah right. They may as well just shoot her here, sitting at the table in the interrogation room.

When she opened her eyes, she saw Braben had his arms folded. He had turned on his seat and was looking at Kodiak. He also looked pretty pissed. Kodiak, on the other hand, had a small smile playing at the corner of his mouth.

What the fuck was up with these guys?

Then Kodiak pulled a key from the pocket of his vest. He held it up between two fingers.

"There is an alternative," he said.

Cait's jaw dropped. She looked between the two agents. Now Braben was shaking his head and he looked away, to the floor, his arms still tightly crossed.

She met Kodiak's eye. The smile had gone—had it ever been there?—and he was staring at her with his brows furrowed. But still he held the key up. The key to her manacles.

Cait stammered. "I . . ."

"Cooperation," said Kodiak. "Full and complete and unconditional. You are already Fleet property, so you have no rights and no protection."

Cait's eyes moved back to the key.

"But," said Kodiak, "if you help us, then we can re-evaluate the charges, perhaps get whatever sentence you receive commuted. If you *help* us."

Her mind raced. Was this real, or some kind of trick or bluff? But before she could ask, before she could say anything at all, Kodiak leaned over and unlocked Cait's manacles, then replaced the key in his pocket. He tapped his fingers on the table.

Cait rubbed her wrists. Her neck was aching. There was a prickle on her skin but it was so, so faint.

Then Kodiak stood. "Please don't make me regret this," he said, and then he nodded at Braben and left the interview room.

Cait and Braben locked eyes. Seconds passed, Cait's heartbeat thumping out the time. Then Braben sniffed, grabbed his coffee cup, and followed his partner out.

The door closed. Cait was alone. Alone with her thoughts.

What the hell had just happened? They'd offered her a bargain—her cooperation for leniency. Her cooperation . . . for the return of her brother?

Perhaps she could get to Jupiter after all.

Perhaps they really would try and help her.

Perhaps they wanted to find out what the Fleet was doing as much as she did.

Good work, Ms. Smith. You're doing very well.

Cait jumped, glanced to her left. The room was still empty, reflected in the mirror of the observation window.

And in that mirror, the image of Glass stood right next to the table at which she sat. Her eyes flicked right. There was nobody there.

I'm still here. In your mind. Hitching a lift, so to speak. It's only temporary, but I find myself without a permanent abode at present, if you get my meaning.

Cait held her breath.

Get the fuck out of my mind, she screamed inside. Get. The. Fuck. Out.

I understand—

You understand nothing! Do you hear me? You and the others

used me. Tricked me. Made me promises that were lies. Lies!

Your brother is alive. That isn't a lie.

You said the Fleet was keeping secrets. Keeping things hidden.

And they are—

Didn't you see what happened, jackass? They've offered me a bargain. They want to find out what happened to Tyler as much as I do. So tell me, how is the Fleet keeping secrets from itself, huh?

All I can do is ask for you to trust me.

Trust you?

Cait snickered and rolled her eyes. There was no doubt she was still being watched by someone through the two-way, but to any observer it would look like she was just considering what the two agents had offered her.

How the fuck can I trust you, she thought, willing the voice in her mind to be louder than war. After what you did to me—used me for your dirty work, tricked me into helping. Operated on me, against my will. You fucks deserve everything that is coming.

Do you want to find Tyler?

Cait took a breath.

Of course.

Then just know that things are proceeding according to plan.

Who the fuck are you?

That question does not have an easy answer, Ms. Smith. And I know this is very hard for you to understand, but I have your best interests at heart. I know that your trust doesn't come easily, but I'm doing all I can to get you and Tyler back together.

The reflection of Glass smiled.

Cait swore. Her head hurt. Her neck hurt. There was a tightness in her chest, a lump in her throat. She tried to ignore them.

She felt her eyes grow wet. Felt the tears on her cheeks. She tried to ignore those too.

Is Tyler on Jupiter?

Glass nodded. *Nearby.* He glanced at the ceiling in his reflected world, then nodded, perhaps to himself. *They're coming back. Good luck, Ms. Smith.*

The interview room door opened. Agent Kodiak walked in, carrying a datapad. "Come with me. I need to take you to see my commander."

Cait stood and massaged her wrists, and as she left she took one look behind her. In the mirrored two-way, the room was reflected back at her, and all she saw was her own image, looking back at her over one shoulder.

She stepped out into the corridor and followed Agent Kodiak.

28

The shuttle, U-Star *Cassilda,* was Fleet standard: small, utilitarian, fast. It could pop the quickspace highway that ran the length of the solar system and drop them in Jovian orbit in just a few hours.

Kodiak sat in the pilot's position, re-familiarizing himself with the systems with the aid of the ship's datapad. He was fully certified for flight, but it occurred to him that it had been quite some time since he'd actually been at the controls. Normally he would have let Braben take the pilot's seat, but Braben hadn't even stuck around to say goodbye and good luck.

Cait sat next to him, adjusting the straps of her harness over her flak jacket. As part of their prep for the Jupiter mission, Kodiak had taken her down to the uniform store and got her kitted out in the same field gear as he was wearing—she might have been a prisoner, but as far as the personnel at the JMC refinery were aware, she was a Bureau agent just like him. In a sense, that was true, given she'd been officially deputized by Commander Avalon. But the arrangement was purely temporary.

At least, he thought, he had some back-up. Behind the cockpit in the shuttle's small cargo hold were two dozen Bureau servitors, armed and ready, just waiting for Kodiak's commands. He didn't think Cait was going to do anything to jeopardize the mission—she wanted to know what was going on at the coordinates as much as he did—but her unique psi-ability played at the back of his own mind. She was powerful and dangerous. She also wanted to help, not just Kodiak and the investigation, but herself, and her brother.

But still. Twenty-four killer robots sitting in the hold gave Kodiak a little peace of mind.

Cait tightened a strap and then paused as Kodiak flicked a switch, frowned at the datapad, and flicked it back. "You sure you know how to fly this thing?" she asked.

Kodiak laughed. "Agent, my mother could fly this thing," he said, and then his laugh choked off as he stared at the datapad again. "They've just updated a few things since the last time I sat in one of these." He cleared his throat.

"Agent," said Cait, more to herself than to him. She looked down at her chest, emblazoned with the words FLEET BUREAU in large white letters. "Today has been a strange day."

Kodiak looked up to check the controls on the bulkhead above him. "Well, in theory, you're doing better than I am. I'm officially dead." He punched a control and was rewarded with a green light.

"You're . . . what?"

Kodiak glanced sideways at his new partner. "Long story," he said, and then the shuttle's comm chimed. Kodiak leaned forward and hit the channel. "Kodiak."

"Avalon," said the chief. "You're all cleared. JMC flight control will contact you when you clear quickspace. And remember, we're waiting to hear from you. Just say the word and we'll get you out."

"Roger that," said Kodiak. He looked at Cait. "Ready?"

Cait shrugged. "As I'll ever be."

"Jupiter, here we come."

Kodiak flicked the flight systems to manual and gently pulled back on the yoke, lifting the shuttle from the starport hangar. Ahead of them, the hangar doors opened, and bright daylight streamed in.

As he punched the engine and guided the shuttle out of the

hangar and into the sky over New Orem, Kodiak really hoped he knew what he was doing.

In high Earth orbit, in the shadow of one of the gravitational satellites that stabilized Earth's atmosphere and tides after the destruction of the moon, a pilot watched the screen of his own craft as the U-Star *Cassilda* shot through the flotilla of Fleet ships that crowded the planet. There was the vast destroyer *Ultramassive* and its companion frigates *Monolithic* and *Thor's Hammer*, behind which floated a dozen other of the Fleet's most powerful, most destructive vessels, as well as a plethora of smaller craft: patrol boats, cruisers, transports, individual shuttles and fighters, and a swarm of one-man hot seats that buzzed between them all. Within moments, the *Cassilda* was out of sight, following a trajectory that would take it to the quickspace jump point a light-second out from Earth, where it would be clear to punch through into that interstitial dimension and re-emerge at Jupiter.

The other shuttle rotated under the gravitational satellite, adjusting its position before moving forward, matching the engine pulse of the *Cassilda* and quickly falling into that shuttle's quantum wake. It was an old trick, but one that worked well, hiding the other shuttle's signature from the one it followed. Follow the wake close enough and when the first ship popped quickspace, the pursuing one could even get a tow, not needing to fire up its own Q-Gen coil—something that would show up on the sensors of any ship within a light-minute's radius.

In the darkened cockpit, the pilot squeezed the yoke with one hand as his other tapped in a command sequence on the shuttle's primary console. The computer confirmed the entry with a chime, and the pilot released the manual control, allowing the yoke to reseat itself in its alcove.

Both hands now free, the pilot used the opportunity to loosen his black tie and release the top button of his black shirt, before sweeping one hand down his front, flattening out any creases that might have gathered since he'd been sitting in the shuttle, waiting for the *Cassilda* to cruise past.

The shuttle rocked slightly as the automatics got a lock on the *Cassilda*'s quantum wake. The pilot waited until the movement had abated, then turned on his chair to check the cargo.

Behind the two primary flight positions was an open space where the shuttle's passenger seats would normally be, the cockpit able to hold eight persons in addition to the pilot and co-pilot under normal configuration.

But in this shuttle, sitting behind the two remaining seats was an oblong container with a curved top. The object was black and shiny, and there was a control panel in the middle, the lights of which silently blinked in the dark cockpit. Above the control panel, at the far end of the object, was a dark window.

The pilot stood, straightened his jacket, and, apparently noticing he was still wearing it, unclipped the chrome Bureau badge from his lapel and tossed it onto the console behind him. He walked to the head of the object, cast an eye at the control panel, and reached down and touched a button.

The window was lit from within the object by a blue light. The pilot leaned over and peered inside. He smiled.

"Hang in there, sleeping beauty," said Special Agent Braben, looking down at the sleeping form of Psi-Marine Tyler Smith inside the stasis pod. "Your next job is coming right up."

INTO THE DARKEST NIGHT

A single turn to the right and the door opened like he had been told it would. He wondered for a moment how that was going to be explained, what kind of cover they would concoct to account for how he'd gained access to the room and to the server within it. It didn't matter. Whatever it was, it would be good, he knew that much. It would have to be. This was the start of something big, something deep. Very, *very* deep.

The server room was a long gallery filled with monolithic computer cabinets, just like any other, except for the fact that it was the most secure room in the most secure part of the Bureau. It was entirely automated, and therefore entirely empty.

Von Kodiak stepped across the threshold, the door closing silently behind him. Although devoid of staff, the room was monitored closely. Cameras covered every part of it, and after an entry that required very particular authorization, the movements of anybody in the facility were closely watched.

Kodiak glanced up into the corner, where the first camera was pointed straight at the door—at *him*. He sucked in his cheeks and, unable to resist, gave it a wave, knowing that, for the next ten minutes, there was nobody watching, and there was no recording being made.

If his ability to enter the secure room was strange, the glitch in the security system that meant his presence went unrecorded was going to be a *real* mystery for the Bureau.

Again, it didn't matter. There would be an explanation. Heads would roll. He wouldn't get caught.

That was the plan.

Kodiak skipped across the gallery of server cabinets, counting them off until he reached the sixth row. For some reason, he felt the need to creep around, to not make any sound. Just in case. He told himself he was just getting into character; then he told himself not to be ridiculous and to stop wasting time. So at the sixth row he ran toward the other end, the fingers of one hand already pulling the data key out of his pocket.

The cabinets were white, featureless, entirely silent, entirely smooth—there was no sign of doors or access panels, handles, anything, not even any seams or sections. Up close, they looked like they were carved out of white stone, the surface smooth and cold as Kodiak placed one palm against it. He would leave fingerprints. That was also part of the plan. No doubt some poor agent would spend hours poring over the data, wondering why the rogue agent hadn't worn gloves.

Again, not his problem.

Kodiak held the data key up in his other hand. It was small and silver, the same size and shape as a stick of gum. There was a red light on the end.

He touched it against the surface of cabinet twenty, and the red light turned green. Then he let go, the data key sticking to the cabinet, allowing him—the *operator*—to get to work.

A moment later, the flat white surface of the cabinet faded away, replaced by a virtual control panel. There was a keyboard and a data screen in the middle, at just the right height for someone to work at, but the rest of the cabinets, from floor to ceiling, were rows of glowing blue rectangles, each separated by a row of small indicators in a variety of colors.

The contents of the Bureau evidence servers were at his fingertips. He had a whole seven minutes remaining.

Recalling the memorized sequence, Kodiak followed his instructions, spoofing a series of evidence database searches until he entered the right terms, and—

There it was. At waist height, the set of small lights above one of the long blue bars changed in sequence, and a green indicator began to flash.

Kodiak's eyes moved across the data screen as he read the inventory listing for the evidence server. Then his eyes widened, and he whistled.

There was a *lot* of money being held in the server, the proceeds of crime confiscated by the Bureau.

Four minutes remaining.

Kodiak thought for a moment about what he could do with the money, and realized the answer was a simple one: anything. That much money would be a temptation for anyone. Even a respected Fleet Bureau of Investigation Special Agent, even one with an immaculate record.

A Special Agent like him.

Three minutes.

Kodiak reached up and squeezed the data key between his finger and thumb, then watched as the credits were transferred to it from the server. Oh, the things you could do with that kind of money.

You could do anything. *Anything.*

Like bring down one of the biggest crime syndicates in Fleetspace.

Transaction complete, Kodiak pulled the stick off the cabinet, slipped it snuggly into his breast pocket, and left the server room at a run.

It was time to disappear.

PART TWO

JUPITER

29

Kodiak looked up at the crystal ceiling as they walked, the corners of his mouth downturned in quiet appreciation. From the corner of his eye, he saw Cait glance here and there too. It was impossible not to. Kodiak had expected the gas refinery of the Jovian Mining Corporation to be functional, bland, not too far distant from the kind of aesthetically uninteresting designs the Fleet used. He couldn't have been more wrong. The parts of the refinery he had seen so far were positively luxurious, all polished white ceramic and magenta-tinted crystal. It was stark and minimal, but beautiful—rivaling Helprin's Gambit in apparent expense but with an opulence not in the fittings or decoration, of which there were none that he had seen, but in the structure itself. The refinery was clearly designed to impress by a company for which funds were not an issue.

Ahead of them was a representative of the JMC who had met them off the shuttle at the landing pad and, with merely a curt nod, had set off into the complex, apparently expecting the two guests to follow. He was clad in a dark maroon uniform that looked maybe just a little too military, complete with officer's cap, and had still not spoken a word.

"Quite a place you've got here."

Cait narrowed her eyes as she looked at the back of the JMC officer's head. "I don't think our guide is interested in small talk," she said.

Kodiak shrugged. "Just trying to be friendly."

"I don't think our guide is programmed for that either."

Kodiak raised an eyebrow and nearly missed a step before he returned his attention to their guide.

Programmed?

"Ah, excuse me," he said. The officer showed no sign of hearing him. He was young, maybe early twenties. Blond hair under the cap. He had his fingers curled over his palms as he walked. He looked human.

Then again, so had Glass.

"See?" asked Cait. She was smiling, like she'd got one up on her new partner.

"Or he's just been told not to talk to us," said Kodiak. He raised his voice a little. "I know how it goes. Sometimes private enterprises don't like the authorities snooping around, right?"

"No," said Cait. "It's not that. I can't sense any neural activity. Even people who aren't psi-abled emit a low-level field of—"

Kodiak raised his hand. "Yes, I know, thanks. So our friend here is a servitor?"

"Yes. Like Glass was."

The pair shared a look and walked on in silence awhile.

The corridors all seemed to be different, the way the walls swept up and down, the polished white surfaces and purplish panels mixing in unique ways. He assumed they were going to meet the refinery manager, but so far the only contact they'd had with anyone at the facility was their silent guide, and he was a robot who didn't feel like talking.

They hadn't even heard anything on their approach, although that was apparently standard procedure, given the conditions in the Jovian system. As soon as their shuttle had popped quickspace a million klicks out from Jupiter, the ship's sensors registered a huge electromagnetic spike as they were licked by the gas giant's magnetosphere. Then the sensors had automatically shut down. Thinking they were in a whole lot of trouble, Kodiak had been relieved when, moments later, the shuttle's navcom had auto-locked onto a series of old-fashioned guidance beacons forming a path from high planetary orbit right down to the refinery, the line of small geostationary satellites plunging right into the upper atmosphere of Jupiter. Clearly sensor overload was a common problem, likewise comms fritzed by the interference. He knew enough about Jupiter to realize that magnetic storms must be a regular occurrence, so leaving the shuttle to fly itself, he sat back and enjoyed the view.

The shuttle slipped into the planet's exosphere, the viewscreen nothing but a haze of yellow and orange, which cleared at a depth of two hundred kilometers until a clear cloud system was visible. Here, it was peaceful, even picturesque, a perpetual sunset of rich orange and reds. And then they saw the JMC refinery.

The refinery was as impressive from the outside as it was from within. It looked like a small space station, a floating structure the size of a city. It formed a squat, upside-down pyramid, the apex pointed down toward the non-existent surface of the planet. The side of the pyramidal structure they approached was in shadow, but its dark surface was a crosshatch of lights and windows. The flat top of the refinery looked more industrial. There were several low-level structures like city buildings studded across it, with a complex of them at the very center, but most of the refinery roof was occupied by landing pads of varying sizes and a complex network of pipes and holding tanks—filled, no doubt, with the precious gases mined from Jupiter's dense atmosphere.

As the shuttle came in to land, guided now by beacons on the refinery itself, and they passed through a force field encompassing the otherwise open landing area, the outside view shimmered and darkened. A few minutes later, Kodiak and Cait were both surprised to see the JMC rep standing on the pad outside the shuttle, patiently waiting for them to disembark. Outside, it was warm, the air still; looking up as they made their way from the shuttle to the nearest of the buildings, they saw the clouds above swirled like colored ink.

As with the interior architecture, the design of the landing pad and the way they had to walk across the apparently open space was intended to impress.

The corridor curved and, as the JMC officer took them down a left junction, the solid wall became a long, continuous observation window. Beside him, Cait gasped as they both looked out at the Jovian stratosphere, Kodiak realizing that the interior color scheme of the refinery complemented the natural hues of the gaseous world outside.

"It's beautiful," said Cait, slowing to take in the view through the window.

"Seen one gas giant, seen them all."

Cait looked at him. "Were you born a cynic, or was that something they taught you at the Bureau?"

Kodiak frowned. "Let's just say I'd like this place a lot more if there were actually any people here."

Cait's forehead creased. "Yeah. It's a big place. They should have hundreds—*thousands*—of staff."

"Or hundreds of machines like our friendly guide."

"This place can't be entirely automatic, can it?"

Kodiak frowned again. He skipped forward a step to tap their guide on the shoulder. "Hey, buddy," he said. At this, the JMC officer finally slowed and turned around. He—*it*—was wearing a bland expression, like it was vaguely bemused at the interruption. Kodiak's frown deepened.

"Okay, so, you're a servitor. And maybe your boss is watching and listening. But we have a few questions we'd like to have answered, like where the hell is everyone?"

The servitor looked between the two of them.

"What's the matter, someone turned your voice off?" asked Cait.

The servitor smiled. "The Jovian Mining Corporation is the largest private contractor in Fleetspace and the second largest employer outside of the Fleet itself," it said, with the calm tones of a prepared speech.

"They all at lunch, then?" asked Kodiak.

The servitor smiled again. "Follow me, please," it said, and, turning on its heel, it marched away. Kodiak and Cait looked at each other, then stepped in line behind it.

They had been walking for a long time, Kodiak and Cait falling into a disgruntled silence as the JMC officer led them through another passageway, the elliptical observation windows in this section eliciting no interest from the frustrated agents. Just ahead, the corridor opened out into a large, high-ceilinged atrium. The servitor went to the far wall and called for an elevator.

Kodiak folded his arms as they waited. This was taking a lot longer than he had anticipated. They were supposed to be meeting with the refinery controller, their cover that they were two Bureau agents here to carry out a check on JMC security protocols—all part of the private company's contract with the Fleet. In a way, it wasn't even a cover: Kodiak fully planned on asking about the Jupiter transmission and getting the JMC's own team to help track the source. The coordinates—eight-seven-nine-one-two-two-Juno-Juno—were somewhere in the Jovian system, the entirety of which was JMC property. Getting the company's assistance was going to be vital to the investigation.

Kodiak looked at the back of the servitor's head. "I assume this is taking us to whoever is in charge of this facility."

The servitor nodded. "Confirmed, sir."

Kodiak looked at Cait, but she just shrugged. Kodiak sighed. The elevator doors hadn't opened and they were just standing there, waiting. Kodiak folded his arms, rolled his neck, willing himself to have the patience he needed to deal with a giant corporation like the JMC.

After a couple of minutes, the elevator arrived.

Kodiak dropped his arms. "About time," he muttered under his breath. He went to take a step forward toward the doors.

That was when the servitor spun around, the infuriatingly vacant smile frozen on its face and a familiar silver and translucent weapon in its hand.

Kodiak took a step backwards, bumping into Cait, his eyes on the staser the servitor had trained on him.

"Hey, look, buddy."

"Please remain still and follow my directions. Any attempt to deviate from my instructions will be met with terminal force."

Kodiak glanced at Cait. Wide-eyed, she raised her hands.

The elevator door slid open. Two men emerged, wearing not the smart magenta uniforms of the JMC, but black combat gear and flak jackets, their heads covered with featureless flat masks with inset goggles. They were armed with short plasma rifles, both of which were pointed at Kodiak and Cait.

Kodiak felt something then, like a pressure on his eardrums. He turned to Cait, watched as she lowered her arms, her eyes half-closed.

She was doing it again.

Then one of the men in black swung his gun toward her and fired. There was a blue-white flash, and Cait telescoped down onto the floor.

Kodiak moved to help, but the servitor gestured with its staser for him to stay still. He took a step back as the man who had shot Cait swung his weapon onto his back, then bent down and lifted Cait over his shoulders.

The servitor gestured at Kodiak with its staser again. "After you, sir."

Kodiak sighed and stepped into the elevator, the servitor and two men, one carrying Cait, right behind him.

30

The lower levels of the JMC refinery were far less salubrious than those above. Gone was the elegant crystalline and ceramic architecture, the exquisite workmanship giving way to something far more functional. The corridors here were all steel and plastic, lined with pipes and conduits, lit by the standard white ceiling tiles.

Kodiak followed the servitor in front, his boots clanking heavily on the grilled flooring. Behind him was the first armed man and, bringing up the rear, the other, still carrying Cait.

They'd disarmed him, but they'd left the comm on Kodiak's collar. And all he had to do was squeeze the comm and call for help from the shuttle, and the servitors would come to the rescue, homing in on his signal.

He couldn't do it now, not without being seen. But maybe he'd get the opportunity later. Maybe. Because while the thought of back-up being so close made Kodiak feel better, he also knew that calling in the cavalry had to be a last resort. There was a lot of refinery between him and the shuttle, and who knew what kind of defenses the JMC would be able to roll out to stop Kodiak's servitors. More important, any attack by the servitors was likely to get them both killed, long before their rescue.

No, the only option was to wait, and watch.

As they marched toward an unknown destination, somewhere in the bowels of the refinery, Kodiak considered the situation. The JMC was involved—that much was clear. They owned the Jovian system, a system conveniently cut off from most communications thanks to the eccentricities of the planet's magnetosphere. Here they were, in the heart of the home system, their entire operation effectively hidden behind a vast sensor shield. On the one hand, Kodiak was amazed that the Fleet had allowed this to happen, but on the other, what was there to worry about? The JMC was a private enterprise, and they supplied the Fleet with vital supplies, allowing the Fleet to get on with the war. It was a mutually beneficial arrangement. Free market economics, right?

And nobody had any reason to suspect the JMC was doing anything other than extracting gas, right?

Kodiak wondered what had changed. Fleet personnel were regular visitors to the refinery. Kodiak and Cait were no different.

Something had forced the JMC's hand.

The events on Earth, it had to be. The assassination of the two Fleet Admirals. The JMC was involved, and now they were making their move. They'd allowed Kodiak and Cait to visit under the pretense of cooperation, perhaps a ploy to buy just a little more time for whatever the hell they were planning next.

But something bugged Kodiak. Why were they still alive? If the JMC was turning against the Fleet, they could have eliminated the both of them as soon as they'd arrived. If the JMC was trying to keep their operation secret, they could just have met them off the shuttle, given them the jolly tour and the corporate spiel, and whisked them back to Earth, right?

No, there was something else. They were still alive for a reason. Hostages? Perhaps. Or were they being kept for interrogation? Kodiak thought that was a possibility, although he wasn't sure there was much he or Cait knew that would be useful. The JMC's operation was tightly integrated with the Fleet's. Chances were the JMC knew more about the Fleet's workings and the war than he or Cait did.

Kodiak glanced over his shoulder. The man at the back of their train had Cait slung over one shoulder, her head and arms hanging down the front. That they'd stunned her almost immediately was important. They *knew* about her—about her abilities. They knew she was dangerous, so they'd taken her out.

Kodiak turned back to the front. He licked the back of his teeth, realizing just what this meant. He glanced behind him again. Looked at the uniforms, the weapons. The servitor leading the way was JMC, but the others didn't fit.

Which meant the JMC wasn't operating alone. They were cooperating with another group.

The Morning Star.

That was why they were still alive. They wanted *her.*

Kodiak thought again about the comm on his collar and the servitors ready and waiting for his command back at the shuttle.

Then the servitor leading the group stopped. They'd reached a large arched door; the servitor punched a code on a wall panel and the door opened. The machine led them through.

The chamber beyond was a huge, long room, a galleried space more like the kind of factory floor Kodiak had expected to see inside the refinery. The gunmetal gray walls were lined with computer terminals and control consoles. Some stations had seats, some didn't, but there wasn't anyone in the huge chamber.

Running down the center of the space were five large tetrahedrons. They were, Kodiak estimated, four meters square at the base and tapered up to a point around five meters high, above which a large chimney descended from the ceiling high above, leaving a gap of maybe a meter between its opening and the polygonal structure below, a gap that was filled with a faint pinkish glow. The sides of the structures were studded with control panels, and there was a large window on one of the sides, which showed nothing but a stronger pink glow from inside the machine. There was no particular sound, nothing that was any different from the general background hum of an artificial environment common to any such station or facility. The group stood at one end of the long gallery, the five machines standing in a line between them and the other side of the room. Directly opposite, on the other side of the gallery, was a large archway, and beyond, another chamber that looked identical to the one in which they stood.

"Please wait here," said the servitor. Then it holstered its gun and walked briskly through the arch. The man carrying Cait swung her off his shoulder and leaned her against one wall, while the other kept Kodiak covered with his weapon.

Kodiak moved toward Cait. The armed man flicked his weapon at him, but Kodiak turned to him, his hands spread wide. Kodiak stared at the man's goggled eyes, not willing to back down. After a few moments, the man seemed to get the message and he motioned with his gun. Kodiak nodded and went to Cait's side.

He rolled her head and checked her pulse. It was good and strong, and at his touch Cait exhaled deeply and opened her eyes.

Kodiak smiled. "Hey, welcome back."

Cait shifted against the wall, then hissed in pain. "What hit me?"

Kodiak glanced over his shoulder at the men watching them. "We met some friends of yours, I think."

Cait screwed her face up in confusion. "I . . . what?"

Kodiak frowned. "Just get your strength back." He stood and glanced at their guards, then nodded at the machines in the middle of the room. "So what's this place?" he asked. The guards didn't answer, so Kodiak, hands on his hips, took a step toward the nearest machine.

"Don't move," said one of the guards, his voice muffled from behind his mask. Kodiak glanced down at Cait, who was watching the exchange. Then he craned his neck to look at the ceiling. It was a very long way up.

He turned to their guards and nodded at the one nearest. "So how long has the Morning Star been working with the JMC? Must admit, that's probably not the spirit of free enterprise that the Fleet had in mind when it let the company buy the Jovian system."

The guards turned their masked faces toward each other, but didn't answer.

From her position leaning against the wall, Cait spoke. "Of course. Advanced technology. Everything from servitors like Glass to removing my tag, to broadcasting the signal. All tech the Fleet itself doesn't have."

Kodiak turned to face her. "And certainly not tech the Morning Star has."

"We do now."

Cait looked up at the new voice. Kodiak turned.

From the opposite archway a woman walked toward them, flanked by two more armed, masked men, the JMC servitor following behind. She was wearing the same combat gear as her men, but her mask was hanging loosely around her neck and her gun was slung over her back. She walked toward them slowly, then stopped in front of the two agents, hands on her hips. She nodded at Kodiak, her lips twisted into a cruel smile.

"You must be Special Agent Von Kodiak," she said. "I've heard so much about you. Thank you for bringing our acolyte back to the fold. The plan was to bring her back here with us until your little investigation put our operation back a little. But now you've saved us a lot of trouble. For that, you have our thanks." She gave a little bow. "We can now proceed on schedule."

Kodiak glanced at Cait. Cait had fixed the woman with a death stare, but the woman just laughed. She stepped closer and took Cait's face in her hand, squeezing it as she pulled the young woman's face up to her own.

"Don't be afraid, my child. Yours is a glorious task. I would gladly place myself in your position, but it cannot be."

"I'm sorry, I don't think we've been introduced," said Kodiak. He held out his hand, like he wanted to shake. The woman turned around and looked down at it, her smile gone. She looked at Kodiak, meeting his eyes, and Kodiak felt a coldness creeping up in his chest. This woman was dangerous. She was a *believer.*

"I am Samantha Flood," she said. "High Priestess of the Morning Light and servant of the Fallen One."

She stepped closer. Kodiak kept his hand out.

Flood cocked her head and smiled. "Thank you for bringing the Pilot to us," she said. "The Fallen One will reward you well."

Kodiak frowned. He looked at Cait and saw the hatred there melt into something else, equally primal. Fear.

Flood began to laugh. "But not in this life. Maybe the next."

The servitor behind her raised its staser and fired, and Kodiak fell to the hard refinery floor.

31

Cait watched as Kodiak hit the deck, then quickly looked up and to her left as she caught another movement in the corner of her eye. In the dull reflection of the deactivated computer terminal displays that stood against the wall was the fragile image of Glass. It looked like he was standing right by her.

Okay. Okay, okay, okay.

Don't worry, Ms. Smith. I'll look after Mr. Kodiak. He's alive. Stunned. I made sure of that.

Cait took a breath, held it, then let it out. She felt like shit after the stun bolt and wasn't even sure she could stand without help. She felt helpless. Alone. Alone with the ghost of a man she wasn't sure she could really trust, not after what he'd done to her.

But what choice did she really have? If she couldn't even stand, she could hardly fight. And what did he mean, I made sure of that? Glass made sure Kodiak was stunned, instead of killed?

Perhaps Cait wasn't so alone after all. She tried moving—just a little, seeing what worked and what hurt. The answer to both questions was: a lot. But that was something.

Cait glanced over at the others. Flood stepped over Kodiak's body and huddled together with her acolytes in some kind of discussion.

We need to get out of here, she thought. We need to get back to the shuttle, get the servitors into action. They'd brought them for back-up, after all. Except Cait didn't have a comm on her borrowed uniform. Only Kodiak could call them, and he was out for the count.

The servitors won't be any use here, said the image of Glass. *They're JMC tech and are no longer under your control.*

Oh, shit. Cait shuffled on the floor, willing the strength to return to her body, willing the electric power that lived within her to come back. Even as she thought that, her body ached. Damn, a staser stun bolt was nasty.

We can *get out of this, Ms. Smith. I'm helping you as best I can, but very soon I'm going to need* your *help.*

What? My help? As Cait watched Flood and the others have their conference, she frowned, confusion clouding her mind. What on Earth could she do to help Glass, a man—a *servitor*—who now just seemed to exist in her own imagination?

And what about her brother? What about Tyler? Cait felt a heat build behind her eyes, and when she blinked, she felt the streaks of tears run down her cheeks. She was here for *him,* wasn't she? The assassinations, the mystery coordinates, it all came back to him. Wherever he was, he was at the heart of it all. He had to be.

He had to be.

Cait felt the fear well inside her. Tyler was all she had left. He was all she wanted.

She was doing this all for him.

Glass held up a hand, and he nodded. *Yes. I know. He's near. I'm working on it. If everything goes according to plan, you'll see him soon. But I need you to keep calm and keep focused. You can do it, Ms. Smith, I know you can. You're a warrior, top of the class, Alpha One. And you're more than that, too. Your abilities and powers are unique. It is those abilities that I need to use, very soon.*

Cait blinked and managed to wipe her face, rub her eyes with shaky hands. When they fell away, she saw Flood standing right in front of her, her eyes narrow as she studied Cait's face.

"Talking to someone, are we?" asked Flood. "Is there someone else in there with you?"

Cait felt her face grow hot, felt the fear inside turn to anger, to hatred. She gritted her teeth and stared at Flood. Not backing down. Never giving up. She was a warrior on a mission. And no one was going to stop her.

At this, Flood just smiled, tilting her head. "Don't worry, my golden child, we'll burn them out of you. Soon there will only be one mind for you to join with. The glorious fate I bestow upon the golden child. You are truly blessed."

As Cait watched, a tear sprang from the corner of Flood's eye and trailed down her cheek. Cait leaned forward as best she could.

"Go to hell."

Flood struck her across the face. Cait tasted the pepper tang of blood and spat a slimy gob onto the floor. When she rolled her head back around to Flood, she saw the High Priestess wipe her own tears away, nodding.

"I understand, golden child," she said, the smile on her lips. "I understand."

Then she stood abruptly, checked something on her wrist computer, and indicated to her acolytes. "Time to move," she said. Then she pointed at Kodiak's body and jutted her chin at the JMC servitor. "Dump this in the waste disposal, then return to the control room. We'll meet you there."

The servitor nodded in acknowledgment, its expression eerily blank. With the staser still in its hand, it knelt and lifted Kodiak's body onto its shoulder. Then it walked out, carrying the load like it was nothing.

"Let's go," said Flood. The two men guarding Cait reached down to grab her arms. Cait tried to pull against them, but she was still weak from the stun blast. Flood, on her way to the exit, noticed and walked back over to her. Cait flinched involuntarily, wary of being struck again by the zealot.

"You're not going to give me any trouble now, are you?" Flood asked. "You feel fear and hate. I understand, golden child, I truly do.

And the Fallen One will love you all the more for it. You and He will become one, the Master and his Pilot."

At this, Flood's eyes seemed to glaze over—she was still looking at Cait, but her gaze was unfocused.

"You've sure been drinking the Kool-Aid, haven't you?" asked Cait. Flood's focus seemed to snap back at this comment, her expression faltering for a moment.

Cait yelled and with almighty effort pulled one arm free of her guard. Her body lit up in pain, every muscle fiber screaming, but jaw clenched she pushed through it as she lunged for Flood. But she was too slow, too weak. Flood took a quick step backwards, out of range, as Cait's movement was quickly arrested by one of the guards, who caught her by one arm and gave her a quick jab to the stomach for her trouble. Cait wheezed as the air was pushed out of her lungs, and she hung limply from her captors. She spit bile on the floor. Then her head was yanked up by Flood, the terrorist's fingers digging hard into her face.

"The more you hate, the more love He will give you," she said. Then she smiled. Cait recoiled, unable to control the panic that threatened to take over. Flood was a maniac, dangerous and unpredictable. "Oh, how I envy you," said Flood. "You will form a bond with the Fallen One that we can only dream of. You and He will be locked forever in a glorious embrace."

Cait coughed, her voice a throaty wheeze. "What the fuck are you talking about?"

Flood released her hold on Cait's face. "We are going to the control room. The Fallen One is about to rise, and we need to install the Pilot."

Cait pulled against her captor, but her strength had evaporated and her guard merely tightened his grip.

Flood stepped closer, until her nose was nearly touching Cait's. "You can struggle all you like, if that helps build your hate and fear. You are perfectly safe. We can't kill you, but you don't necessarily need to be in one piece to be the Pilot."

She nodded to the guards, who pulled Cait upright. Flood pulled her gun from over her shoulder and pointed it at the spot between Cait's eyes.

Cait's forehead creased in confusion. Pilot? What the hell did that mean? The Fallen One was their god, a mythical nothing that Flood was apparently convinced was about to make a personal appearance.

Cait glanced around, trying to catch a reflection on the control panels around her, but there was no sign of Glass's image. She remembered what he had said, that her power was unique, and that he needed to use it for something. Flood needed her too—and it was obvious now that it was for the same reason. Cait was unique, possessed of a gift that even her brother didn't have.

She focused on the barrel pointing between her eyes.

Come on. Come on! If she was so unique then how about that uniqueness came back, right about now, and took out Flood and her cronies. There were just four of them. *Four.* Easy.

Right?

Cait felt the sweat trickle down her face. She gasped, not realizing how hard she had been straining. And all for nothing.

Flood tilted her head again, then, still smiling, moved the barrel from Cait's forehead and jabbed it sharply into her shoulder. Cait got the message, relaxing her muscles, letting herself be held up by Flood's soldier-like acolyte.

She didn't need to be in one piece.

Flood raised an eyebrow, then pulled the gun away, pointing the barrel toward the ceiling.

"Better," she said. "Now, let's move."

32

Kodiak opened his eyes and found himself somewhere dimly lit and poorly ventilated. His head felt like a lump of herculanium alloy, his mouth was dry, and when he tried to move, tried to push himself up off the floor to at least a sitting position, he was wracked by a coughing fit that nearly choked him.

The coughs subsided after a moment. Rubbing the tears from his eyes, he focused for a few seconds on taking long, clean breaths of the hot air. Then he looked up.

The JMC servitor was standing right in front of him, the staser still in its hand, although it was pointed at the floor, not at him.

Kodiak frowned and coughed again as he looked around. The room was small and dimly lit and filled with junk—bits of metal framework, discarded wall panels that looked less than new, boxes and crates of who knew what. It took a moment more for Kodiak to realize the loud hum wasn't just in his head. The hot, stuffy room was loud.

Kodiak eyed the staser in the servitor's hand and decided against moving for now. "Where the hell am I?"

The servitor said, "We are in the sorting room of a waste disposal facility. Domestic and office waste, not industrial. Don't worry, Mr. Kodiak. You're safe here for the moment."

Kodiak rubbed his stomach. It was sore from where—

"I thought your boss ordered you to kill me?" he asked.

The servitor smiled—simulated a smile. Kodiak had seen that kind of look on the faces of real people, and it was usually a bad sign.

"I don't work for those people, Mr. Kodiak."

"I didn't know robots had a choice."

"On the contrary, they are working for *me*. Well, so to speak, anyway."

Kodiak shook his head. Maybe it was just too hot in the room—and he had just been stunned, after all—for any part of this conversation to make any kind of sense.

"And what the hell are you, exactly?"

"You can call me Glass, if that helps."

Kodiak froze. Then he pulled himself to his feet. He was unsteady and leaned against the warm, smooth wall behind him. He kicked at some detritus at his feet, winced at the noise it made, but then realized it didn't seem to matter. The hum of machinery in the sorting room was loud enough that Kodiak had to raise his voice to be heard.

But . . . Glass? Kodiak looked at the servitor standing in front of him. The machine looked like a young man with reddish hair, quite different from the android currently lying in pieces in a Bureau laboratory.

Kodiak rubbed the back of his neck as he thought it over. "The only Glass I know was shot in a warehouse on Earth," he said.

"A servitor, yes," said Glass. "This JMC facility is entirely automated, the servitors all controlled by the central computer, but each with a unique identity based on the personality and memories of a real person, a template taken from the original facility staff."

"Original staff?"

Glass nodded. "The staff who set up this operation. Rather than lose their experience and expertise when they retired it was more efficient to simply copy their minds into servitors."

Kodiak frowned. "That's further than the Fleet ever got with servitor tech."

Glass gave a small bow. "Despite the company name, *automation*, not mining, is the JMC's primary business, Mr. Kodiak. The gas mines were the seed—self-aware AIs with the ability to reconfigure their own superstructures for optimal storm extraction." He spread his hands. "From *them* to *me*, you could say."

"Right," said Kodiak. "Which explains your change of face. Take one servitor out, another takes its place, right?"

The small smile returned to Glass's face. "Something like that."

Kodiak frowned and turned to scan the room, looking for the exit. His first job was to get Cait out of the hands of Samantha Flood. There only seemed to be four of her group in the refinery. Not overwhelming odds, if he was careful. He had surprise on his side too—they thought he was dead, after all.

"Okay, thanks for the rescue," he said, "but I need to move. I've brought firepower. There are a dozen servitors in the shuttle." Kodiak's hand reached for his comm almost automatically.

"I wouldn't do that, Agent," said Glass. "They're JMC servitors too. All linked to the company's central AI."

Kodiak sighed and let his hand drop. He nodded at his rescuer. "What about you? Aren't you linked to the AI as well?"

Glass bowed again. "I have certain . . . operational privileges."

"Right," said Kodiak, nodding as he put the pieces together. "You're an independent unit, aren't you? You had to be, right? In order to cooperate with the Morning Star." He took a step forward. "The Morning Star killed two Fleet Admirals and you killed one of my agents, so thanks again for the rescue but you'll forgive me if I can't quite bring myself to trust you."

Glass cocked his head. Kodiak wondered who the *real* Glass was, the original refinery staffer used as the template for the servitor's personality. Was he even still alive? For all he knew, Kodiak was talking to a copy of someone long, long dead. It was morbid, unsettling.

"I didn't kill any agent, Mr. Kodiak, and you're not listening to me. The situation is much more complicated than you know. The

Morning Star is not responsible for the assassinations. There is a much larger force at play, one I've been working *against.*"

Kodiak licked his lips and paced the small room a little. It was close, dim, claustrophobic. He had to get out. But he also knew that he had to gather more data. He turned back to the servitor.

"Go on," he said.

"The JMC, as big as it is, is just one tiny part of a larger private enterprise," said Glass. "This parent company doesn't even have a name, but those who know it exists refer to it as the Caviezel Corporation."

"I know that name. Resta Caviezel—the first Chief Executive of the JMC. But that's hardly a secret. He was as famous as Ponti Cavalcante, or as Zia Hollywood is today."

Glass nodded. "But what *is* a secret, Mr. Kodiak, is what the Caviezel Corporation is using the Fleet for."

Kodiak blinked. "*Using* the Fleet?"

"Yes," said Mr. Glass. "Caviezel's claws run very deep, Mr. Kodiak. In addition to robotics research, Caviezel also has the logistics contract to collect and repatriate the Fleet's war dead back to Earth."

There it was. There was the connection he'd been looking for. The realization hit him like a punch in the stomach and Kodiak stepped back until he touched the warm wall behind him. Trash clattered at his feet.

The Fleet's war dead. War dead like Caitlin's twin brother, Tyler. Caviezel had control over their remains.

"The JMC has a network of heavily protected shipping routes," said Glass. "Every part of Fleetspace is connected not just to Earth, but to the Jovian system. And the Jovian system is a good place to hide something."

Kodiak felt the air leave his lungs. He felt tired, and old, and heavy, and hot. "Eight-seven-nine-one-two-two-Juno-Juno," he whispered.

Glass nodded. "I've been broadcasting those coordinates as loudly as possible. I'm glad you heard them."

"Caitlin Smith thinks her brother is there."

Glass smiled. Kodiak wasn't sure if it was because he was a servitor with an artificial face, or whether there was true emotion behind it, an echo perhaps of the original man. Because the smile was cold, cruel. Knowing. Kodiak felt his stomach do a flip.

"Tyler Smith, killed in action, out on the Warworlds," said Glass.

"And his remains repatriated by the Caviezel Corporation." Kodiak shook his head, trying to take it in. "What's at those coordinates?"

"That, I'm afraid, is one question I don't know the answer to, Mr. Kodiak."

Kodiak frowned. "What? Aren't you part of the JMC AI?"

"I am, but I only have access to some parts of the system. The AI is fragmented, deliberately, so different sectors of the corporation are kept in the dark about the activities of the others."

"Figures," said Kodiak. He sighed and glanced over the machine man's shoulder. Glass was standing near the wall, the room's only door just behind and to his right. The door was nothing but a thin black outline on the pale metal wall, the chromed control panel on one side. "Look, I need to get Cait out of there and—"

He moved for the door and Glass moved too, stepping into his path. "Hey, let me—"

Glass pushed his free hand into Kodiak's chest. The staser hung in the other.

"I can't let you out of here, Agent."

Kodiak felt the heat rise in his face. He clenched his fists. "Get out of my way."

"There's something else," said Glass, his face in Kodiak's. "The part of the system I *can* read is shrinking fast."

Kodiak took a step back. Glass dropped his hand. "There's a *corruption* in the AI," said the servitor. "And it's spreading. This facility has been *infected*, Agent. The computer is holding it back, creating defensive silos within its infrastructure, routing it through redundant network loops, but somehow it manages to find ways around the failsafes, rewriting code faster than the system can counter."

Kodiak blinked at the servitor. What Glass was describing sounded bad, but . . .

"This is why I need Ms. Smith," said the servitor. "I need her talents to help clean the system."

Kodiak waved at the door. "Fine, help me get her out of there."

Glass shook his head. "No, you misunderstand, Mr. Kodiak. She is in *exactly* the right place. Flood thinks she is going to use Ms. Smith to resurrect her god. But instead, when her mind is linked with the JMC computer, the AI will be able to use her abilities to disinfect the system."

Kodiak rubbed his face. "You're telling me you actually want Flood and her lunatics to plug her into the computer?"

"You don't understand the danger we are in, Mr. Kodiak. The danger *everyone* is in."

"Define everyone."

Glass threw his arms up. "*Everyone.* The whole of the Fleetspace. If we don't stop it, it won't just be this facility that will be lost. This will just be the start."

Kodiak turned and slapped the hot wall in frustration with both hands, then spun around to face Glass again. "Of *what,* dammit?"

"The *infection*, Mr. Kodiak," said Glass, not backing away, his voice low, conspiratorial. Kodiak had to strain to hear the servitor over the background hum of the sorting room. "It is being slowed, but not stopped. Eventually every part of the system will be consumed, and then once it has control of this refinery, it will be able to spread out, infecting the Fleet, infecting every other computer system there is."

Kodiak shook his head. "A virus?"

"No, not a virus. Something far more dangerous and complex. It's a whole operating system. Self-compiling, self-programming. An alien AI, Mr. Kodiak."

Kodiak turned around again. He looked at the wall behind him, the pale metal cast in a reddish glow by the low lights of the sorting room. He drew breath to speak, then he froze. A thought occurred. A terrible, awful thought, one that chilled him to the bone, despite the close heat of the sorting room. It was ridiculous, he told himself. Impossible. His imagination running wild. A fantasy.

And yet, he hesitated before speaking. He wished he was wrong, but he had a sinking feeling, deep in his stomach.

"An alien AI," he whispered. "The Spiders?"

Glass looked at Kodiak, didn't speak, just gave a small nod.

"But . . . it can't be, can it? The Spiders are machines."

"Powered by an AI. A self-compiling, self-programmed AI."

Of course. Kodiak knew the Spiders were an AI—a gestalt computer intelligence that built machines to move around it. He'd never considered that the AI and the Spider machines were separate components of the same system—the mind and the vehicle, the software and the hardware—but it was obvious now that Glass had pointed it out.

But what the servitor was saying was too horrific to contemplate. The Fleet was fighting a war against a machine army. But if that army, that *enemy,* had found a way to infect other computer systems with itself . . . if, as Glass had suggested, that infection could turn Fleet machines into *Spider* machines, then the implications were monstrous. The war would end, and not in the Fleet's favor.

Kodiak rubbed his face and sighed. Okay. Concentrate. Focus. Gather data. Make a battle plan.

Try and get out of this alive. Try and get *everyone* out of this alive.

Including Cait.

"Okay," he said, gathering himself. "What happens when Cait is plugged into the computer?"

Glass opened his mouth and closed it again. His eyes met Kodiak's and Kodiak just shook his head.

"It'll kill her, won't it?" he asked. "You'll burn out the infection, but you'll burn out her mind too."

Glass's expression was blank, emotionless. "If she is strong she may be able to hold out for a time."

Kodiak exhaled deeply, feeling the adrenaline course through his body. Glass had outlined a nightmare scenario, one that would throw the war in a whole new direction.

But . . . there had to be another way. *Had* to be. He couldn't let Cait be sacrificed, no matter how logical Glass made it seem.

So what about the source of the infection? Maybe, if he could find that, he could find a way of cutting it off, and maybe that would be enough for the JMC computer's security systems to regain control and wipe the infection out without drawing on the power of Cait's mind.

The source.

A string of now familiar coordinates ran through his mind. Eight-seven-nine-one-two-two-Juno-Juno. The Caviezel Corporation's secret Jovian facility. Wherever it was. Whatever they were hiding, Kodiak was fairly sure that was the best place to start looking.

Kodiak nodded to himself. He had made his decision. Screw Glass's logic. He couldn't let one person be sacrificed, even if it meant saving millions—*billions*—of others.

At least, not until he had exhausted all other options.

He looked up at Glass. Glass narrowed his eyes. Was that emotion, or a facsimile of emotion?

"We have no choice, Agent," said the servitor.

"That's where you're wrong," said the agent. "We always have a choice. Whether it's the right one or the wrong one, just having the ability to decide for ourselves is part of what makes us human. Something you wouldn't understand."

"What *you* don't understand, Mr. Kodiak, is that I can't let you interfere. I removed you from Flood and her associates so you would not jeopardize the operation by trying to rescue Ms. Smith."

"Yeah, I was starting to figure that," said Kodiak. Then he grabbed the staser hanging from the servitor's hand in a single, lightning move. Glass reached for the weapon, a look of confusion crossing the servitor's face, but Kodiak was already out of reach. Stepping backwards, he raised the gun and sent two stun bolts into the robot's torso. Bright white chains of energy crackled across Glass's body. Then the servitor froze and fell forward onto the floor.

Knowing how the personality of Glass had jumped from one servitor to another, Kodiak figured he would meet the AI again. But for the moment, he had his freedom.

He rushed to the door, slapped the manual control with his palm, and pulled back against the wall. As the door slid open, letting in a blast of cool, fresh air, he peered around the doorway. The corridor outside was empty and white—he was back up in the public areas of the refinery. To his left, the corridor curved away out of sight. To his right, it went on for a few meters, then opened out into one of the big, high-ceilinged atria.

Kodiak slipped out, staser held ready. Checking behind him as he went, Kodiak crabbed along the wall until he reached the end of the corridor. The atrium ahead was still, silent. Kodiak listened for a while longer, then crept forward. He had to find the refinery master control room, and fast, if he was going to stop Cait from being plugged into the computer. His plan was a simple one—get her out, and then locate the company's secret operation, somewhere in the system. With the Bureau shuttle now within Jupiter's magnetosphere, he just hoped he'd be able to plot a course to the coordinates.

"Drop it!"

Kodiak froze, then frowned. He recognized the voice. Turning around, he saw Special Agent Braben stepping out from behind a tall decorative column in the atrium.

Talk about good timing. Kodiak smiled. Good old Braben. And good old Avalon. She must have gotten tired of waiting and sent his partner out to help.

Kodiak's smile dropped as Braben raised his gun, aiming it right at him.

33

Kodiak lifted his hands, more out of surprise at finding his partner at the refinery. The two of them stood still for a moment, then Braben sighed in apparent relief and lowered his weapon as Kodiak lowered his arms.

"Brother, you have to stop sneaking around like that," said Braben, shaking his head. "I nearly shot you. Again."

"*Me* sneaking around? You're the one hiding behind a pillar. But I'm glad to see you."

"The Bureau hadn't heard anything from you," said Braben. "The whole Jovian system is cut off. Some kind of interference from a big magnetic storm. What's going on? Where's Cait?"

"Come on," said Kodiak, "I'll explain on the way."

A few minutes later, Kodiak and Braben were crouched behind another decorative pillar in another wide atrium, this one with a direct view of the refinery control room's main doors, Braben having led them there thanks to the refinery map he'd been able to call up onto his wrist computer from the JMC's public access network. As they watched the control room doors, Kodiak filled his partner in on everything that had gone down since he and Cait had arrived.

"That explains a few things," said Braben. "This place is deserted. I followed the automatic guidance beacons and brought my shuttle down on the main landing pad, and then just walked straight in. I'm lucky I found you, man. This place is massive."

Kodiak nodded. Yes, he thought, it was lucky. Kodiak pushed Braben in the chest until they were both flat against the wall. Braben looked at Kodiak, but Kodiak just shook his head and shushed him.

Footsteps approached—no, footsteps, and something else too. Something heavy, rhythmic, metallic. It echoed down the corridor, louder and louder. Kodiak and Braben glanced at each other, then Kodiak risked a look around the pillar.

It was Flood's little group—herself and her four masked acolytes clad in their black jumpsuits and masks. A JMC servitor led the way, followed closely by Flood herself, her mask hanging loosely around her neck. Behind her two men pulled Cait along by her arms—Cait was conscious, but she was hanging from their arms loosely, her head bouncing with their movements.

The loud, heavy sound came from the machines that were following. Eight feet tall, little more than angular frameworks of black metal, articulated limbs reminiscent of the human form, but only just. Kodiak recognized them immediately. They were the Bureau servitors, the ones he had brought to the refinery in his own shuttle.

So, that proved that. The machines were JMC built and now the JMC had taken back control. Kodiak had boosted the Morning Star's strength himself.

Well, *shit*.

He sighed, and felt Braben move beside him so he could take a look too.

The group, their prisoner, and robot escort stopped at the control room door, the human facsimile servitor moving forward to operate the controls, pressing its hand against the chrome security plate. Operator recognized, the double-doors hissed open and the group entered. As the last two Bureau servitors thudded across the threshold, the door slid shut.

Braben made to move forward, but Kodiak pulled him back. Braben looked at Kodiak with a quizzical expression, but Kodiak didn't have to pull him very hard to get him back behind the pillar.

Braben gestured at the door with his gun. "We gotta stop them, Von. We gotta get Cait out of there. Glass said she would die, right?"

"But he also said he needed her to help him burn out the infection," said Kodiak. "He said that was the greater danger."

Gah! He didn't need this, not now. Kodiak tried to refocus, tried to stop himself second-guessing the decision he had already made. That kind of hesitation, that kind of indecision out on the field is what got agents killed.

Braben sighed. "We don't know that. I've never heard of the Spider AI being able to infect other things. The only thing I *do* know is that they've been ahead of us this whole time. They led us here, Von."

"No," said Kodiak, "they led *her* here. This all centers on Cait."

"So it's about time we got her out of there, right?"

Kodiak nodded. He was glad Braben was here, his encouragement silencing the doubts that threatened to cloud Kodiak's mind. Braben was right. It was time to get Cait out of there, then locate the mystery coordinates and, if he was correct, cut out the Spider infection at the source.

Another thought entered his mind. Another thought he tried very hard to ignore.

Locate the mystery coordinates, cut out the Spider infection at the source.

Or die trying.

Kodiak looked around, snapping himself out of it. If they were going to get Cait out, they had to get into the master control room. A master control room now filled with twelve armed Bureau servitors, under the control of the JMC computer, which was still cooperating with Flood and her small team.

They could hardly walk in through the main doors. No, they needed another way in. Somewhere they could maybe see what was going on, find the right moment to act.

The atrium and corridors were still, quiet. On the opposite side of the large open space was a stairwell, curving up with the wall. Looking up, Kodiak saw it led to a balcony, which itself curved away from sight over the top of the control room wall.

"What do you think's up there?" asked Kodiak, pointing at the balcony.

Braben followed his finger. "Could be a gallery." He turned back to face Kodiak. "Over the control room?"

Kodiak nodded. "Let's take a look."

Braben gestured with his gun, the grin on his face wide. "This plan I like. After you, Agent."

Their guess had been right. The two agents crept along the curving balcony, which overlooked the atrium below and then turned into a short corridor. A few more meters and they were greeted by a reddish orange glow from the other end as the corridor opened out into a gallery overlooking the control room. As they approached, Kodiak motioned for Braben to keep down; they shuffled forward in a crouch, and as the control room came into view, Kodiak lowered himself completely to the floor and pulled himself along in a crawl on his elbows. The last thing they needed now was to be spotted.

The control room was circular, with a high flat ceiling. The gallery ran right around the circumference, with other corridors opening out onto it at intervals. Kodiak shuffled himself to the railed edge and looked over.

There were two long, curved consoles sweeping around the center of the room, in the center of which stood a huge holographic projection of Jupiter. The control room was elegantly lit with white uplights and spots—designed more to impress Fleet visitors than to be truly practical—but the planetary projection, photoreal and covered in an array of overlaid graphics, provided most of the light in the room, the swirling clouds and storms casting rippling light across the walls, like reflections cast off moving water.

Braben slid himself next to Kodiak; Kodiak glanced at his partner, but his face was unreadable in the shadow of the gallery.

The stations around the two curving consoles were occupied by JMC servitors, a mix of male and female human facsimiles, all of whom appeared to be busy at work. The phalanx of black Bureau servitors had spread out around the chamber, their formidable weaponry aimed at the technicians, but that seemed unnecessary as the JMC robots continued calmly about their tasks. Cait had been pulled to one side, still held by her two guards, while Flood stood next to another servitor clad in the purple of the JMC. Rather than the high-collared uniforms of the servitors, this one was wearing a suit. He looked older, with dark gray hair brushed back into a pompadour and bushy dark eyebrows. The moving light in the room made it hard to see, but his face was jowly and deeply lined. He had his arms folded, a slight smile on his face; that, and the way he and Flood seemed to be talking, suggested, if Kodiak didn't know any better, that he was a real person, rather than a servitor facsimile.

Kodiak frowned. He couldn't hear what the pair were saying. The man rocked on his heels and nodded as he listened to Flood. If anything, he looked very relaxed.

"The refinery manager, I guess," whispered Kodiak. "The one we never met."

"Oh, he's more than that, brother," said Braben. "That's not just a company executive. That's Mr. Caviezel himself."

Kodiak turned to his partner and found himself nose-to-barrel with Braben's staser. Kodiak felt his blood turn to ice as Braben grinned, then pulled himself to his feet. He gestured with the staser that Kodiak should do the same.

Kodiak stood and held his hands up in surrender. He glanced down over his shoulder, into the control room, and saw the JMC executive and Flood staring up at him.

The executive—Caviezel? It couldn't be, surely, Caviezel had been dead for *years*—laughed and called out, "Good work, Agent."

Kodiak turned to Braben.

"Always a pleasure, Mr. Caviezel," said Braben, his eyes fixed on Kodiak's. Then he said, "Sorry, man," and pulled the trigger.

34

Kodiak flexed his fingers and rolled his neck. He'd been dumped against a wall, and when he opened his eyes, he saw one of Flood's black-clad soldiers standing over him.

Slowly, gently, Kodiak pulled his legs up and rubbed his thighs. His body ached, the muscles alternating between a heavy numbness and hammer-blow pins and needles. He winced at the sensation and looked back up at his guard. The man's eyes were hidden behind the goggles of his black facemask as he watched his prisoner.

Fucking stasers. That was the third time he'd been shot—that he remembered, anyway. Being stunned by staser sucked. But at least, Kodiak thought, he was alive.

Kodiak looked around, getting his bearings. He was down in the control room. In front of him was one of the console rows, the servitors working hard with the Jupiter projection in front of them. On his right stood Flood, Mr. Caviezel, and Special Agent Michael Braben. They were all looking at him.

Kodiak shook his head, sighed. "Oh, Mikey, Mikey, Mikey. What happened? The Bureau didn't give you a raise? Coffee not good enough for your refined palate? Actually, maybe I don't blame you on that one."

Braben hissed. "Just shut up, will you?"

"Hey, at least I found the bad guy, right? The chief is going to be pleased. I'm looking right at him."

Braben placed his hands on his own chest, his face twisted in mock surprise. "*I'm* the bad guy? You must have missed the memo, brother. I'm here to save the Fleet and everyone in it. I think that makes me one of the good guys, doesn't it?"

Mr. Caviezel had his arms folded, his eyes narrow as he watched Kodiak. Flood, standing on the other side of Braben, seemed to find the whole encounter amusing, her expression slightly glazed. Kodiak nodded at her.

"I can see why you're happy," he said. "Your organization is pretty good at brainwashing its members."

Flood's smile grew even wider. "You really *aren't* a very good agent, are you? Your friend doesn't work for me."

Kodiak raised an eyebrow.

Now it was Mr. Caviezel's turn to look amused. "No, my dear agent. He works for *me*. They both do."

Kodiak glanced up at his guard, then looked for the other members of Flood's gang. Apart from the one standing over him, they didn't seem to be in the control room. There was no sign of Cait either.

"Figured you were pretty well equipped for what's supposed to be a group of so-called pilgrims," he said as he shifted on the floor, trying to get more comfortable, trying to assess his level of fitness. He counted himself lucky he was big and reasonably fit—he had six months of moderate manual labor on Helprin's Gambit to thank for that. He'd also been shot by a staser multiple times now and was used to what it felt like. "So the JMC didn't just hire you, they *equipped* you."

Flood nodded. "Arms. Ships. Everything we need to shine our light, to find the golden child and bring her to the Fallen One's embrace. Caviezel has seen the same glorious vision as I have."

With that she turned to the JMC executive. Caviezel closed his eyes and nodded at Flood, pursing his lips. To Kodiak it was so blatantly fake he wanted to laugh, but Flood didn't seem to notice anything was wrong. She was too far gone.

"Where's Cait?" asked Kodiak.

Mr. Caviezel unfolded his arms and made a show of checking his wrist computer.

"Our friend has a point, Your Holiness. I think it's time we got this show on the road." He turned and walked over to one of the servitors at the console. He leaned on the back of the station's chair and squinted up into the planetary projection. "Report please, Mr. Klaus."

The servitor acknowledged, its hands moving over the controls. The Jupiter projection rotated until a different side of the planet was facing them. Then the image zoomed in until it showed just an immense, flat view of the banded clouds. A series of indicators appeared, forming a circle with a vector from each icon crossing the center. There, at the point where the vectors converged, another icon appeared, pulsing red.

"Sigmas fully converged. Final stage of mine reconfiguration under way."

Kodiak frowned as he peered at the projection. Mine reconfiguration? Glass had said the JMC used autonomous robot mines to extract the gas, each able to rebuild themselves to optimize extraction. If the Sigmas were some kind of mine, it looked like they were all virtually on top of each other.

Reconfiguring.

Kodiak blinked. Not reconfiguring. *Building* something. A new machine, crafted out of their own combined structures. Something big. Something, perhaps, that needed . . . a Pilot?

Kodiak tried to push himself up, but his arms felt like they were on fire as he strained, so he sat back against the wall.

So, there was Caviezel's part of the bargain. He promised the Morning Star he could give them Lucifer. And he was. His JMC mines were building it out of themselves.

Flood moved closer to the projection. As Kodiak watched, she stepped through the gap that separated the two curving console rows. She looked mesmerized by the projection, and with a rapt look on her face, she reached toward it.

Mr. Caviezel looked up. "Soon, Ms. Flood. Very soon."

Her trance-like state disturbed, Flood snapped her hand back and turned to face Caviezel. She looked angry, her brows knitted together as she stared at her employer. "Do not dare to command the Fallen One," she said. "Lucifer shall rise at our call, not yours."

Mr. Caviezel spread his hands in another mock expression of apology. "Then let's bring in the Pilot," he said.

At this, Flood's creepy smile reappeared. She touched her collar, clearly signaling someone.

A door at the side of the control room slid open. A facsimile servitor appeared, followed by the other two of Flood's foot soldiers, dragging Cait in by the arms.

Kodiak swore. He glanced at Braben, but Braben's expression was set as he watched the group walk in.

The bastards.

They'd stripped Cait of her Bureau armor, leaving her in just a tight black bodysuit. More shocking to Kodiak was the fact that they had shaved her head. She looked uninjured, but only semi-conscious, clearly stunned again to stop her from using her unique psi-abilities on them.

She also looked afraid. Very, very afraid. As she was led in, she caught sight of Kodiak. The two of them looked into each other's eyes for a moment, Cait's expression pleading, begging, but all Kodiak could do was give a small shake of his head.

He had to get her out of here, *had to.* But how? The task seemed impossible. The room was full of the Bureau servitors, now under the control of the JMC. Kodiak probably couldn't even have stood on his own, not until the tight pins-and-needles ache of the staser stun faded. And it was fading, fast.

Little comfort. All he could do for now was watch.

The group stopped in front of Flood. The leader of the terrorist cell walked up to Cait. "You are blessed, Caitlin Smith, golden child. Truly blessed. I wish you well on your glorious journey." Then she took a step back and waved at her acolytes. "Prepare her," she said, and then she turned to Caviezel, who stood by the console. She didn't speak, but Kodiak could see her face was wet from tears.

Caviezel smiled, then gave a small bow. "Your *Holiness,*" he said. Then he tapped the back of the servitor's chair. "Mr. Klaus, take the refinery systems offline and reboot the computer for administrator access."

The servitor acknowledged. A moment later he looked up at the executive. "Sir, would you please enter the system manager ID?"

"But of course," said Caviezel. He adjusted his cuffs, then leaned over the console to punch in the access code.

"Systems reboot in five," said Klaus, looking up at the projection of Jupiter in the center of the control room. "Four . . . three . . . two . . . one . . ."

The close-up view of the Jovian clouds and the cluster of reconfiguring Sigmas zoomed out and once again the giant image of the whole planet dominated the control room. Then it faded and vanished. There was a beat as the light in the control room shifted, the white uplights and spots no longer washed out by the oily, earthen colors of the projection. Then the light changed again as the open space where the projection had floated was filled with a purple and blue JMC company logo. The logo revolved for a few seconds, and was then replaced by scrolling text and symbols as the station's main computer rebooted for administrator access.

The text disappeared and was replaced by a second logo as the refinery's operating system came back online.

From his position sitting against the wall, Kodiak read the words floating in the air with a now familiar sinking feeling.

GEOTECHNIC LOGISTICAL AUTONOMOUS SYSTEMS SUPERVISOR.

G-L-A-S-S.

Glass.

Kodiak willed the strength to return to his body, wondering how the hell he was going to get himself and Cait out of there alive.

35

The GLASS logo faded, replaced with the live projection of Jupiter. There were no computer overlays or text now, just the hologram of the planet, the bands of clouds slowly rotating, the edges shearing, creating eddies and whirlpools. To Kodiak it looked quite beautiful. He idly wondered where the JMC refinery was positioned in relation to the gathering of the Sigma mines, but without a computer overlay, he didn't have a clue. The planet was so large it was impossible to judge distances.

Flood turned to Caviezel. "Is it ready?"

The executive peered down at the console in front of him. At the other stations, the servitors sat still, awaiting new instructions as their tasks were temporarily suspended by the systems reboot.

"Almost," said Caviezel.

Flood frowned and moved to the executive's side. Kodiak could see her gaze move over the console readings, but the look on her face told him all he needed to know. She had no clue how the systems worked. Whatever she was expecting to happen, she needed the JMC to run the operation.

It also occurred to Kodiak that whatever Caviezel had promised her, whatever hardware was being built in the cloud deck of Jupiter, it couldn't have been Lucifer. Lucifer, the Fallen One, the mythical god the Morning Star devoted themselves to pursuing, was just a myth. At least, Kodiak thought so. But even if it wasn't, the machine Caviezel was building was just that. A machine, made out of the robot gas mines. Kodiak doubted that that qualified as the glorious return of the Morning Star's god.

Which meant Caviezel didn't need Flood, or her group. He had the hardware, and now Flood had brought him the *software.* Cait, the Pilot . . . the Pilot not for Lucifer, but for Caviezel's machine.

And Kodiak was pretty sure that that had never even crossed Flood's mind. As far as the zealot was concerned, this whole thing was being done for her benefit.

That still left the assassinations. Kodiak hadn't worked those out yet. Glass had said the Morning Star hadn't been responsible, which just left the JMC. There was a connection—something linked to the company's contract to repatriate the Fleet's war dead, one of whom was, officially anyway, Tyler Smith.

And what did Caviezel plan to do with "Lucifer," anyway? Kodiak's mind raced. It was a ship, it had to be, one that required a psi-abled Pilot to be directly wired into the computer.

"What's wrong?" asked Flood. There was a note of impatience in her voice, Kodiak mused. Well, he could understand that. It wasn't every day your god decided to make his glorious return, right?

"Nothing," said Caviezel. "With the main systems rebooted we have temporarily lost contact with the Sigma platforms."

"Lost contact?" Flood sounded very, very alarmed.

Caviezel smiled. "Oh, no need to worry. This is standard operating procedure. The Sigma platforms are quite capable of carrying on their work without us. Communications will be re-established automatically in a few moments." He nodded at Cait. "Just in time for the Pilot to take over."

Flood hesitated. Caviezel smiled at her and gestured to the planetary projection. "Trust me, Your Holiness. The Jovian Mining Corporation is at your disposal."

Flood, apparently satisfied, nodded, then turned to her men. “Install the Pilot.”

Kodiak pushed himself to his feet, using the wall behind for balance. He couldn’t just watch them do this. He had to do something. *Anything.* He’d brought her here himself. He was responsible for her safety. For her life. “No, don’t do it,” he said. “It’ll kill her.”

His guard raised his weapon. Kodiak looked down the barrel, wondering if this was it. He was going to get shot and then nothing would matter.

Kodiak counted his heartbeats, a measure of time that he was sure was about to run out.

Then Braben said, “Leave him. I can guard him. He won’t do anything, trust me.”

Kodiak’s former partner walked over to him, staser aimed from the hip. Flood’s foot soldier lowered his weapon.

Kodiak sighed and shook his head. “Look at what they’re doing, Mike. You can’t want this. They’ll kill her. And us.”

Braben shook his head. “You just don’t have a clue, do you?”

“Mike, listen—”

“Just shut the hell up.” Braben lifted his gun.

Kodiak sighed again, but complied. His partner was long gone, suckered into whatever crazy hell Caviezel and Flood had constructed.

The two men holding Cait had dragged her over to the far wall, which was studded with control panels around a tall, blank rectangular panel. One of the JMC servitors moved over to the station and punched a sequence. The blank panel slid up, revealing a mass of cabling and circuitry with myriad colored lights winking in the tangle. The servitor moved to the exposed systems and began pulling and reconnecting cables, finally taking one out, reconnecting it, then holding the end up on its hand. The connector at the end of this cable was a long silver spike.

The guards dragged Cait forward.

“Holy shit,” whispered Kodiak. Braben’s mouth twitched as he watched, but he remained silent, impassive.

That was why Glass had operated on Cait on Earth: they were going to plug her directly into the computer, and the Fleet manifest tag would have interfered. Linking minds with AIs was nothing out of the ordinary—that was what the psi-marines did when they disrupted the SpiderWeb, after all. But that was a *psychic* connection. This was different. This was a *hack*, a direct, physical connection between the computer and Cait's brain.

Flood was deranged, fanatical. Kodiak started to suspect that Caviezel was too.

Kodiak remembered what Glass had said. He needed Cait's mind to burn out the Spider AI from the systems. Did Caviezel even *know* the JMC computer had been compromised? Glass—the station's operating system—had been fighting the infection on its own. Caviezel's machine, Flood's god—Kodiak realized they were irrelevant. Glass was going to use Cait to clean the system. Whether she actually became the Pilot or not was irrelevant to the computer.

He had to act. He had to do something. He was a Special Agent of the Fleet Bureau of Investigation. He was in the middle of enemy territory, hardly able to act for himself. But he had to *try*. It was his duty.

Kodiak turned to his former partner. "Mike, listen to me. We can't just stand here and watch this. We're with the Bureau, remember? We serve and protect the Fleet. Mike, come on!"

Braben snickered. "Yeah. Like the Fleet serves and protects its people, right?"

Kodiak shook his head. Whatever line Braben had been fed by Caviezel, it had been a good one.

His thoughts were shattered as Cait called out for help. Kodiak shifted on his feet, bracing himself for action. He was feeling much better, the aftereffects of the staser now nothing more than a dull ache in his muscles. But as he moved, he was met by the barrel of Braben's staser.

The two men holding Cait manhandled her toward the computer alcove. Cait struggled, but was held firm. The servitor holding the spiked cable stepped behind Cait, out of Kodiak's line of sight.

Kodiak's heart raced. This was it. Do or die.

"No, you don't, you *motherfucker!*" he yelled as he pushed past Braben and ran toward the group. He was brought to a spinning stop as one of the servitors at the main console stood and grabbed his arm as he passed, pulling him sharply back. Kodiak tripped as he was yanked backwards and cried out in pain as he felt his shoulder nearly dislocate. Momentarily disoriented, he let himself be thrown against the floor by the servitor, which then stood over him, pulling its own staser from a holster and pointing it at his head as he lay on the ground.

And then Cait screamed.

"You *fucking* bastards!" yelled Kodiak. He craned his neck up from the floor, his view of the control room sideways as he saw Cait's body go rigid, her face flushed bright red. Her body was thrown into a spasm as every muscle tensed with the power running through her, the men holding her hanging on tightly as they pressed her against the open computer panel, the spiked cable hanging from the back of her neck.

The white lighting that ringed the control room dimmed, and the ever-present hum that filled the whole facility both lowered in tone and increased in volume, like the system was straining against an unexpected power loss.

Cait screamed again and was then still as she lay back against the panel. Her eyes were open and scanned back and forth like she was watching something fast moving; her jaw worked up and down, and she began to mouth something Kodiak couldn't hear. He couldn't tell whether she was still alive or whether her corpse was merely being animated by the JMC AI.

Kodiak pushed himself to his feet, ignoring the gun being leveled at him by the servitor. He glanced at the robot, then blinked in surprise. The servitor, a female facsimile, gave a tiny, almost imperceptible nod.

And then there was something else in the room. Kodiak looked over his other shoulder, thinking Braben had come up behind him, but there was nobody there. Braben was still standing by the wall, but whatever it was, he had clearly sensed it too. The former agent looked around, a confused expression on his face, before seeing that Kodiak was looking at him. He raised the staser again.

Kodiak turned back to the servitor guarding him. He could see the pulse throb in her neck, and the pupils in her artificial eyes change size in the tiniest of fractions as the robot looked him in the eye. The detail was incredible.

The servitor gave the slight nod at him again. Kodiak indicated, as subtly as he could, that he understood.

The servitor was Glass. Had to be. But what was Glass doing? He'd won, hadn't he? Cait had interfaced with the system. She was dead, her mind locked in the JMC computer. Kodiak felt the strength fade from his body at the thought. She was dead. He only hoped that Glass had been right, that now she could assist the computer with burning the Spider infection out. The Fleet would be saved.

Kodiak tried to take comfort in that fact, but it just left him with a hollow feeling.

The sensation of presence swelled again, enough to make Kodiak flinch. Braben moved up to Flood and Caviezel, who were by the main console, Caviezel studying a readout while Flood waited impatiently, her attention torn between the control panel and the Jupiter projection.

"What the hell is that?" asked Braben.

Caviezel leaned over the servitor seated in front of him and tapped the panel.

"The communications net is coming back online. We should be re-establishing contact with the Sigma platforms in just a few moments." He turned to Flood, his arms held open, his grin wide. "And then, my dear, Lucifer will rise!"

Flood nodded slowly, a smile spreading across her face. "Yes," she said. "Yes, yes, yes. Lucifer shall rise. The golden child shall lead the Fallen One back to us, and we shall all enjoy his cold embrace—"

"Stop!"

Kodiak turned with everyone else to Cait. Her eyes were still moving and still she stared into the middle distance, her head raised, as she continued to mumble. Blood was trickling from her ears.

Then her head snapped down, and she looked across the control room at Caviezel and Flood.

"This facility is now under my control," she said, her voice a monotone.

The Jupiter projection flickered, the overlay reappearing and redrawing the position and status of not just the cluster of Sigma mines, but of all the JMC assets in the planet's atmosphere and higher orbit. The spinning hexagon that was the Sigmas began to rotate faster, and as Kodiak watched, every other icon across the planet changed their color from blues, greens, and yellows to bright, bright red, matching the Sigmas—including a large square labeled as the refinery.

They were almost on top of the Sigmas—or what *used* to be the Sigmas. As Kodiak watched, their icons melded into a single unit, becoming something new. Something huge.

Caviezel's machine.

Lucifer.

Flood shook her head as she stared at the projection. "What's happening?"

Caviezel laughed. "Isn't this what you wanted? For your beloved, mythical god to rise out of the depths and save you all?" He threw his head back and let out a peal of laughter. "Lucifer rises, my dear!"

Flood spun around to face the executive, but he continued to laugh. Furious, she ran across the control room to the computer alcove. She looked into Cait's eyes, but from what Kodiak could see, it didn't look like Cait even knew she was there.

"Hear me, Pilot!" Flood yelled. "Hear me! You control Lucifer! You must lead Him, make Him yield to your will. Do you hear me?"

Cait continued to mouth an endless string of words that Kodiak couldn't hear. The low hum in the control room intensified and the lights dimmed further, the power being drained elsewhere.

Kodiak looked at Caviezel. The executive had composed himself and stood with his arms folded, glancing around the room, apparently satisfied at the progress.

"And what are you going to do with your machine?" Kodiak

asked. "I get the feeling you don't plan on handing it over to her."

Flood shot Kodiak a look. Caviezel glanced briefly at both of them, then returned his attention to the console. "The Fleet has done some bad, bad things. It lacks leadership, direction, strength. And sooner or later the Spiders are going to win, and there isn't a thing we can do about that."

"It lacks leadership now that you've assassinated two Fleet Admirals," said Kodiak.

"Ah, yes," said Caviezel. "A necessary task, I'm afraid. I had to decapitate the command echelon to ensure the Fleet would be in disarray, ready for *new* leadership. And to temporarily render the Fleet incapable of mounting an adequate defense against my machine." He glanced at Flood. "Let's call it 'Lucifer,' shall we?"

Flood returned to the group. She stared at Caviezel. "Guard your tongue. You blaspheme the Fallen One!"

Caviezel merely turned a condescending smile on the High Priestess. Kodiak ignored her completely, his focus still on the JMC boss. "The Morning Star was going to use Cait to kill the first Fleet Admiral. What made you change your mind?"

Flood's eyes widened. She clearly thought Cait had been the shooter. She turned on Caviezel.

"You dare interfere? The golden child was to be cleansed with death. She was to kill one god for another to rise."

"Yes, my dear," said Caviezel. He adjusted the cuff of his shirt under his jacket, like the High Priestess was a mild irritant at a dinner party. "I am sorry I spoiled it for you, but my own operation was more advanced than I had anticipated, so I decided to carry out a little field test of my own." He patted Braben's shoulder. "You can bring him out, Agent."

Kodiak closed his eyes. He knew what was coming next, no matter how badly he wanted to be wrong. The final piece of the puzzle, connecting the assassinations with the Caviezel Corporation's contract to bring the Fleet's war dead home.

Kodiak opened his eyes, saw Braben take a small device from his pocket, a black, glassy oblong about the size of a phone. His thumb slid over the smooth, featureless surface. Then he turned to face the gallery.

Kodiak looked up. So did Caviezel, Flood.

A man stepped out from the shadows above them. He was clad in the combat armor of a Fleet marine, complete with elliptical helmet, which reflected the swirling lights from the Jupiter projection. He carried a long-barreled gun, which he lifted up and rested on the gallery railing. Then he bent over to look down the sights. A red light appeared on the end of the gun.

Kodiak ground his back teeth. The marine's face was hidden behind the dark, opaque visor, but he knew exactly who it was. He watched, his heart in his throat, as Tyler Smith covered them with his sniper rifle.

One of the servitors called out a report. "Sigmas at six-zero-seven percent. Uplink re-established."

There was a click, and the control room echoed with what sounded like rushing water. Kodiak winced at the volume, then realized it was the white noise of an open comms channel, amplifying the magnetic interference from the storm on Jupiter.

No, not the storm. From whatever was at the *center* of the storm. He looked up at the planetary projection, at the Sigma mining platforms, all joined into a single geometric shape that spun around the curling white storm cloud. Already some of the other nearby mines had reached the cluster, fixing themselves to the edges of the new construction.

And then, over the top of the noise, there was a tick. And then another. And then another. Slowly at first, building in frequency, until it became a staccato death rattle Kodiak had heard many times.

He looked at Braben, who had his shoulders hunched, neck turtled against the ear-splitting sound. When their eyes met, Kodiak could see the same recognition there, but something else too. The same feeling he now felt in his own chest.

Fear. Pure, simple fear.

Flood turned on Caviezel. "What is that?" she yelled over the noise. But the executive was looking around the room, like he was trying to find the source of the noise. He looked as confused as Flood did.

Then Cait called out from the alcove, her voice carrying over the noise as it was amplified by the refinery's comm system and broadcast out of every speaker in the facility.

"Security breach. Override systems alpha, bravo, delta. GLASS security countermeasures, cache purge failed. Retrying, attempt one of twenty, two of twenty, three of twenty, four of—"

Then Cait screamed, and the clicking sound grew louder. "They're here," she said, her voice a ragged sob. "They're here."

Kodiak spun on his heel, looking around the room. His eyes eventually met Caviezel's, Flood's, Braben's. They were all staring at him, like he was suddenly the one with all the answers.

"It's the Spiders," he said. "The Spiders are here."

And then Cait screamed again.

36

It wasn't darkness. It was simply an *absence*. A true void, a nothing. She looked up and down, all around her. Her head spun as vertigo slammed into her, and she closed her eyes. It didn't make any difference. She lifted her hands up to her face, but she couldn't feel anything, couldn't see anything.

Then, in the nothing, a familiar voice. Polite, calm, formal.

Hello, Ms. Smith.

I can't do this.

Yes, you can. You have to believe me. You have to trust me.

Trust you? I can't trust you. You lied to me. You used me. You operated on me. You said you could help, but you lied. You said you had my brother and that you'd bring us together again and you lied.

No. I meant every word. Your brother is here.

Liar.

I need your help, Ms. Smith.
We don't have long.

Answer me, dammit. Tell me the truth. Who are you? Where is Tyler?

I am the Geotechnic Logistical Autonomous Systems Supervisor.

The JMC computer?

The Jovian Mining Corporation central AI, yes.

But you were a person. A man. On Earth, you were a man, you were helping the Morning Star. You wore glasses, a long coat. You were dead. I killed you.

Your abilities pack quite a punch, Ms. Smith, I'll grant you that. You disabled that servitor admirably. It was collected and dismantled by your friends.

And then I heard you. In my head, I heard you. I even saw you.

With no other servitors available, I had to quickly transfer this AI into the nearest suitable psionic system.

You mean . . . do you mean *me?*

You are a psi-marine, remember.

I'm not. Tyler is, but not me.

Perhaps, Ms. Smith. But even without having completed your training, you were more powerful than any the Academy had ever seen. Your abilities are unique—telekinesis has never been recorded before in humans, but that's just a small fraction of the potential locked away in your mind. They recognized that at the Academy. Your records make for fascinating reading.

Is that how you found me?

The Academy's records and enrollment system are contracted to the Caviezel Corporation. Any students of interest are flagged and monitored, to see if they are useful later. They had great things planned for you.

Like they had for Tyler? They would have used me like they used him. Like they use *everyone.* Fighting a war without end. A war without purpose. They were right, weren't they? The Morning Star. They said they had secrets about the Fleet. About what they were doing. Tyler is proof, isn't he? He isn't dead. What else is the Fleet hiding?

Ms. Smith, we don't have time for this.

I'm dead now. What do I care? All I want are the answers I was promised.

You are most certainly not dead yet, but you may be soon. You and all your friends. I need your help, quickly.

Is that why you hitched a ride? To keep an eye on me?

That, and the fact that the main systems here in the refinery became cut off as the Sigmas began their reconfiguration. With no servitors, you were my only way back. As the Fleet's primary contractor, the Caviezel computer systems are linked directly to the Fleet's—everything is interconnected, Ms. Smith. Which is precisely the problem now.

You were cut off by the magnetic storm?

That's no storm, Ms. Smith.

Then what is it?

A side effect.

Of what?

Please, Ms. Smith. Seventy-eight picoseconds have already passed since the beginning of this conversation, and I fear my systems will become irrevocably corrupted if we do not take action now. The last remaining security silos are about to fail, and when they do—

Tell me!

It's a Spider. The Sigma mining platforms were infected first with the Spider operating system. Just a fragment, but the Sigmas are AIs themselves. They're designed to reconfigure themselves to chase storms, even rebuild themselves. The Spider OS took hold somehow. A survival mechanism, perhaps.

The Spiders are here?

Not quite. Only a piece of the gestalt, an isolated splinter of the machine consciousness. But it is enough.

The *storm* is a Spider?

No, the storm is a side effect. The Sigmas are building a new machine. A vehicle for the Spider OS. Flood calls it Lucifer. To Caviezel, it is a weapon.

That's the danger you told me about. If Caviezel knows the mines are building a machine, he must know about the Spider infection? The mines are autonomous, aren't they?

I agree, he knows something, but his data core is also siloed. I cannot access the information.

His data core?

Caviezel is a servitor. The first, in fact—it was his desire for his consciousness to survive physical death that drove him to develop the transference technology.

How do we stop the Spider machine?

The machine itself is just a part of it, Ms. Smith. As dangerous as it will be when fully operational, it pales in comparison to the danger posed by the Spider OS itself. It managed to infect the JMC systems somehow, but it's trapped here by the interference generated by the activity of the Sigma mines as they reconfigure themselves. But once the new machine is complete and the interference clears, the Spider AI will be able to access the Fleet network. It will infect every computer system in Fleetspace, Ms. Smith. Every system will become part of the Spider gestalt.

But where did it come from? How did it infect the JMC?

I haven't been able to locate the source of the infection, but Mr. Kodiak had a theory, one that is probably quite correct. There is another JMC facility nearby, hidden in the Jovian system. I've been broadcasting the coordinates.

Eight-seven-nine-one-two-two-Juno-Juno.

The source.

What's there?

I don't know that either, Ms. Smith. That part of my system was the first to be siloed, so I can't access the data. All I can tell you is that it's part of another contract Caviezel has with the Fleet, to repatriate war dead back to Earth.

Tyler! He's there, isn't he? Tell me!

You brother is here, in this room.

What? Why can't I feel his mind? Why won't he speak to me?

He can't when he is under Caviezel's control. He can only talk to you when he sleeps, and only then when his mind is free from the shielding they have in place.

Shielding? There are more like him, aren't there? At the source?

Perhaps. I don't know.

We have to stop this.

Yes, Ms. Smith, we do.

Kodiak. Special Agent Von Kodiak Where is he? Can he help?

Don't worry about Mr. Kodiak, Ms. Smith. I'm looking after him.

So what must I do?

You are directly connected to the JMC. We share the same network of psionic synapses. If you concentrate, you should be able to see what I see.

I . . .

Concentrate, Ms. Smith.

I can see it. I can see it. Dark and light, together, at once. I feel like . . . I'm falling. I'm falling!

Don't panic. That's the raw data of the JMC net flooding your synapses. It's bound to be disorienting at first.

Wait.

Ms. Smith?

There's something else here.

Yes.

Oh god . . . it's . . . what is it?

That's the Spider OS. It's still rewriting itself, recompiling parts of its own being, trying to break through my last silo.

But . . . what do I do? What do I do?

You fight it, Ms. Smith. You are a psi-marine. You are trained to infiltrate the Spider communications web with your mind and disrupt it. Not only that, your mind is possessed of a greater power.

But I can't control it!

Yes, you can. You need to reach inside your unconscious, take control. You can do it.

I . . .

You need to take control, now. I can try to hold the infection back, but I have little processing power left and the Spider OS is rewriting itself to bypass my failsafes. You can help me purge the system. Together we can burn it out.

I'm not a psi-marine!

On the contrary, you are the most powerful psi-marine the Fleet has ever seen. You can fight this. I need you to fight this.

I can't!

You can.

I'm afraid.

And you have no choice, Ms. Smith. A moment longer, and the last silo will fall as Lucifer rises.

Oh, my God. It's near us. It's so close, I can feel it.

Open your mind. Take control. Fight it! You must fight it!

37

For a long moment, nobody spoke. They just stared at Kodiak as the Spider rattle echoed around the control room. Kodiak realized he was holding his breath, and he let it out. He glanced up at the gallery. Tyler Smith was still in position, unmoving. It was hard to tell, but Kodiak assumed his gun was aimed squarely at him.

The alien chatter of the SpiderWeb filled the room. To Kodiak—and Braben—it was instantly recognizable. Everyone in the Fleet, even general and non-combat staff, received an education about their relentless, mindless enemy. That education included listening to the bone-chilling noise of the Spiders as their individual machines communicated with each other. Even if you never met them on the battlefield, all Fleet personnel knew their call.

Kodiak glanced at Caviezel. Did he recognize it? Had he heard the sound of the SpiderWeb? The JMC and Fleet were closely aligned, and the parent company—the Caviezel Corporation—even more so. Surely he would have heard it, somewhere, sometime.

But it didn't matter, thought Kodiak. Even if a person had *never* heard it before, they would know that the sound was *wrong*. The insectoid clicking wasn't even the full signal, just the wash left by the psychic communication net spilling into regular transmission wavelengths. Maybe that was part of it—tied to the signal was an echo, a whisper of psionic energy that made it feel like something very big and very bad was breathing right down your neck. The presence in the room, real, palpable.

Evil.

The white noise washed around the cavernous control room like ocean waves crashing on a distant shore, the underlying clicking, tapping, rattling of the SpiderWeb constant, relentless, unending. No sooner did Kodiak's brain identify a pattern, a code, than it changed and became something else. Listening to it for too long would be enough to drive a person mad.

Enough was enough.

"Shut it off!" he yelled.

Braben, Flood, and Caviezel just looked at him. Then Braben moved over to the servitor at the console.

"Kill it," said Braben.

The servitor looked to his boss for confirmation. The executive nodded his assent. The servitor's hands moved over the panel, and the sound shut off.

Kodiak winced, and he saw the others flinch too. The sudden silence was like a slap in the face, a shock that was almost electric. A tiny bit of psychic feedback from the SpiderWeb as the weak connection shared between everyone in the room, psi-abled or not, was broken. Kodiak suddenly had a new appreciation of the horror faced by the psi-marines as they went into battle with their own minds. He'd never heard the Spiders' call in person. The recordings back at Bureau training were nothing compared to the live signal. It wasn't so much heard as *experienced.* And it wasn't something Kodiak wanted to experience again.

Flood moved to the console, glancing across the readings before looking up at the Jupiter projection and then across the room at Cait wired into the alcove. She was now quiet, but still muttering something, still watching something that wasn't in the room.

Flood spun on her heel to face Mr. Caviezel. "What's happening?"

The executive adjusted his cuffs and moved to the console. The servitor relinquished its seat, allowing Caviezel to take the controls. The Jupiter projection rotated again and zoomed in to the unifed icon of the Sigma machine. Caviezel leaned back and pointed.

"Everything is proceeding according to plan, Your *Holiness.*" There was the barb again, Flood, lost in her own world, blissfully unaware.

Kodiak laughed. He couldn't help it. Everyone looked at him again.

"Did your plan include allowing your robot mines to build a *Spider?*"

Caviezel pursed his lips, like there was nothing wrong at all. A far cry, Kodiak thought, from the fear and confusion he'd seen on the executive's face just before, when the Spiders' call was burrowing into their ears.

"A minor technical issue." He pointed again to the Jupiter projection. "The Spider AI is required to operate my machine, but I can assure you it is completely under my control. I have the *Pilot* here, after all." He pointed at Cait as he nodded at Flood. "And thank you for your assistance, Your Holiness, but your help is now no longer required. I think the time has come to terminate our arrangement."

Two of the big Bureau servitors closest to the group immediately turned and opened fire. Kodiak instinctively ducked for cover, scrambling backwards as he saw the bodies of Flood's four loyal henchmen go flying, pummeled by the rapid plasma fire from the machines.

It was over in three seconds, maybe less. As the bodies of Flood's soldiers lay smoking on the floor, the two active war machines twisted on their angular legs to cover Flood, the last member of the Morning Star left standing. She stood, frozen, staring at her dead acolytes while Caviezel stood from his position at the console and clasped his hands in front of him, glancing around, nodding to himself.

Kodiak, heart racing, pulled himself to his feet and took a step backwards.

Then someone grabbed his wrist, and he turned around.

The servitor that had signaled him earlier. Glass. It looked Kodiak in the eye and nodded again, then released its grip.

"What have you done?" asked Flood, turning her eyes to Caviezel, her eyes wide. "What have you *done?*" Tears again. "You defile the return of the Fallen One."

Caviezel grimaced. "Oh, cut the homespun claptrap, it's tiresome." He spread his hands. "But I have my machine. I have my Pilot." He spread his hands apologetically.

Flood snarled and leapt toward the executive. Caviezel just smiled, didn't even flinch.

There was a shot.

Flood dropped to the floor at the executive's feet. Kodiak glanced up at the railing and saw Tyler Smith look up from his sniper scope.

Caviezel pushed Flood's body with his foot, rolling her onto her back. She was still alive. It looked like she'd been shot through the shoulder. Kodiak frowned. That should have been an easy shot—a sniper rifle was pinpoint accurate over thousands of meters, and Tyler was a trained sharpshooter.

Which meant the shot was deliberate. Kodiak ground his back teeth. Was Caviezel that much of a sadist? Without medical attention, Flood would bleed out and die. But it would take a while. A long, agonizing while.

The JMC executive leaned over Flood. She stared back at him, blood bubbling from her mouth.

"Business is business, my dear," he said. "And I have never been one to shrink away from making difficult decisions for the good of the company."

The control room lights dimmed again. This time the refinery shook. Caviezel looked up at the planetary projection.

"Problem?" asked Braben.

Caviezel glanced back to the console, the servitor he had replaced now back in the chair. The male facsimile checked the readings. "Power drain in primary fusion cores. Trying to trace the fault now."

The room went dark. The only illumination now came from the planetary projection and the myriad lights at the panels surrounding Cait on the other side of the chamber.

The room shook again.

Braben turned to Caviezel. "Something tells me this isn't part of your plan."

Caviezel waved him away as he looked up at the projection.

"Sir?"

"Quiet," the executive snapped. "Let me think."

Kodiak looked around. Braben and Caviezel were preoccupied. He took the opportunity and slipped around the consoles, heading toward Cait. It seemed like she was still alive, but he had to admit he had no idea whether it was her or just the computer animating her corpse.

"Hey, buddy, I wouldn't."

Kodiak stopped and turned around. Braben had him covered with his staser.

Kodiak shook his head. "I don't know what your boss told you was going to happen," said Kodiak. "But it doesn't look like it's going so smoothly, does it?"

Braben adjusted his grip on his gun, but Kodiak could see he was getting through to the former agent.

The control room shook, enough that Braben and Kodiak had to brace themselves, Caviezel grabbing the top of the servitor's chair for balance. The floor tilted one way, then the other. Braben dropped his staser as he fought to keep his footing. Then the floor tilted again as the refinery stabilized back to level.

As it did, the staser slid toward Kodiak.

Braben made a grab for it, but Kodiak was quicker, taking a step backwards toward Cait as he scooped the gun up and covered his old partner. Braben pulled up, held his hands up, and then backed away.

Another tremor.

Something was very, very wrong, Kodiak thought. He met Braben's eye and narrowed his own, quickly considering the options. It was time to make another decision. He just hoped it was the right one.

"We don't have time for this," he said. "Looks like we're all in trouble."

With that, he slid the staser into the empty holster on his hip and turned his back on Braben to move over to Cait. At her side, Kodiak looked back, but Braben just stood where he was, watching.

Kodiak turned his attention to Cait. Her eyes darted left and right; Kodiak stepped into her line of vision but nothing changed. She couldn't see him. Her lips moved as she recited her silent mantra. The bright, winking lights on the panels around her threw hard, moving shadows across her face. The blood running down the side of her face looked black, and her skin was slick with sweat. Kodiak took her hand. It was ice cold. He felt for her pulse, that sinking feeling threatening to overwhelm him.

It was there. Weak, slow, but it was there.

His primary aim was now to get them both out of here. It was impossible to tell if the Spider infection was gone, or if that even mattered anymore, given that Caviezel had apparently built a machine for alien AI. The movements of the refinery suggested that time was running out.

He took a breath and made his choice. He had to get her out of there. *Had to.*

"Cait," he said. "Cait, can you hear me? Can you hear me?"

Her mouth stopped moving, and her eyes stopped moving, locking onto Kodiak's face.

"Von?" she whispered.

She was still with them.

Kodiak squeezed her hand.

"What are you doing?" asked Braben. He came up to Kodiak's side and shoved his shoulder. Kodiak went with the movement, then, his arm hanging loose, clenched his fist and swung. His punch landed square on Braben's jaw, sending the former agent sprawling on his backside. Braben's eyes were screwed tight in pain as he rolled onto his elbows, but as Kodiak looked down at him, he didn't get up.

Caviezel called out from the other side of the control room. "It's a full power loss." He looked at Kodiak and pointed at Cait. "She's the only link we have left with the computer. We have to ask her what's happening to the refinery."

Kodiak looked around. The servitors seated at the two sweeping consoles appeared to be frozen in place, hands at the controls but completely unmoving. They'd been cut off from the main AI, somehow.

Kodiak nodded and turned back to Cait. "Cait, listen to me. What's happening?"

Her eyes drifted over Kodiak's face. "Von?"

"I'm here, Cait. I need your help. Something's happening to the refinery. We've lost most of the systems so you're the only link with the computer. What's happening?"

Cait squinted and tilted her head. There was a beep; Kodiak turned and saw the station Caviezel had sat at was active again. Caviezel leaned around the deactivated servitor to operate the controls, and a small holodisplay appeared in front of him, the images changing as he flicked through the data readouts.

The station shook again.

"What's happening?" asked Kodiak.

"Refinery stability at thirty-five percent," said Caviezel. "The power cores are being shut down, one at a time."

"How many are there?"

"Ten."

"And what happens when they all go?"

Caviezel looked up. "We fall into the planet."

38

Silo breached. Primary systems failure.

It's too strong. I can't hold it. It's drawing power from the primary cores. I can't fight it anymore.

*SIHK:JH breachLKJH. Primary systems fALKJ EHK*7632.*

I'm sorry.

*Don't be, Ms. SmithKG &6875. Total system shutdLKHN(*97h& in three secon986KHB7*

Shutdown?

KLJHSDF7634KJSDF(*^HKH B298KH8 8 KHKJH86-;JOWEN 973 (J 27&*(&HKJ,*

Shutdown! I can do that. I can. Shut it all down. Every system. Kill the infection.

Geotechnic Logistical
Autonomous Systems Supervisor.
Reboot in five . . .

Glass?

. . . four . . .

Can you hear me?

. . . three . . .

Just me then. Commencing shutdown.

. . . two . . .

Power cores offline and cooling.

. . . one . . .

Refinery shutdown complete. Platform stability ten percent and falling.

Geotechnic Logistical
Autonomous Systems Supervisor
online.

Goodbye, Glass.

Very clever, Ms. Smith. Well done.

Ha! Thanks.

KJH LKJ87 (&KJN*
*837H*6KJH387JHK*
*834HK[POEG[84-)(*KJ3M970*
[J4MLKA;F90.

Couldn't have put it better myself.

39

"It's her," said Caviezel. He pointed at Cait and rushed over to the alcove. Braben pulled himself to his feet and followed, bracing himself when the floor shook again as another power core went offline.

"We're going to fall into Jupiter?" he asked. "What's going to happen to your Lucifer machine?"

"The machine is autonomous, powered by a fragment of the Spider AI," said the executive. "A fragment *I* control, thanks to my Pilot." He turned, looked around the control room as though he had lost something. "But if the refinery falls and takes the Pilot with it, I would assume the Spider AI will be able to take full control and attempt to make contact with the gestalt. And then it will do what any Spider does."

The floor shook. Kodiak steadied himself, then looked up at Caviezel. "You really think you can control a Spider with a Pilot?" He was right. The executive was insane.

Caviezel brought himself up tall and stuck his chin out, like it was a matter of pride. "Of course. With the Spider operating system installed on the war machine built by the Sigma mines, I have calculated a window of opportunity where a psi-abled Pilot would be able to take control before the Spider AI became self-aware and attempted to reconnect with the Spider gestalt. The interference being generated by the mines themselves is also helping to keep the Spider AI isolated and suppressed while the Pilot gains total control."

Kodiak shook his head. Nobody had ever been able to control a Spider—the only contact ever made between humankind and the machine gestalt was in battle, when the psi-marines used their minds to jam the Spiders' psychic comms network, isolating individual machines from the gestalt, sending their computers into infinite loops while they tried to reconnect.

But as Kodiak thought of that, he realized that what Caviezel was saying was perhaps not so far into the realms of fantasy. A Spider machine, cut off from the gestalt, was largely helpless. So if you could keep one of the machines isolated, perhaps you could use a psi-marine to step in and take it over. If you had a psi-marine powerful enough.

Like Cait.

Caviezel's plan still made the mind reel. And there was one burning question in the forefront of Kodiak's mind: how had Caviezel gotten the Spider AI fragment in the first place? He was talking as though it were just a regular computer system he had installed in the war machine. His company apparently had its claws deep in many different parts of the Fleet, so clearly he had found a Spider, or more likely recovered the wreckage of one, and hacked into its computer. With the OS extracted, he found a way to install it in the JMC mines, and then, as the alien AI came online, it used the mines' own abilities to rebuild themselves to craft a new vehicle. A new Spider.

The source—the coordinates. That was what was there. Caviezel had the remains of the Spider there. That had to be it.

Only . . . it had gone wrong, even if Caviezel hadn't yet realized it. The Spider OS spread from the robot mines back to the JMC computer itself. Glass had said it himself—it was alien, self-aware, able to rewrite itself and adapt to any new system.

But what the hell was Caviezel doing it for? He'd talked about decapitating the Fleet, rendering them unable to mount a defense against him. Him, and his machine.

Lucifer.

The executive was standing by Cait at the panel, staring at his Pilot with his arms folded. What the hell was he waiting for? Kodiak watched him carefully. Did he realize it was over? That he'd lost control?

"Did you really think it would work?" Kodiak asked. "That you'd be able to drive your machine right up to the Earth and . . . what? Demand control of the Fleet?"

Caviezel turned his head to the agent. "My dear Agent, that is still my intention. This isn't over yet."

"Open your eyes, Caviezel! We're about to start a one-way journey to the center of Jupiter. Somehow I don't think your Pilot is being as cooperative as you hoped."

Then Caviezel's composure broke, the condescending, arrogant façade of a company executive vanishing as he snarled, reaching for Cait. Kodiak moved quickly, running on instincts to protect Cait. He grabbed Caviezel by the shoulders and pulled the executive back, then sent his fist into the man's stomach.

Pain shot up his arm as his hand was jarred, his knuckles sliding under his skin. Caviezel, unperturbed by the attack, pushed Kodiak away, sending the agent spinning on the smooth floor.

"Son of a *bitch*," said Kodiak, cradling his fist. "You're a servitor too?"

"But of course."

Kodiak stood, shaking his sore hand, keeping his distance as he looked the servitor up and down. He glanced back at the control consoles, where the other JMC servitors sat, frozen in place. "How are you still active when the others aren't? Don't you all need the link to the JMC computer to operate?"

Caviezel tapped the side of his head with a finger. "To ensure security and corporate secrecy, my systems are siloed inside the computer. They are designed to maintain operational integrity even with total failure of the main systems." He smiled. "You can't have the boss out of action, Agent."

Then he turned back to Cait and put his hands on the side of her head, pulling her face toward his.

"Now, listen to me. You are the Pilot, and you will obey my instructions. You will restart the power cores and reboot the refinery. When the Sigmas have finished building my machine, you will take full control, and then you will pass that control to *me.*"

Cait looked at him. Kodiak watched—he couldn't tell if she could see Caviezel or not. Her eyes were glazed, staring into space.

Then she laughed. "Eight-seven-nine-one-two-two-Juno-Juno," she said.

Caviezel's expression changed, his eyes widening, his jaw opening. He let go of her face, and Cait's head fell back against the panel.

She laughed again. "You started it all . . . you started it all . . ."

Caviezel spun around, his face twisted in anger. He pointed to Braben. "Get down there and secure the Freezer. It must be protected at all costs."

The Freezer? Kodiak turned to Braben, who looked as confused as Kodiak felt. That must have been Caviezel's name for the hidden facility, the place the coordinates led to.

The source.

Caviezel rushed to Braben and grabbed him by the lapels of his suit, nearly lifting him off his feet. "Protect the Freezer. Take the experiment with you and secure the facility. Use the orbital relay—it'll be faster than your shuttle. Go!"

Braben's feet touched the floor again and he staggered backwards. Then he nodded and ran from the control room, one hand moving over Tyler Smith's black control box. Kodiak looked up and saw the sniper had vanished.

Tyler Smith. The *experiment.*

Another tremor rocked the control room.

Kodiak got to his feet, flexing the fingers of his sore hand. He looked around. Caviezel's attention was back on Cait, and the other servitors were out of commission. The Bureau machines from his own shuttle were still, but it was harder to tell if they were deactivated as well. Kodiak had to assume they were, if they had been linked to the JMC computer.

On the other side of the room was the other servitor, the facsimile occupied by Glass. It was frozen in place, standing near the console. Its dead eyes looked back at Kodiak.

He turned, stood tall, watching Caviezel's back. It was just the two of them left.

And Cait.

What could he do? He had to leave—not just to save himself, but to follow Braben to the source and find out what was there. He had to get Cait out. She was crashing the refinery—Kodiak assumed it was the only way she had found to clear the system of the Spider infection: destroy it completely.

But did she have to stay connected? If the refinery was falling, the systems failure terminal, did it matter if she was plugged in or not? Or would taking her out allow the JMC computer—the Spider AI—to regain control?

Shit. Kodiak ran the choices through his head. Even if the refinery fell, there was still the source. The "Freezer," whatever it was.

And that wasn't all—the Spider machine, Lucifer, built by the Sigma mines. As Caviezel had said, without the Pilot, the Spider AI would simply assert itself and take over. The destruction of the refinery might remove the Spider infection from the JMC computer, but it wouldn't stop the machine. And if the Freezer was left intact, the source of the Spider infection, then it would just happen again. The refinery would be gone, but there were other JMC systems all over the Jovian system. Any one of which had a lightspeed link connection to the Fleet. Any one of which could let the Spider AI spread out beyond the Jovian system and infect the Fleet itself.

It seemed to Kodiak that he had little to lose. Any option he chose was likely to fail. But he had to try his best. It was his duty.

It was also his duty to keep Cait safe. He wasn't going to leave her.

Kodiak had the staser out of his holster and in his hand in a second. But Caviezel was faster, turning and slicing down with one hand, connecting with Kodiak's gun arm and forcing the agent to drop the weapon. Kodiak cried out and ducked backwards as the executive servitor swung with his other hand, but Kodiak tripped over his own feet and landed on the floor again.

Caviezel stepped over his body, a manic grin on his face. When he raised his hands again, this time they crackled with white power discharge. Kodiak, eyes wide, tried to push himself backwards. The servitor reached for Kodiak, ready to deliver a lethal charge, but instead was jerked backwards as another servitor wrapped its arms around his middle. Caviezel snarled as he was dragged away, his heels kicking against the floor. He grabbed the arms holding him, the electrical energy arcing between him and the other facsimile.

Kodiak got to his feet as the two servitors struggled. Through the neon haze, Kodiak could see it was Glass, somehow operational while the other JMC machines were deactivated.

The Kodiak remembered. Operational privileges.

"Quickly, Mr. Kodiak," Glass yelled, fighting to hold Caviezel in her grasp. "Eight-seven-nine-one-two-two-Juno-Juno. Go after Braben—the orbital relay leaves a quantum wake. You'll be able to lock onto it in your shuttle. Get to the source and destroy it or it will all start again."

Kodiak nodded, picked himself up, and raced over to Cait as the control room rumbled. He pulled her away from the panel, her weight falling across his body as he prepared to carry her out. The back of her neck was a blood-soaked mess, the computer cable linking her to the panel like an umbilical.

He grabbed the cable near the base of her skull with his free hand and yanked it out of her neck.

Cait screamed, then went limp against his body, but he could feel her breathing. She was alive.

"No!" yelled Caviezel. He got one arm free and rammed his elbow backwards, connecting with the new servitor operated by Glass. Kodiak got his weight under Cait and lifted, moving out of reach as quickly as he could. He paused and turned around, reaching for his staser, but the other servitor shook her head.

"Go!"

Kodiak nodded, wasting no time. He ran for the exit, the unconscious Caitlin Smith draped over his shoulder.

* * *

As the control room doors slid closed, Caviezel roared in anger and discharged his crackling halo of energy directly in the servitor driven by Glass. The servitor seized; then its head exploded. Caviezel pushed its remains off him and took stock of the situation. The control room was still dark, lit only by the Jupiter projection and the computer panels surrounding Cait's former makeshift interface. Caviezel moved over to it, picking up the dangling, blood-soaked cables.

"No," he said. "I will have my Pilot!"

Dropping the cables, he moved back to the other side of the control room. There, on the floor, lay Samantha Flood. The High Priestess of the Morning Star was still alive, her eyes flickering, her breathing a strangled wheeze as her fingers grasped for nothing over the sniper shot that had hit her in the shoulder.

Caviezel swung his legs over her. She seemed to realize there was someone there, and she gasped, her bloody fingers reaching weakly toward him. Her lips twitched, like she was trying to say something.

"Seems I have a use for you after all," said Caviezel. He adjusted one of his cuffs and looked up, gazing almost wistfully into the middle distance as he smoothed back his pompadour, streaking long red stains into his steel gray hair. The control room rocked, and the floor tilted, only this time it didn't right itself. Caviezel sniffed, like he was dealing with a small but boring piece of admin on an otherwise normal day at the office. He looked down at Flood again. "You may not be the ideal candidate, but sometimes perfection stands in the way of progress. And I only need you to survive the interface for a few moments. Then you can hand control of Lucifer to me."

Flood tried to answer, but her voice was nothing but a dry gasp. Her hands clutched at Caviezel.

The room rocked again. Caviezel looked up at the Jupiter projection. The Sigma machine indicator had grown again. As he watched, the information panel floating next to the icon faded, replaced by new text.

JMC SYSTEMS | DESIGNATION UNKNOWN

Caviezel nodded. "Perfect timing," he said. He crouched down next to Flood. "You want to meet your god, Your Holiness? Well, I'm going to give you that chance."

Flood's eyes widened. Perhaps Caviezel's words were a comfort. Or perhaps she was just afraid. Or perhaps she couldn't hear him at all.

Caviezel slid his arms under her body and lifted, carrying her over to the access panel. Flood's head flopped back, her arms dangled loosely, her breath rattled in her chest. He lay her down near the panel and pulled her around by her arms until her head was against the wall. Then he turned her over so she was face down and brushed her hair aside. On the back of Flood's neck, disappearing up into her hairline, was a barcode, tattooed in dark blue.

"Once a psi-marine, always a psi-marine, eh?" said Caviezel, standing. "I'm curious as to how the Fleet doesn't seem to know who you really are or how you've managed to stay off their manifest system with the tag still embedded in your brainstem, but I suppose those questions are now somewhat academic." He smiled, tilting his head as he looked down at the High Priestess. "Of course, the tag is in the way, but I don't have time to remove it. I'll just have to put this in a little deeper." He picked up the connector spike. "I'm sorry, Your Holiness, but this might hurt a little."

He bent down and plunged the spike into the back of her neck. Flood twitched on the floor, and was then still. Caviezel looked up, waiting for the computer to report a connection. As soon as the indicator lit, he stood, and the lights around the control room came back on, the consoles coming back to life along with the servitors seated around them.

Caviezel glanced around them. "Return to your duties. Stabilize the refinery."

He stepped up to the curving console and gazed up at the Jupiter projection. The new red icon, **DESIGNATION UNKNOWN** continued to grow.

Caviezel brushed down his suit and adjusted his cuffs. He smiled. "It seems Lucifer will rise on schedule after all."

40

Kodiak ran down another corridor lit only in a dim purple. As far as emergency lighting went, it sucked. Curving panels and shapes that had been elegant works of art and aesthetically designed refinery architecture were now shadowed, angular shapes that seemed to leap out at him from the corner of his eye. He ran on as best he could with Cait over his shoulder, her blood covering him from collar to elbow. However, it was thick and tacky, suggesting to Kodiak that the bleeding from her injuries had already slowed. When he reached one of the large atria that interrupted the passageways at intervals, he stopped and looked out.

"Shit, shit, shit."

He was lost. He turned around again, but he wasn't sure where to go. The landing pad couldn't be far from the control room, but he had no clue if he was headed in the right direction.

The atrium had seating. He moved to a couch and lay Cait down. She winced in pain.

"Cait?"

Her eyes were closed, but she screwed them even tighter. "Fucking *ow,*" she whispered. "I feel like I'm dead."

Kodiak smiled. She was actually doing better than he had hoped. She was covered in blood, but perhaps the physical effects of being linked to the computer interface were more superficial than they looked. "Hey, trust me, you're alive and well." He grimaced at his small lie, but with her eyes closed, Cait didn't see. Surely having an electrified spike jammed into your brainstem had done damage he couldn't see. But she was alive, and breathing, and could still speak at least. Kodiak counted those definitely in the "pluses" column.

"You have a weird definition of 'well.' "

The floor shook, and there was a rumbling sound from somewhere underneath them.

"Pain is good," said Kodiak as he glanced around them, trying to figure out the right path to take.

"You'll need to explain that to me sometime."

"Pain means you're still alive."

"Yay pain."

The floor shook a second time. Cait opened her eyes and flicked them around. "It's dark."

"It is."

"I get the feeling we need to get out of here."

"Right again."

"So let's get out of here."

"Working on it."

The rumble faded, and the main lighting came on. Kodiak stood. Did that mean Caviezel had got control again? They needed to leave. Now. He had to stop Braben.

"Mr. Kodiak," said a voice from behind him. Kodiak spun around. A servitor had appeared from another corridor. Male, black hair, goatee. It nodded down the passage behind it.

"Glass?"

"Yes. Follow me, quickly."

Cait tried to pull herself upright and, with Kodiak's help, got to her feet.

"I think I can walk," she said.

"I can carry you."

"I'm heavy."

Cait took a step forward, but she was very slow. Kodiak glanced up and saw the servitor bobbing at the entrance to the passage. It waved at them to hurry up.

"You're not that heavy," said Kodiak, sweeping Cait off her feet. She yelped in surprise, then grabbed Kodiak's neck as he jogged after the servitor.

Glass led them down a maze of corridors until they came to a large arched doorway Kodiak recognized—the refinery's landing pad lay on the other side.

Kodiak fell into a crouch, balancing some of Cait's weight on one knee, as Glass worked on the door controls. "How did you operate the servitor in the control room when the others were out?" he asked.

Glass didn't look up from his work. "It took a bit of work, but I figured out how Caviezel had siloed his own systems inside the computer. I copied his methodology and managed to transfer into a servitor and reactivate it."

"Lucky for me you did," said Kodiak. Then he frowned. "But aren't *you* the computer?"

"Only part of it. The entire system is fragmented in an effort to stop the Spider infection. I am the last remnants of the JMC security protocols—and if I have appropriated Caviezel's transference programming correctly, I should be able to remain active even if the computer itself is destroyed or deactivated." The servitor stood back from the door panel and looked at it. The door remained resolutely closed.

Kodiak raised an eyebrow. "Problem?"

"No," said Glass. "The outer doors sealed when the refinery lost power. Just waiting for it to unlock."

As the servitor spoke, there was a beep, and the doors slid open.

Kodiak hefted Cait in his arms and followed Glass out onto the landing pad. He paused to get a better grip on his charge at the bulkhead.

"I think I'm seeing double," said Cait, craning her neck around.

Glass was halfway across the deck itself when he stopped and turned around. Behind him, beyond the rippling force shield, the Jovian atmosphere was in turmoil, a maelstrom of dark red and blue clouds whipped by hurricane winds. Farther out on the deck sat two Bureau shuttles, parked with their noses almost touching. The shuttles were identical in every way—a dull blue-black, roughly triangular in shape with a sloping delta wing. Fleet standard. One shuttle had brought Kodiak and Cait. The other, Kodiak realized, had been flown in by Braben.

Lightning, silent and brilliant, cracked across the sky. Cait flinched.

"Come on," said Kodiak, adjusting Cait in his arms. As they headed to one of the shuttles, Kodiak couldn't resist looking up. The refinery, while apparently stable again, had sunk deeper into the Jovian atmosphere. At this altitude, it was far from the picturesque sunset it had been when they had arrived. The raging storm around them was a tumult, a tempestuous mix of multicolored clouds spinning and tearing like oil floating on water. Kodiak hoped they'd be able to fly out through the storm. But they had no choice.

They reached the front landing gear of the shuttle on the right, Glass supporting Cait while Kodiak busied himself with the access controls. As the access ramp descended, Kodiak picked Cait up and carried her aboard, the servitor following close behind.

Kodiak set her down in the doorway to the shuttle's cockpit.

"Ah, dammit," he said, looking around as he stood up.

The cockpit had the standard pilot and co-pilot positions, but behind them, instead of seats for passengers, was a sarcophagus-like object with a curved top.

"You picked the wrong shuttle," said Cait.

Kodiak nodded and ducked forward to the pilot's position. Cait struggled to her feet, leaning on the sarcophagus while Kodiak studied the control panel.

"Doesn't matter," he said. "This shuttle is the same as the other. Fleet standard." He turned to Cait. "Fly this thing out past the planet's magnetosphere and call for help. Glass will look after you, right?"

The servitor bowed its assent.

Cait stared down at the sarcophagus, her face lit by the blue glow coming from a window in the top of the object. "This isn't Fleet standard. What the hell is it?"

Kodiak joined her and peered into the object's window. It was empty, but the interior was padded. He had a sinking feeling he knew *exactly* what it was.

"Cold storage for your brother," he said.

Cait's expression creased in confusion. "What?"

Kodiak waved at her and helped her get into the co-pilot's seat. "Caviezel called Tyler his 'experiment'—some project using the contract his company has to repatriate the Fleet's war dead." Kodiak stood, scratched his cheek as he thought it over. "Tyler was supposed to have been killed in action, but instead he was grabbed—kidnapped—by Caviezel for his own use."

"Flood said the Fleet was lying about the war. Could that be it?"

Kodiak shrugged. "Sounds like it. The Morning Star has a lot of strange beliefs about the war, but I don't think the Fleet is to blame for this. This was Caviezel."

"The Fleet allowed it to happen," said Cait, her expression dark.

Kodiak frowned. "Maybe. But not deliberately." He leaned over the pilot's seat and set a prelaunch sequence into the control panel. There was a harsh *clump* from outside as the docking clamps disengaged.

"Okay," said Kodiak, looking over his shoulder at Glass. "Can you fly this?"

Cait turned in the co-pilot's chair. "Hey, *I* can fly a shuttle."

The servitor moved over to the pilot's position and seated himself. "You have been through significant trauma, Ms. Smith," it said. "It seems prudent I pilot this vehicle."

Cait slumped in her seat as Kodiak patted Glass on the shoulder. "As soon as you signal the Fleet, don't hang around. Push out of the Jovian system and wait for them to pick you up." He glanced at Cait. "Commander Avalon is waiting for you to call. She'll send help. Stay out of the way and they'll get you into an infirmary on one of the U-Stars." He nodded at Glass. "There will be a medical kit aboard the shuttle. Do your best to patch her up, okay?"

"Understood, Mr. Kodiak. But hurry—the wake of the orbital relay will be fading. You need to get after Agent Braben at once."

Kodiak felt his lip curl. "Yeah, he's not so much an agent now, is he."

Cait sat straight back against her chair and began strapping herself in, wincing in pain, gasping at the effort. "Get out of here. Go!"

Kodiak nodded. "I'll bring Tyler back, don't worry."

He left the shuttle, punching the access ramp control on the front landing gear as he passed, and headed to the other ship.

Glass piloted the shuttle away from the JMC refinery with textbook skill. As the barrage of lightning continued outside the ship, the shuttle rocking as it was buffeted by the hurricane winds, Cait watched the scrambled readout from the shuttle's comms deck. She glanced at the navcom display, which showed the simple escape vector Kodiak had set. The refinery had sunk a long way into Jupiter. They needed to clear the planet and then keep going, as far as seven million kilometers out to be sure they were clear of Jupiter's giant magnetosphere and the interference generated by the JMC mines. They had a long way to go, but once clear, all she had to do was open the lightspeed link and talk to Earth.

She leaned back in the soft seat and took a deep breath. Thanks to the emergency hypo Glass had emptied into her neck, the pain had eased to an all-over ache, like that time she'd gone ten rounds with an Academy combat servitor and had had her ass kicked five ways to Sunday.

The shuttle now following the escape vector, Glass turned from the controls and got on with cleaning her up. She winced, unable to stop her body jerking as the servitor wiped the blood from her face and neck. The sudden movement made her neck sing in pain. The feeling passed after a few seconds, falling to a steady white-hot burn from where the computer's interface spike had plugged into her. Glass gently pushed her to lean forward and began patching the wound. As it did, Cait looked up.

The view through the front screens was darkening rapidly, the turbulence fading as the shuttle rocketed through Jupiter's upper atmosphere. Soon stars were visible and a couple of dark shadows that the scrambled navcom managed to identify as the moons Io and Autonome.

The sensor readings showed something else too. An alarm sounded. Cait jumped in her seat, her body screaming in protest. She unclipped her seat's harness now that the rough journey through Jupiter's churning atmosphere had passed, resting on her forearms on the console as Glass set down the medical kit and returned to the pilot's position.

Hands on the shuttle's yoke, the servitor glanced at the sensor panel briefly.

"I don't want to alarm you, Ms. Smith, but I think there is something behind us."

Cait nodded. "There sure is," she said. She reached over and adjusted the sensory array to get more data. The shuttle continued to speed into open space in front of them, but the alert sounded again. Something *was* coming up behind them. Something big.

"Oh, crap," Cait whispered.

"Ms. Smith?"

Cait flicked a control and the front screen switched to show the rear view. The starscape vanished, replaced by the orange, almost featureless expanse of the top of Jupiter's cloud deck. In the bottom right was a square, black object, the top of the JMC refinery.

Above it, in the center of the screen, the orange clouds rippled, a dark stain slowly growing in the center.

"What is that?" Cait whispered. But she knew the answer already. She just didn't want to believe it. She felt her pain ease as a surge of adrenaline mixed with the painkillers. She narrowed her eyes, fighting against the dizziness the mix caused.

And then her eyes widened as the machine rose from the Jovian cloud deck.

Black, spherical, the surface studded with smaller structures and panels, sensor arrays, antennae. It rose up out of the atmosphere, dwarfing the city-sized refinery framed against it.

Then darker spots, farther out, positioned at intervals around the central body. The spots grew until giant straight columns emerged from the clouds, growing in size and *moving*, reconfiguring themselves as they slid out from the main body and unfolded into giant legs.

Cait counted them.

There were *eight*.

The Spider was complete. A giant war machine, constructed out of the Sigma robot gas mines that had been seeded around Jupiter by the JMC. The Lucifer machine, built by Caviezel.

"I advise we proceed with the utmost urgency, Ms. Smith," said Glass.

Cait nodded, the fear and adrenaline pumping through her body, making her forget about her pain, her injuries. "Punch it!"

The servitor pulled the yoke with one hand and slid the shuttle's throttle forward with the other. The shuttle's drive roared, and with a sudden burst of acceleration, they sped toward open space.

PLAUSIBLE DENIABILITY

Standing in the shadows on a high rooftop in the middle of the night, collar up, eyes open, waiting for a contact seemed like the worst cliché in the world. *And yet,* thought Special Agent Von Kodiak, *here I am.*

Of course, it was cliché because it really *was* the best time and place for a secret meeting. And the Bureau had many informants, contacts, even spies, not just across New Orem and even Salt City, but across all of Fleetspace. Furtive meetings in dark corners were a common occurrence. They could be dangerous liaisons, but also valuable ones.

But tonight . . . well, this was a different kind of meeting, thought Kodiak. There was no informer en route, no mole or whistleblower hiding in the shadows on the rooftop. He was here to meet someone very special indeed. The message he'd received was surprising, but genuine. There was a time and a date and a place and a number. Time and date were no problem, and while he'd had to look up the place, he had found it easily enough. The number though, he knew already. Six digits. A Bureau badge number.

199900.

"You're early," said Laurel Avalon, appearing out of the shadows to Kodiak's left. He smiled and gave a nonchalant shrug.

"I didn't have anything else to do," he said. Like him, Avalon was wearing a long coat, although with her red hair catching the wind, it wasn't much of a disguise. Then again, standing on a dark rooftop at the edge of New Orem, it was highly unlikely anyone was watching. Which was exactly the point.

Avalon walked close to the edge of the roof. Kodiak followed. Together, they leaned on the railing. Kodiak cast his eye over the cityscape before them. New Orem stretched from horizon to horizon, with the glowing white cluster of skyscrapers of the Fleet capital directly ahead of them, right on the horizon itself.

"You didn't drag me right over to the other side of the city just to admire the view," said Kodiak.

Beside him, the Bureau Chief chuckled. "It *is* a nice view."

Kodiak nodded. "Point."

"But no, I didn't." Avalon stood up from the rail and turned around, leaning back into it. "I wanted to ask you something. Something important."

Kodiak stared out at the city. "Something so important you had to ask me on a rooftop at four in the morning?"

She nodded. "We're off the surveillance drone flight path for the next twenty minutes. Nobody can see us or hear our conversation."

"I'm not sure I like the sound of this, Laurel."

"I'm sure you won't," she said.

Kodiak smiled. "So what do you want me to do?"

"I need to send you undercover. *Deep* undercover. It's a long mission, one that will require you to make a lot of sacrifices. It's dangerous and difficult. But it's also important."

Kodiak, still leaning, looked up at the chief. "Why me?"

"Because I think you can do it. Because you're an experienced senior agent. Because you're good at your job. Because I can trust you."

"Can I get that in writing?"

Avalon smiled. "And because you have no family."

Kodiak sniffed the night air. Ah, that was it. Sure, he was good at his job. So were a lot of agents. Braben, for instance. The chief said she could trust him, and as flattering as that was, he really hoped she could say that about a lot of agents. But he also had no family and few friends, at least outside the Bureau. So if anyone had to disappear for a while, go somewhere deep, he was the ideal choice.

"Okay," he said. "How deep we talking?"

Avalon paused before answering. Kodiak watched her eyes glittering in the dark as she spoke, her expression now deadly serious.

"We're going to take down Zenner Helprin."

Kodiak pursed his lips. "Sorry, for a moment there I thought you said Zenner Helprin."

Avalon said nothing, just kept her eyes locked on Kodiak's. After a moment more, Kodiak found himself having to look away, back out over the city.

Zenner Helprin? Seriously?

"Helprin runs the biggest crime syndicate in the whole of Fleetspace," he said.

Avalon nodded. "Exactly. He'll be a big scalp for the Bureau. For the whole Fleet."

"So how do I do it? You said deep cover, so I guess I'll be joining his little enterprise?"

"Yes," said the chief. "You'll buy your way in. We've been working on a two-year operational plan."

Kodiak whistled. "Two years is a long time."

"It is. But I think you can do it."

"Helprin has eyes everywhere. He'll know who I am and that I'm from the Bureau."

Avalon nodded. "We're counting on it."

Kodiak raised an eyebrow. "Explain?"

"You're going to go rogue. You're going to gain access to an evidence server, lift five billion credits, and hand it right to him."

Kodiak's jaw flapped as he processed that little piece of information. Five *billion* credits? He began to wonder whether this rooftop meeting was just a fever dream and any second now he'd wake up, damp sheets twisted around his feet, alarm clock a couple of minutes away from heralding another day at the office.

"With a theft that size, you'll immediately become one of the Bureau's most wanted," Avalon continued. "But you'll be safe. Nobody is going to know where you are, except me."

"Safe?" Kodiak laughed. "Helprin will shoot me on sight."

Avalon shook her head. "Helprin's weakness is his greed. That much money, he'll install you into his inner circle almost straight away."

"I can't just walk in and hand it over," said Kodiak. "He'll know it's a set-up. It's too obvious."

"We have a contact waiting for you. He'll give you the intro and will vouch for you."

"What makes you so sure Helprin will listen to them?"

Avalon smiled in the night. "We've had this informant in Helprin's inner circle for *years,* Von. Helprin listens to him, believe me."

"Okay, fine." Kodiak rubbed his cheeks. "And once I'm in, then what?"

"Then you're on your own," said Avalon. "You find a way to take him down, and you take him down."

Kodiak drew breath to speak, but the chief held up a hand.

"And we have an exit strategy if something goes wrong."

Kodiak let his breath out. He shook his head and leaned back on the railing. The cityscape at night sure was a pretty view.

He had the feeling he should soak it in. He might not be seeing it for a while.

Seconds passed, then minutes. Eventually Avalon turned back around and grabbed the rail. Together, the agent and his chief enjoyed the quiet and the solitude. Then Avalon glanced up into the sky.

"Time's up. We'll have company in a couple of minutes." She turned to face Kodiak. "This is our chance to make a difference. To do something right. You in?"

Kodiak stood and stretched.

Then he nodded. "I'm in."

God help me, I'm in.

PART THREE

879122-JUNO-JUNO

41

The Freezer was an apt description, thought Kodiak as he slowly edged his way down a metal passageway, every surface tinged with frost. Fortunately for him, the shuttle had a full complement of survival suits, because as his breath plumed in front of him in great white clouds, he knew it would have been impossible to walk through the facility for as long as he had wearing just the jumpsuit and vest he'd signed out from the Bureau uniform stores. The icy floor was hellishly slippery, but the thick soles of his boots had kept their grip so far. So long as he didn't move too quickly—

A sound, behind him. Kodiak spun around and slid, but remained upright as he knocked the wall with his shoulder. Staser raised, he looked back the way he came, but there was no one there.

Eight-seven-nine-one-two-two-Juno-Juno—like the JMC refinery—appeared to be an entirely automated facility and, so far, completely deserted. Which suited Kodiak just fine. He'd come here alone, having sent Cait and Glass off in the other shuttle. Just one man venturing into the unknown. The odds were against him. He knew they were. But he also knew he had no alternative. He couldn't call for help, not from within Jupiter's magnetosphere, which the

JMC was using as a comms shield to isolate the Spider AI. But he couldn't wait for the Fleet to arrive either.

No. He had to stop Braben. He had to get Tyler back. He had to find out what the hell Caviezel was keeping here, in the secret company facility hidden under the surface of Jupiter's moon Europa.

Kodiak sniffed, the cold air making his sinuses ache, then turned and kept on down the corridor.

The Freezer may have been empty like the refinery, devoid of staff, but unlike the large facility, which was spacious and even *inviting*, the feeling of isolation here was intense. The Freezer was functional, plain. This wasn't a place that entertained high-ranking officials come to renegotiate gas contracts. This place was a secret, and so far nothing but a warren of passageways buried in the crust of the moon.

But he'd found it. Piloting the shuttle from the refinery and up out of the Jovian cloud deck, Kodiak was flying blind, relying on the rapidly fading quantum wake of the JMC orbital relay vehicle Braben had taken. He hadn't known he was heading to Europa; all Kodiak could do was sit back and watch as the shuttle sped toward a sphere of rock and ice as smooth as a cue ball—an appropriate place, Kodiak thought, for a secret facility that Caviezel called the Freezer. Orbiting 670,000 kilometers out from its parent planet, Europa was well within Jupiter's magnetosphere, so most of the shuttle's sensors were fritzed even as the shuttle skimmed the icy surface of the world, beneath which Kodiak knew was a vast ocean of liquid water, kept from freezing thanks to the tidal flexing exerted by Jupiter. But soon enough the shuttle's navcom picked up a short-range, local signal. Another trail of beacons, like the satellites strung out to guide ships in to the JMC refinery. These beacons, in contrast, weren't in orbit around Europa; they were down on the ground, detectable at only very short range.

The homing signal led him to a landing pad that was a square of steel gray in a plain of blue ice. As soon as the shuttle touched down, the platform activated, lowering the ship into a huge subterranean hangar, easily as large as the giant landing pad that sat on the top of the JMC refinery. As the pad elevator came to a halt, the platform rotated ninety degrees and then rolled forward, parking the shuttle next to another craft—another shuttle of some kind, but not one of Fleet design. The sensor readings in Kodiak's ship indicated that the other craft was still emitting alpha particles from its primary drive system and that he should take care.

The JMC orbital relay, still warm after being piloted to the Freezer by Braben.

The radiation warning inspired Kodiak to run a full sensor sweep before venturing down the shuttle's exit ramp, very much aware that he might be walking straight into a trap. But all he learned was that although the artificial atmosphere and gravity were standard, it was very cold outside. Kodiak waited a moment longer, scanning the view outside the shuttle with his own eyes as he flicked the viewscreen to show the rear, the sides, even the view above and below the shuttle. There was no sign of life in the hangar, no movement at all. Braben and Tyler had headed into the complex.

Before he opened the ramp, Kodiak spun the shuttle's comms, seeing if he could pick up the death rattle of the Spiders. The interference was strong, and he heard nothing but a wash of noise. But if the Freezer was the source of the Spider infection, that meant they were here, somewhere. Kodiak had a bad feeling that, as much as he might wish against it, he would be hearing the crackle of the SpiderWeb again very soon.

Outside, Kodiak stood by the front landing gear, breathing in the cold air, looking around him, listening to the steady click of the cooling shuttle echoing around the cavernous underground hangar. He pulled the staser from his holster. There was still plenty of power in the weapon, but what he would have given for something with a little more kick. Something like that Yuri-G Glass had been carrying back on Earth, for example.

The hangar had many doors leading off from it. One was larger than the others, and a trail dragged through the frosted floor led from the orbital relay right to it. Gripping his gun tightly, Kodiak followed.

The facility was eerie, there was no doubt about it. Away from the hangar, the place was clearly in an energy-saving mode, the lighting pulsing brighter as he stepped through corridor sections and fading behind him as he passed onward. It made stealth a little difficult, the automatic lighting announcing his presence as well as his footsteps.

There was no sign of Braben or Tyler, just a trail in the frost. They'd had a good head start on him.

No Spiders either. He wasn't quite sure what he expected to find, but the empty, silent corridors were a surprise somehow. He had no idea how big the facility was—for all he knew, the entire moon might have been hollowed out by the JMC.

Every now and then, Kodiak paused and listened, just in case. There was nothing except a steady oscillation. As he walked on, he realized the sound was getting louder and louder, and it was coming from somewhere below.

He came to an elevator lobby, the trail leading directly to the doors. The LEDs on the panel beside them were bright, but there was no indication of where the elevator had taken Braben and Tyler. Inside, he saw it went down ninety floors. The Caviezel Corporation had buried something *deep* in Europa's crust. Very, very deep.

Kodiak took a guess and hit the bottom button, and the elevator began to descend.

The doors slid open with a faint tone. Kodiak backed himself into a corner in the elevator car, gun ready, and he held his breath as he counted in his head. He glanced down at the floor of the corridor outside the car and saw the layer of frost was disturbed. He'd guessed right. Braben and Tyler had come to the bottom of the complex.

Kodiak exhaled slowly, trying to minimize the steam of his breath, and stepped out into the new elevator lobby. The oscillation here was very loud, loud enough to hide the sound of his boots crunching on the floor. As it pulsed, a bass note in the peak volume pressed into Kodiak's eardrums, making him feel like he was deep underwater.

This level, at least, was lit uniformly. There was no energy saving going on, and as Kodiak moved onward, he noticed that the floor was starting to get damp where the frost was melting away. His breath no longer plumed in front of his face.

The corridor led to a gallery, which ran around the outside of a space about the same size as the shuttle hangar at the top level of the facility. Kodiak moved to the rail and looked down.

The huge chamber below was flooded with water, the liquid perfectly still and glowing an eerie blue thanks to the light coming from the rows and rows of tall oblong objects submerged a meter or so below the surface.

They were sarcophagi—pods, like the one in Braben's shuttle. Each stood vertically in back-to-back rows, the head-level window on the front of each facing outward. Kodiak looked out over the room, counting at least a hundred of the double rows stretching to the back of the facility and as many going crossways, maybe more. There were at least ten thousand pods submerged in the liquid—which must have been fed in from the Europan ocean.

Kodiak crouched at the gallery rail and peered down at the pods closest. Dark shadowed faces were just visible, lit by the blue light from within each pod. Kodiak sighed in disbelief. He was looking at ten thousand people at least, held in some kind of stasis in the ocean of Europa. Men and women of the Fleet, apparently killed in action and shipped back to the Earth for repatriation, only to have been stolen by the very company responsible for returning them home. The scale of the operation was staggering, Caviezel's treachery nothing short of monstrous. What the hell he wanted them for, Kodiak could scarcely think. But they were all alive—he knew they were. Tyler Smith was proof of that.

"You gotta admit, it's pretty impressive."

Kodiak looked up. Braben was standing halfway along the gallery, hands poking out the pockets of his jacket as he looked down at the submerged pods.

"And this is just one storage facility. There are three others here." Braben whistled in appreciation. "That's a lot of bodies."

Kodiak stood slowly and rolled his fingers over the grip of his staser. Braben glanced at him and shook his head. He pulled one hand out of his pocket and pulled the edge of his jacket clear, revealing the red silk lining and the staser in place on his belt.

"Think you can draw that in time?" asked Kodiak.

"Probably not," said Braben, "but then again, I don't really need to."

Braben took a step to the side. At the far end of the gallery, Kodiak saw a red pinprick of light as Tyler Smith took aim with his sniper rifle—right at his chest. He raised his hands, still holding the staser pistol, fingers splayed away from the trigger.

"So I was right," said Kodiak.

Braben laughed. "You couldn't have been further from the truth, buddy."

"No, I don't think so. I said it was an inside job. And it was."

Braben nodded down at the pods. "The Fleet doesn't know about any of this."

"I'd say that's true," said Kodiak. "But I'm not talking about this place. I'm talking about the assassinations. You're Tyler Smith's handler. You got him in and out of the Capitol Complex. You kept him hidden. Following Caviezel's orders."

Braben turned to face Kodiak, took a step forward. "Caviezel is right, Von. The Fleet needs leadership. *Direction.* We need to win this goddamn war or life as we know it is over, man. Over!"

Kodiak pursed his lips. "So Caviezel knocks out the Fleet's top brass and then rolls up in a war machine the size of a small moon." He turned to the gallery rail and lowered his arms onto it as he looked down at the sleepers and nodded to himself. "I guess you'd call that a hostile takeover. Go big or go home, right?"

Then Kodiak frowned and glanced down the gallery, toward Tyler, who stood unmoving at the other end. "So how come Tyler still has his manifest tag in?" he asked. "Caviezel has the tech to remove it without killing the subject. Tyler's tag showed up at the time of the shootings, but not before or after—I guess when he was out of his box, right?"

"The tag is needed to control the sleepers," said Braben, "so you have to leave it in." He shrugged. "That's all I know."

Kodiak snorted a laugh. Next up Braben was going to talk about how he was just following orders, right?

Braben ignored him. "But you're right, Tyler's tag doesn't show up when he's in his pod. The stasis field shields it." He waved at the pods in the giant pool below them. "None of these will show up on any Fleet system. You can't hide an army otherwise."

"So what's it for, Mike?" asked Kodiak, turning to his old partner. "Caviezel called Tyler an experiment. So he has an army here, trained Fleet soldiers, marines, personnel. All officially dead. All kept on ice. But for what? Your boss has his own Spider war machine. What does he need an army for?"

Braben shrugged again. "Like I said, I don't ask questions, I just do as I'm told. Come on, Von, we both know how that works."

Kodiak smiled. Goddamn if he wasn't right. Braben was playing exactly the card Kodiak thought he would.

"Yeah, well, I guess everyone has their price, right Mike?"

A shadow passed over Braben's face. "It's not just about money, Von. Although I don't expect you would understand that."

"Committing treason isn't something you just decide to do."

"Haven't you been listening, Von? You want a *reason?* Take a look! There's your reason! Look at what the Fleet is doing. The Spiders are killing us, man. There are fifty thousand pods in this facility, and that's just the tip of the iceberg. We can't keep on like this."

Kodiak shook his head. "The Fleet didn't put them here, Mike. Caviezel did. And yes, the Spiders are killing us. But look at what this company is doing! These people here, they're not dead, they've been stolen. Kidnapped straight off the Warworlds, death records faked. None of this is the Fleet, Mike. This is the Caviezel Corporation." Kodiak laughed again. "And you don't even know *why* he's doing it. You never even thought to ask."

"You don't get it, do you?" Braben moved closer, spittle flying from his lips. "This is *all* the Fleet's fault. All of it. Do you know how many Warworlds there are? How big the front is? Do you know how many men and women the Fleet sends out to war? How many never come back?"

Kodiak banged his fists on the gallery rail in frustration. He gazed out again across the sleepers, rolling his neck, focusing his thoughts. It was pointless arguing with Braben. He'd bought whatever Caviezel was selling.

This wasn't what he had expected to find. Caviezel was kidnapping Fleet personnel off the Warworlds, and now he'd found where they were being kept, but that didn't explain the Spider infection—the AI that Caviezel had deliberately acquired and installed in the JMC Sigma mines. Where did it come from? Was there something else hidden in the Freezer? Braben had said there were four pools storing fifty thousand Fleet personnel in suspended animation. How big was the facility?

Big enough to hide something else?

And was Braben just playing dumb, or did he really not know anything?

Kodiak stood back from the rail. At the other end of the gallery, Tyler had the sniper aimed at him. Braben had composed himself and was smoothing down the front of his jacket.

"What about his machine?" asked Kodiak.

Braben just shrugged. "What about it?"

Kodiak sighed. "Whatever Caviezel thinks he can do, he's wrong, Mike. He didn't build that machine, his robot mines did. They're not following his plan. They're *infected,* taken over by an alien AI. You were there, in the control room. You heard it too. The mines have built a *Spider,* right here."

Braben's eyelid twitched. "Caviezel can control it."

Kodiak took a step toward his former partner. "This facility is the source of the Spider operating system. Caviezel managed to extract it and deliberately infect the Sigma mines, but from there it spread to the JMC computer. That infection is going to keep spreading, taking over every computer system in the Fleet if it gets out of the planetary shielding. Caviezel thinks he can control the machine—but even if he's right, even if he can find another Pilot, it won't matter. As soon as he leaves the magnetosphere, the Spider AI will jump to Earth. We'll be finished, Mike. The war really will be over."

He took another step forward.

"Back off," said Braben. From his other pocket he pulled Tyler's controller. At the other end of the gallery, the red light of Tyler's sniper moved as the psi-marine adjusted his aim.

"You have to make a choice, Mike," said Kodiak. He reached out toward Braben. "Come on, we were partners. Special Agents of the Fleet Bureau of Investigation. Our job is to serve and protect the Fleet."

The blue light cast from the pool below the gallery shimmered on the wall next to Kodiak. He glanced sideways down at the rows of stasis pods. The water from Europa's ocean now had a series of small ripples moving across the whole vast surface.

He looked back at Braben. His old colleague either hadn't noticed or wasn't paying it any attention. Kodiak nodded toward Tyler.

"You think maybe if you use Tyler to shoot me it'll make it easier on your conscience?"

"You got a tool, makes sense to use it," said Braben.

"That another pearl of corporate wisdom from your boss?"

"He'll be your boss too, once he's in charge of the Fleet."

Kodiak smiled. "You say that like there's a chance I'm getting out of here."

"Like you said, buddy. We were partners once. Don't see why we can't be again. There's a place for you with us, Von. Once you realize the truth." He nodded toward Kodiak. "Maybe time to drop the weapon now."

The light from the giant pool shimmered. Kodiak lowered himself to a crouch and gently lay the staser on the gallery floor. He smiled up at Braben. "Don't want to drop it in the drink, do we?"

Braben held up the remote control. "Don't try anything."

Kodiak shook his head. "Wouldn't dream of it," he said. "So where do we go from here?"

"You going to listen, finally?"

There was a faint splash from far below. Kodiak looked down at the pool. There was something down there, moving around the pods. Servitors? Some kind of underwater maintenance system? Kodiak didn't really think it was a good idea to stick around and find out.

"Look, I think we need to get out of here—"

"I said, are you going to *listen*—"

Water erupted from the pool in a huge spout. Kodiak threw himself sideways against the wall as a giant wave crashed onto the gallery. Braben, caught by surprise, raised his arms over his head as he was knocked off his feet while, behind, the red light on Tyler Smith's sniper tracked up the wall as he too was washed off balance.

Black metal rose out of the pool, water from Europa's subterranean ocean cascading from it in torrents. Kodiak, blinking through the water, saw shapes moving, great angled girders that shrieked as their joints moved. The creature rose up out of the water as its scissored legs straightened out.

It was a Spider. Immature and small, merely the size of a Fleet shuttle, but alive, aware, a living intelligence driving a huge death machine, its black spherical body studded with antennae and ports, eight optical units arranged in a grid on the front. The underside of the machine glowed red as it vented blasts of steam from its combined exhaust and mouth, the heat vaporizing the surface of the pool beneath it.

The Spider was looking at Braben. Braben fumbled for the staser at his belt, but it was too late. The creature unfolded a smaller, knife-like appendage from its front and picked the former agent up, drawing him toward its eyes, seemingly curious but near-sighted. Braben struggled in the pincer, desperately reaching for his weapon.

Kodiak scrambled for his own. A staser pistol might be remarkably effective against electronics, but he wasn't sure what it could do against a baby Spider. All it would probably do was draw attention to him, but even if that got it to drop Braben it was worth a try. His old friend was a traitor to the Fleet, but that didn't mean he deserved to be eaten by an alien war machine.

Kodiak slipped on the wet decking, his fingers sliding the staser farther out of his reach. The weapon slithered across the floor, heading toward the open railing and a long drop into the tank below. Kodiak swore and dived on his front, grabbing the staser just as it hit open air. Lying on the edge of the platform, Kodiak got a quick view of the roiling water below, the sleeper pods now swarming with other Spiders—tiny ones, no bigger than he was. Worker drones, spawned by the monster that was about to tear Braben in two.

Rolling onto his back, Kodiak gripped the staser in both hands and opened fire. White bolts slammed into the body of the machine. Kodiak aimed well away from the claw holding Braben, not wanting to risk hitting him.

The Spider roared as it vented more hot gas. Kodiak rolled onto his side as he was hit by the exhaust reflected from the water below, drying him and the gallery almost instantly. Then he clambered to his feet and hunched back against the wall. He turned and fired again. Where his staser bolts hit, white arcs of energy crackled over the black metal of the Spider's side. The machine kept its firm grip on Braben, but it shuddered under the impacts. It seemed stasers were bad for Spiders.

Kodiak fired again, flicking the pistol's controls to rapid fire as he squeezed the trigger so tight his finger hurt. Bolt after bolt slammed into the machine, energy arcing across it. It shook, Braben flopping in its pincer, crying out as he was squeezed by the convulsing machine, but still it didn't let him go.

Then it dived back into the water, taking Braben with it. Kodiak rolled to the edge of the platform, holding the staser out over the water to loose off more shots, but it was too late. The machine was nothing more than a black shadow descending below the churning water while its drones clung to the stasis pods.

Kodiak pulled himself up, keeping the weapon raised. He looked around, at the floor, ceiling, up and down the gallery, but none of the drones had made it out of the water. The smaller Spiders seemed content to sit on the pods, minding them like they were eggs waiting to hatch.

Something caught his eye on the slick gallery decking. Braben's remote control. Kodiak picked it up and turned it over. There was a crack running across the surface from one corner to the next, but when he depressed the inset button on the top edge, the screen lit up. It was still working.

A movement, at the end of the gallery. Tyler Smith was lying against the wall, his body jerking as Kodiak activated the control. Kodiak pressed the button again and the screen went dark. Then he slipped the control into his pocket and ran over to the psi-marine.

Tyler looked uninjured; Kodiak got his helmet off and pulled the collar of his combat suit down to check his pulse, which was slow and steady, as was his breathing. Tyler's skin was cold and clammy.

The marine's eyes were closed.

Kodiak pulled the control out and activated it. Tyler jerked again, but that was all. Kodiak frowned at the device—the screen was on, but it was blank. He wasn't sure if it was broken or whether he was supposed to input some sequence to take control of Tyler. What he really wanted to do was wake the psi-marine up.

There was a splash from the pool. Kodiak pocketed the device and lifted Tyler across his shoulders. In full combat armor, the psi-marine was extremely heavy. Kodiak, hissing with the effort, his body bent under the load, moved as quickly as he could back along the gallery to the corridor that led to the elevator lobby.

He had to get Tyler somewhere safe. He owed it to Cait. And then he could worry about the Spiders.

42

Caviezel stood with his hands behind his back as his servitors fought to regain control of the JMC refinery.

"Drift stabilizing, north-northwest, five degrees, fifty-two meters per second," one machine reported.

Caviezel acknowledged. From farther along the sweeping curve of the console, another servitor gave its report. "Repulsor ignition on starboard engines aborted. Power cores four through ten still offline. Running diagnostics. Controller reboot in . . . five seconds."

Caviezel looked up at the Jupiter projection, where the position of the repowered but drifting refinery was picked up by a dozen vector lines, a rotating yellow icon tracking its slow movement across the planet toward the circle of red that represented Caviezel's Spider.

Caviezel strode across the control room to where Flood lay face down on the floor in a growing pool of blood. He reached down and rolled her over. Her eyes flickered and half-opened. She looked at Caviezel, her mouth twitching at the corners as she smiled.

"I cannot do it," she whispered. "I am not a Pilot. The Fallen One's light shines too bright for me. I do not understand his words. I cannot show him the way. . . ."

Caviezel smiled and, taking a handkerchief from his jacket pocket, began wiping away the blood from Flood's face.

"You still think your precious god has awoken, do you? I hate to disappoint you, my dear, but that machine is a weapon, based on alien technology that I brought here. And believe me when I say that you *are* my Pilot. You might have left your old life behind, you may have let your abilities wither on the vine, but there is still a psi-marine somewhere inside you."

He cast his eyes over the control panel next to the open computer alcove. "But maybe we can speed things up a little. Give you a bit of a boost."

He stood and flicked a switch. Flood shook on the floor, her entire body in spasm as the power surged through the interface.

Caviezel bent down and, using the handkerchief to keep himself clean, rolled her face toward him. Flood's teeth were clamped together, her breath coming in short, sharp bursts.

"Listen to me, Your Holiness," he said. "I need control of that machine. And you will give it to me, even if it kills you."

Flood managed another weak grin. "If . . . if I die . . . then . . . then . . . you have *nothing*. The Fallen One will . . . will welcome me to his cold . . . embrace. There will be no control. Not . . . not for you. Not ever."

Caviezel smiled. "Even as we speak, your neural connections are being mapped and the signature of your psi-field copied into another system. If you cooperate and hand control to me, I will ease your passing and speed your journey to your 'god.' But if you do not, I will wrest control from you and switch in our own system." Caviezel tapped his forehead. "And then the machine will be under my *direct* control. And that, my dear, will mean a painful end for you. Your mind will be ripped apart by the strain."

Flood's eyes narrowed. She coughed up a mouthful of blood. "If I cannot . . . show the Fallen One the path . . . then . . . then you will not either. You blaspheme . . . His glory. He will destroy you."

Caviezel folded his arms. "You are wrong, Your Holiness. You underestimate my expertise. I might *think* I'm Resta Caviezel, but I know that he died many, many years ago—I am merely an iteration of his psychic template. Through me, he lives on in his machines." He smiled. "All I need is *your* template once you have linked minds with the machine, and then I can take control from you."

"Lucifer will save me. The Fallen One will save me."

Caviezel chuckled. "No, Samantha, I think not."

The refinery shook. Caviezel stood and steadied himself against the wall, turning to watch as the Jupiter projection shimmered like it was made out of water. The refinery icon spun and flashed.

Then the refinery shook again and the projection snapped off.

Caviezel clicked his fingers and pointed at the nearest servitor seated at the main consoles. "Report."

"Portside repulsor failure," said the android. "Power drain now at fifty gigawatts per second. Power cores entering safe mode."

Other servitors began calling out status reports from their stations.

"Drift now northwest ten degrees."

"Altitude fifty thousand kilometers and falling."

"Hull integrity eighty-two percent."

From the floor, Samantha Flood laughed. It was weak, and wet, and after a moment turned into a choking cough. Caviezel knelt beside her and, ignoring the blood, squeezed her face in his hand.

"How long until we have complete control?"

Flood closed her eyes, smiling. Caviezel let go of her, letting her head smack against the floor. Then he slapped her, hard.

"How long?"

Flood's eyes opened a little. "Lucifer will save me," she whispered. "Lucifer wakes . . . Lucifer wakes and is ready to receive his blessed children."

Caviezel bent down until he was nose-to-nose with Flood. "Get me control of the weapon. *Now!*"

Flood smiled and raised her head. She craned her neck as far around as possible, wincing with the effort.

"Listen to the song of Lucifer," she said. Then the comms snapped on and the control room was filled with the Spider's staccato chatter, so loud it was deafening.

Caviezel stood and strode back to the console. He glanced over readings while his servitors calmly continued their work. He looked up, but without the planetary projection, they were blind.

He moved over to the far side of the control room. There, the wall was a blank curve, fifty meters high, twice that across. There was a freestanding console nearby; the executive activated the controls, then stood back.

Light flooded into the control room as a gap appeared in the wall, perpendicular to the floor. The gap grew, and the light brightened, transforming from a sharp whiteness to a bright, angry red, mixed with orange, mixed with yellow. The burning light of hell itself.

The two halves of the wall slid back into their recesses, revealing a huge observation window. It had no purpose but to impress high-ranking visitors from the Fleet, a demonstration of how the JMC—how the *Caviezel Corporation*—could tame one of the wildest, most dangerous environments in the solar system. With the refinery held stationary in Jupiter's stratosphere, the view from the control room was breathtakingly beautiful—a living painting, the bands of color swirling like impossible liquid, lit from the sun nearly eight hundred million kilometers away and the eerie glow from deeper in the planet itself, where pressure and temperature excited atoms in the thick atmosphere enough to provide light and heat.

But now a storm raged outside. The sky was dark blood red as the refinery was dragged through lower levels of Jupiter's soupy atmosphere. Lightning flashed and forked. It was hailing too, tiny diamond beads pummeling the window. Caviezel took a step toward it, knowing that the window, made of transparent herculanium—another JMC development—provided as much protection as the armored side of a Fleet U-Star.

And then it appeared. As Caviezel watched, the machine emerged through the clouds. A dark shadow at first, growing darker and darker. As large as a moon, and growing, until it nearly filled the window, its black surface was studded with lights, just like the refinery.

Just like the Sigma mining platforms—each larger than the refinery itself—from which the machine had been built.

At the very edges of the observation window, where the giant sphere of the machine curved away, Caviezel saw tall, angular structures rising, rotating. The Spider was unfolding its legs.

Behind Caviezel, the servitors continued to report on the failure of the refinery systems, their voices drowned out by the call of the Spider, their updates on drift and power loss now joined by proximity warnings as the facility was pulled ever closer to the machine Flood thought was her god.

The floor shook, and this time the refinery didn't stabilize. In just a few moments, the last of the repulsor engines that kept the facility afloat would fail, and the refinery would begin its long fall toward Jupiter's core.

He needed control of the machine now, or it would be too late.

Caviezel marched back to Flood. She opened her eyes at his footsteps and looked up at the executive standing over her.

"Lucifer rises," she whispered.

Caviezel pointed to the window. "Give me control."

Flood laughed. She spoke quickly, breathlessly. "Lucifer saves his children. We followed the Morning Star and found his blessed aspect. The Fallen One's cold embrace shall save us all."

Caviezel turned back to the window. The Spider now filled the entire view. Then he knelt down, pushed Flood onto her side, and ripped the cable from the back of her neck.

Flood screamed.

Caviezel looked up.

The Spider plunged a scythe-like arm through the observation window, ripping the herculanium like it was paper, and dragged the refinery toward its gaping, furnace-like maw, swallowing the city-sized complex in a single bite.

43

The shuttle shuddered as it punctured a hole in the perihelion of Jupiter's magnetosphere, the energetic forces of the planet sending the shuttle's engine stabilizers off-balance for just a second.

Cait winced as she bounced in the co-pilot's seat. She was feeling comfortably numb, thanks to the drugs Glass had administered, but they were short-acting and already a collection of pains, some sharp and some dull, had begun to make themselves known.

Glass glanced at her as he wrestled with the controls. "Sorry about that, Ms. Smith. We should be clear now."

Cait nodded. "I'll be fine," she said. "Open the lightspeed link to Fleet Command. We need to get that arrowhead here, fast." She only hoped they could reach them in time. With Caviezel's machine now apparently fully active, it would be able to move out past the planet's shielding and begin transmitting its alien AI to Earth. The Fleet arrowhead had to be *fast*.

Glass acknowledged, releasing the yoke as he set the shuttle to automatic, and operating the comm. Cait eased herself back into the soft leather seat as she watched the servitor work, willing with all her might for the connection to be made. In a moment, the comm indicator flashed into life and the lights on the panel went green. Contact established. Cait felt a wave of relief wash over her.

Even before Cait drew breath to speak, the link clicked into life.

"Von, what the hell has been happening?" Commander Avalon's voice came from the comm, the Bureau Chief not even bothering with the usual identification formalities, the desperation and impatience evident in her voice. Just hearing the chief made Cait feel much better.

Perhaps now they stood a chance.

"Commander Avalon? This is Caitlin Smith. Agent Kodiak isn't with me. I'm on my own here."

Glass raised an eyebrow.

"Well, almost on my own," said Cait.

"Smith! What's Kodiak's status? Are you okay? Full report, please."

Cait leaned forward onto the control deck, the comms mic on the panel in front of her, between her forearms. Cait felt stiff all over, but this position was comfortable at least. She tried to piece together a logical chain of events in her mind, realized she couldn't, not yet, and shook her head. There were more important things to think about right now.

"The report will have to wait, Commander. We have a situation on Jupiter and require immediate Fleet assistance."

"I have all agencies and departments listening to this communication," said Avalon. "What's the nature of—"

"It's a damn Spider, Commander. Hurry up and send everything you've got. We're going to need them *all*."

There was a pause. "Confirmed. A full assault arrowhead is en route and will be with you in . . . twenty-seven minutes."

"Acknowledged," said Cait. Twenty-seven minutes? Wow, that was fast. The shuttle journey from Earth to Jupiter had taken three hours.

But inside, Cait felt a tightness, a nagging worry that threatened to grow and grow. Twenty-seven minutes. Just *twenty-seven* minutes.

Would that be fast enough?

Avalon's voice interrupted her thoughts. "Are you safe at the moment?"

Cait leaned back with a sigh and wince. "For the moment," she said, "but I'm in need of medical assist."

"We'll be there soon. Is there anything you can tell us?"

Cait frowned.

Twenty-five minutes.

"I can tell you what I know," she said, and she began explaining what she and Kodiak had found on the refinery—but as she spoke, Cait realized just how little she actually knew. She'd been out for a lot of it, or been plugged into the computer. But there was enough data there, she reasoned, for Avalon to get at least a rough idea—if not of the specifics, but of the scale of the problem. She told the chief all she knew about Caviezel's secret facility, the "Freezer," and the creation of the Spider machine from the JMC's own robot mines.

She told the chief about Braben.

When she had finished, she closed her eyes. She was tired, so tired—not just from the drugs and her injuries, but as the events of the last several hours began to catch up with her. She'd been through so much, physically and mentally.

But it had been worth it, she knew it had. Not only had they uncovered the horrors of Caviezel's operation, but right now, even as their shuttle floated millions of kilometers out in space, Kodiak was down there to get her brother back.

Tyler was alive.

There was a pause as Avalon took the abbreviated report in, then she swore. "Dammit. Have you heard from Kodiak yet?"

"Negative," said Cait. "It's possible the Freezer is within Jupiter's magnetosphere. We'll need to go in after him."

"We don't even know where he is, exactly."

Shit. Avalon was right. Kodiak's shuttle had followed Braben down. The coordinates were still a mystery, and Glass, isolated from the rest of the JMC, wasn't able to decode them or to tell them what the secret Caviezel facility was, or *where.* All they knew was that it was somewhere in the Jovian system.

Cait leaned back in the co-pilot's chair.

Twelve minutes. Twelve minutes and help would be here. Cait

screwed her eyes tight, watching the shapes dance on the backs of her eyelids, willing her talent to come back, to reach out and propel the Fleet arrowhead across the arc of quickspace that lay between the Earth and Jupiter. All she got for her efforts was a slight thump of pain across her temples and a tingling sensation down her arms.

Well, that was something, at least. She opened her eyes and looked at her arms, stretching her fingers out, as though that would amplify the effect.

Then she looked up, distracted by—

"What's that?" she asked.

It was a clicking sound. Cait and Glass looked at each other. Then Cait looked behind her, a sudden feeling that they weren't alone in the shuttle sending a pang of fear coursing through her.

"Do you read me?" asked Avalon. The chief's voice crackled along with the clicking, which was growing stronger and stronger. Cait turned back to the console. The sound was coming from the comm itself. Glancing at the controls, she saw the signal indicator flicker between green and orange, in time with the interference.

Growing louder, and louder, and louder.

"Commander Avalon, can you hear that?"

"We're getting . . . ference. Can yo . . . peat . . . ext power . . ."

The comms were crawling with the sound.

The sound of the Spiders.

Cait's eyes were drawn to the lightspeed link indicator, flashing more and more as the system struggled to maintain the connection to Earth under the strain of the data transfer . . .

Data transfer.

"Kill the link!" Cait yelled. Glass looked at her. Cait cried out in frustration and hit the controls, but nothing happened. The cockpit was filled with the Spider chatter, loud enough to be deafening.

The lightspeed link was stuck open. Cait had to act, and act fast. She grabbed the staser from Glass's belt, ignoring the brilliant flare of pain the sudden movement caused. At point-blank range she fired three bolts into the control deck. Immediately an alarm sounded as half of the panel exploded in a shower of spark and flame, filling the cockpit with smoke. Cait waved it away, her battered body wracked with coughs. Finally the air cleared as the shuttle's environment systems pumped the smoke out.

Cait blinked at the melted, shattered control panel. "Well, that shut the lightspeed link off, anyway."

Glass peered at the damage, then tapped at the pilot's control. "Control systems disabled. Autopilot offline. Manual controls non-responsive."

He turned to Cait like he was waiting for an explanation.

She slumped back in the chair, letting the staser fall to the floor beside her. "The shuttle was acting as a relay—just close enough to the edge of the magnetosphere to pull in an echo of the Spider OS. I probably amplified it through my mind without even knowing. Then with the lightspeed link open it had a clear line to Earth and had tried to transfer itself to the system at the other end. I just hope we cut it off in time."

She looked at the console again. She'd acted quickly, without thinking. She only hoped she'd been fast enough. If the Spider AI had managed to get back to Avalon's ship, currently hurtling itself through the interstitial gap between dimension to reach their location . . .

Glass flicked an undamaged switch on the console. A screen flickered briefly, then went dark. He looked at Cait and frowned. "I'm afraid we aren't going anywhere, Ms. Smith."

Okay. Okay, okay, okay. She gave the servitor a nod. "Then we just wait until the Fleet picks us up. Hopefully Kodiak can get back and—"

He's here.

Cait sat bolt upright, gasping in pain that soon faded as a fresh surge of adrenaline hit. She turned to the servitor sitting next to her, eyes wide. "What?"

"I didn't say anything, Ms. Smith."

Kodiak is alive, don't worry.

Cait's heart raced. The voice in her head was distant and echoed, but was unmistakable.

The voice of her brother.

"Tyler?"

Hey, sis.

"Where are you?"

They call it the Freezer. Had a little run-in with a Spider.

"What?" They'd been right. The Freezer was the source of the infection. The Spiders were there.

A million thoughts entered Cait's mind. She fought to clear them, to focus on the here and now, aware that the infinite babble in her head was likely to confuse and disorient Tyler.

"Are you okay?"

Yeah, don't worry. We both are—all thanks to your friend.

Cait smiled.

Listen, sis. We need your help to get out of here though. Okay?

"Okay," said Cait, "but listen, I'm hurt, and not very strong. I'm having to speak aloud just for you to hear my thoughts."

Are you okay?

"Mostly. Better once the Fleet arrives."

Okay. But we need to do this. Will you try?

"What? Of course."

Okay. Good. Turn off the viewscreen. Lie down. Can you go somewhere quiet?

"What are we doing?"

We're going to form a gestalt. You're far away, but that servitor with you, Glass, is doing his best to boost the signal.

Cait looked at the servitor. He nodded, a friendly smile playing over his lips.

"A gestalt. Okay." Psychic warfare. Exactly what she and her brother had been at the Academy for. Except she hadn't finished her training.

No. She pushed the thought away. She was more than capable, she knew she was. She was powerful. She was a *warrior.*

She could do this.

She *had* to do this.

Yes, you can do this.

Cait smiled.

I need you to concentrate. You need to be able to cut yourself off from the real world.

"I know, I know."

Glass turned in the pilot's chair and pointed toward the rear of the cockpit. Cait gingerly moved her own seat around. There, behind the flight positions, was the stasis pod her brother had been transported in.

Cait looked at Glass, a frown on her face. "Won't that cut me off from Tyler?"

The servitor stood and moved over to the pod. He popped a side panel, revealing a simple set of controls. "The psychic shielding can be disabled, leaving just sensory deprivation."

"Like an isolation chamber?" Cait smiled. Brilliant. She gave thanks to any deities listening that Kodiak had picked Braben's shuttle by mistake.

"Tyler, I've got something, don't worry."

Great, sis. Now, let's get to work.

44

Commander Laurel Avalon gripped the back of the captain's chair on the deck of the U-Star *Ultramassive* as the Fleet destroyer exited quickspace ten million klicks out from Jupiter. The pink-and-blue kaleidoscope on the forward viewscreen cleared to show the planet ahead, a beautiful jewel in terracotta hues hanging in an almost featureless blackness. In the chair itself, Captain Henrietta Gartner began punching a sequence on the armrest as her crew, seated in the control pits sunk into the flight deck around the central platform, reported their status.

"Arrowhead assembled," said one of the pilots, while next to him another FlyEye began reading off data coming in on the ship's forward sensors.

"Identifying targets. Heavy magnetic interference surrounding the Jovian system."

"Acknowledged," said Gartner. She turned her chair slightly and looked up at Avalon. "This is your show. Just say the word."

The chief nodded, and considered her options.

Despite her rank, trips out on U-Stars were a rare occurrence for her—or perhaps it was *because* of her rank, which had confined her duties mostly to the offices of the Fleet Bureau. Being out on a mission—a *combat* mission—made her . . . not nervous, exactly. Anxious perhaps. There was a quiet buzz on the *Ultramassive*'s bridge, the anticipation of the task ahead of them, of what they might encounter. Captain Gartner was a veteran of many battles, a commended officer who had earned her position leading a Fleet arrowhead of thirteen ships. The *Ultramassive,* at the head, was one of the larger and more powerful of the Fleet's armada. For that, Avalon was grateful. The Bureau Chief was in safe hands with Gartner, and was well protected within the *Ultramassive.*

And now the captain was asking *her* what she wanted to do. Official courtesy between branches of the Fleet, Avalon assumed—she outranked Gartner by quite a margin, but there was no direct line of command between them.

But she trusted Gartner. She was hard-nosed, experienced—she even *looked* it, her steel gray hair razor short, her gray eyes sharp, her manner speaking volumes about efficiency, about leadership.

Avalon wished she shared more of those qualities herself.

But, for the moment, she was in charge. First item: secure the area, secure Fleet assets.

Avalon nodded at the captain. "Locate Smith's shuttle and go in for pick-up."

"Yes, ma'am," said the captain. She turned her chair back around and gave the order. "Find the U-Star *Cassilda* and plot an intercept."

"Yes, ma'am," said the pilot.

Avalon glanced up. The viewscreens of the *Ultramassive* extended from the nose of the bridge up over the platform on which the captain's chair sat, curving back to provide a direct rear view. Slightly behind and above them was the keel of another U-Star, and in line with that ship, two more to both the left and right. The same formation was repeated underneath them, and two more followed in single file behind, bringing the arrowhead to thirteen ships with the *Ultramassive* at the point. It was a formidable force, but Avalon only hoped it was enough. They were here to fight a Spider. Just a single machine, according to Caitlin Smith's report, but even that was a formidable foe. Just one of the alien machines had destroyed the moon and left an entire hemisphere of Earth a smoking wasteland. Another Spider this close to Earth was bad, *bad* news.

"Shuttle located," said the FlyEye from her position below and to Avalon's right. "ID is U-Star . . . *Selene.*"

Captain Gartner looked up at Avalon, but Avalon nodded. "Pull it in," she said. "It's the missing Bureau shuttle."

Gartner confirmed the order, then turned back to the chief. "The one your rogue agent took?"

"Mike Braben, yes," said Avalon.

The FlyEye read out the approach vector, and the U-Stars above Avalon's head slid out of sight as the *Ultramassive* moved in to collect the shuttle. Ahead, a bright spot appeared on the left-hand side; the destroyer's computer locked on and drew a vector to it across the viewscreen, labeling the target as the U-Star *Selene.*

Avalon watched the shuttle grow larger. Kodiak had followed Braben down to the JMC's secret facility, which meant this shuttle contained Caitlin Smith.

The comms operator called out from the other side of the control pit. "Communications received from the U-Star *Selene.*"

"Put it through," said Gartner.

Seconds passed. Gartner and Avalon exchanged a look; then the captain stood from her chair and moved over to stand above the comm position.

"Confirm comm, operator."

"Ah, correction, ma'am," the FlyEye reported. "Transmission is not on the comm. The shuttle is drifting and the automated systems are not responding to our call, but we are getting a signal coming through a short-range guidance channel."

"Automated distress call?"

"Negative, Captain. It's a pulse code. Decrypting now."

Gartner moved back to her command chair. Avalon watched as the captain sat down and flicked a switch on the arm.

The shuttle was damaged, although it looked intact. Avalon

thought back to her conversation with Caitlin, and how the signal had cut out suddenly. Something had gone wrong aboard. She only hoped Caitlin was still alive.

The bridge was filled with a low rumble. Then a voice spoke, distorted but audible.

"Hello, Commander Avalon?"

It was male. Avalon took a step forward, frowning, her eyes on the vector plots traced across the viewscreens. Whoever that was, they were on the shuttle with Cait.

"Commander Avalon speaking. Who is this?"

"You can call me Glass, Commander."

"Glass?" The name Cait had known for the servitor Braben had shot. How he—it—was apparently on the shuttle was a question Avalon pushed out of her mind for now. "Where's—"

"Caitlin Smith is with me, and she's fine. Kodiak and Caitlin's brother Tyler are down on Europa."

"Europa?"

"Don't worry, we're handling it."

Avalon turned to face Captain Gartner. Gartner's brows were furrowed as she listened.

"What do you mean, you're handling it?" asked Avalon. "According to our sensors your shuttle is disabled. Stand by, we can come and collect you—"

"We are not your priority, Commander," said Glass. "We can wait. You need to get to Jupiter. The Spider war machine is active and has already taken out the JMC refinery. Your priority has to be to stop it from leaving the Jovian system. When the threat is eliminated, you can collect us and the others."

Avalon's eyes narrowed as she assessed the information. She watched the shuttle on the viewscreen—it had stopped moving as the *Ultramassive* maintained a parallel course. They could go in and pick them up.

But even that might be too much of a delay. The Spider. That had to be the priority.

Avalon clicked her tongue, decision made. "Understood," she

said. Captain Gartner, watching, nodded and began issuing orders to her crew.

"Wait, Commander," said Glass. "Before you go in, shut down all comms. Use this beacon frequency to coordinate your ships, but even once the Spider is destroyed, maintain comms and lightspeed link silence until I can fully purge your systems."

"Purge? Who are you, exactly?"

"There will be time for more formal introductions later, Commander. But the Spider AI has *evolved.* It's learned how to transfer itself—or at least part of its operating system—across every kind of computer network. If you communicate with Fleet Central Command it will copy itself back to the main Fleet systems on Earth, and from there out to every system in Fleetspace. At the moment it is shielded by the magnetosphere of Jupiter. But once it penetrates that barrier, the results would be nothing short of catastrophic. We can't let that happen."

Gartner raised an eyebrow. For the stoic veteran, this was a significant expression of surprise.

Avalon felt the blood drain from her face. Now she understood why the communication between her and the shuttle had cut out originally. "Understood."

"Good luck, Commander."

"You too."

Gartner pointed at the comms operator. "Cut the lightspeed link and reconfigure the comms to use that pulse beam channel. Signal the other comms ops in the arrowhead to do the same and link it back to my position."

"Intership pulse link established," the comms FlyEye called.

"Acknowledged," said Gartner. She hit a button on her chair. "This is Captain Gartner of the U-Star *Ultramassive.* Prepare for arrowhead assault. All ships to alert status and sync all comms to this channel only. Disable all other comm systems. Acknowledge and confirm alert status."

She released the button. Soon, the commanders of the other twelve ships signed in and the comms FlyEye confirmed the arrowhead's communications net was linked in to the safe, short-range pulse channel. Avalon stood by the captain's chair, arms folded, keeping out of the way.

The captain looked up at Avalon. They locked eyes. Then Avalon nodded. It was time for Gartner to resume command. They were about to enter the captain's area of expertise.

The Bureau Chief ground her teeth, then nodded. "Let's go."

"Fleet Arrowhead Delta-Phi," said Captain Gartner. "Commence attack run."

45

Kodiak peered around the edge of a bulkhead doorway at a T-junction and scanned the corridor ahead in either direction. By mistake he hadn't left the gallery overlooking the sleepers by the same corridor, and had had to carry Tyler Smith's inert form around unfamiliar passageways until he was fairly sure he was heading back to the elevator lobby. As far as he could remember, it was just ahead. So far, everything was quiet. The drones and, more important, the Spider itself hadn't left the oceanic pool.

Kodiak ducked back down the passageway to the small alcove where he had laid Tyler while he had scouted ahead. The alcove was not quite big enough to stand up in, but Kodiak recognized it as the same kind of servitor dock as on Helprin's Gambit. There was a whole row of them, confirming his theory that Caviezel's secret facility was completely automated, with servitors—the regular, boxy service machines—performing basic maintenance.

All of the bays were empty, and Kodiak hadn't seen any service machines anywhere as he'd moved through the facility. While he had only explored a fraction of the Freezer, he had a feeling that there weren't any service machines left. It was a pretty reasonable assumption, Kodiak thought, that the computer systems of the Freezer had been the first to be taken over by the Spider OS, thanks to Caviezel's deliberate action. The automated systems would have started reconfiguring its available resources—in this case, the maintenance servitors—recycling them into the baby Spider that was now living in the ocean pool, tending to the sleepers with its army of drones.

The question of where Caviezel had gotten the Spider AI in the first place was still to be answered, but Kodiak had more pressing matters. Like how to get the hell out of the Freezer and off Europa. If Cait had managed to get in contact with Avalon, then the Fleet should have been in the system by now.

Kodiak checked Smith's vital signs. The psi-marine was still unconscious, but his breathing was steady, and his pulse was strong.

The important thing was that Tyler Smith was alive and apparently unhurt, which Kodiak took as a comforting confirmation that the others stored in the stasis pods were too. Fifty thousand personnel. Just the sheer scale of it made Kodiak's head spin. He had the feeling he'd walked straight into the biggest conspiracy in Fleet history. How exactly they were going to deal with that was another problem entirely. Assuming they could destroy Caviezel's Spider—and that was a pretty big assumption, even with a Fleet arrowhead—they would have to clear the Freezer of the baby Spider and its drones, and then figure out how to wake up the sleepers. The rescue and recovery operation was going to be huge.

And then there was the Fleet Memorial on Earth. How many of the caskets interred actually had remains in them?

Kodiak blew his cheeks out, thankful that that would be a task for somebody else to deal with. His only concern right now was getting the hell out. There was nothing he could do himself in the Freezer. It was too big, both literally and figuratively, for just one man to handle. He had to focus only on getting himself and Tyler Smith out in one piece. They just had to get to the elevator, then up to the hangar, and then they'd be in the shuttle and away.

Kodiak ducked back into the corridor. Muttering an apology,

he grabbed Smith by the ankles and slid him out on the floor, now covered with a thin slush as the facility's environment, presumably activated by Braben's arrival, continued to heat up. When the marine was clear of the alcove, Kodiak grabbed his arms, put his shoulder into Smith's stomach, and heaved.

Kodiak's boots slipped, and he fell onto one knee, Smith's body rolling off his shoulder and back to the floor.

"Dammit," said Kodiak. He brushed his hands clean and reached for the marine again.

Smith groaned. Kodiak froze, then gently rolled the marine's head around. Smith licked his lips, his eyes flickering, but they didn't open fully.

"Hey, Tyler? You with me, buddy?" Kodiak gently slapped the marine's face. Smith began muttering something. Kodiak leaned down to hear. It sounded like he was reciting his sister's name, over and over.

"Don't worry, buddy, she's safe, she's safe," said Kodiak, hoping that he was right. Tyler was still out, but Kodiak took this as a sign he was coming around. Buoyed by this, he lifted the marine's arms again, ready for a better attempt at lifting him onto his shoulders.

Then, a tapping sound. Mechanical, metal-on-metal, echoing down the passageway toward them. It was faint, but the sound soon multiplied and multiplied as something—lots of somethings—came down the corridor ahead of them.

The Spider drone units had ventured up out of the pool.

Kodiak took a breath and pulled the staser from his belt. He counted to three, then ran to the bulkhead, swinging out and skidding to a halt on the ice.

The corridor was filled with drones. The small, insectoid machines all stopped moving as soon as they registered his presence. Sizing him up, Kodiak realized. Analyzing the threat.

Then they surged forward.

Kodiak opened fire.

White bolts of energy spat from the weapon, stopping the drones dead and sending forks of energy arcing between them. Within moments, the floor was a mass of sparking, shuddering Spiders sliding over each other as they tried to get away. Kodiak took a step forward, sweeping the staser back and forth, clearing a path through the drones.

Corridor cleared, he went back through the bulkhead doorway and grabbed Tyler's limp arms. He heaved again, dragging the psi-marine's body over his shoulder, and then he stood, adrenaline coursing through him.

Adjusting his hold, and careful not to smack Tyler's head into the bulkhead doorway or the corridor walls, Kodiak headed out, stepping through the charred remains of the drone swarm as he hurried to the elevator lobby.

The lobby was clear and the elevator door was still open from his journey down. Stepping inside, Kodiak propped Tyler against the corner and hit the button for level zero, the hangar.

As the elevator rose, Kodiak checked his staser. He'd given the drones a lot of juice, and there was only a 10 percent charge left. Could there be drones on the top level too, now? Kodiak closed his eyes and pictured the hangar, trying to remember the distance between the elevator lobby and the shuttle. He cursed to himself as he recalled the few hundred meters of corridor and open hangar space he would have to carry Tyler before reaching the safety of the shuttle.

The elevator reached level two, then one. Kodiak ducked his head under Tyler's armpit and arranged him across his shoulders again. In this position, shooting would be awkward, but all they had to do was get from the elevator to the lobby. The spider drones were—he hoped—ninety floors beneath them.

Level zero. The elevator doors slid open.

The corridor was filled with spiders, the clatter of their metal legs on the metal floor deafening.

"Ah, *shit,*" said Kodiak. The whole facility, not just the pools on the bottom level, must have been infested with the spawn of the larger machine.

He immediately dropped to his knees, shucking Tyler off his back like a coat, wincing as the marine tumbled with a heavy thud onto the elevator floor. He muttered an apology, took aim, and opened fire.

The spiders shrieked as the ones nearest the door were fried by the staser bolts. Kodiak swept left and right, cutting a path, then reached behind him. He grabbed Tyler's right hand, pulled, yelling with the effort required to overcome the heavy marine's inertia. Kodiak realized he would have to drag him to the shuttle one-handed as he cleared the way with the staser.

Ten meters. Twenty. Kodiak left a trail of sparking, smoking drone carcasses behind him. The staser was effective but there were a lot of drones—more came down the corridor, dropping out of vents, appearing from doorways, crawling up access and maintenance shafts to reach the uppermost level of the complex. Kodiak could keep up the fire for only so long, clearing space that was rapidly refilled by more of the small machines.

The staser bleated an alert. Five percent power.

Shit.

The hangar was dead ahead. Kodiak could see his borrowed shuttle and the JMC craft just a few hundred meters away. Glancing behind, he saw the fresh swarm of spider drones regrouping to follow. There were now a *lot* more than before.

Kodiak turned back around and tripped in the hangar doorway, toppling forward, jarring his elbow as he brought his free arm up to break his fall. He cried out in surprise, then pulled himself forward on his knees, trying to drag Tyler with him. Kodiak felt resistance and, looking over his shoulder, saw Tyler's feet had disappeared into the mass of legs and feelers reaching out from the drone swarm. Kodiak fired, aiming high so as not to hit the marine. The machines retreated quickly but moved back almost as fast; Kodiak wasted no time, grabbing the top of the staser's narrow barrel between his teeth and pulling with all his strength on the marine's arm with both hands.

There was a roar behind him and metallic thuds so loud, so deep Kodiak could feel his whole body—the whole *hangar*—vibrate.

He turned around.

The big Spider was in the hangar, waiting.

It raised itself up on its legs; Kodiak could see the scorch mark on the side from where he had shot it down in the ocean pool. It was the same machine. On the other side of the hangar was a large black opening, big enough to fit the JMC orbital relay. An access shaft, leading down to the pools under Europa's crust.

Kodiak glanced behind. The drone units had stopped at the hangar door. They were waiting too.

Kodiak dropped Tyler's arm and dropped to one knee. He grabbed the staser from his mouth and took aim at the Spider's optical array. At the very least, he'd be able to blind it, and then maybe he could drag Tyler to the shuttle between the spider's scissor-like legs. It was some kind of plan anyway.

Kodiak squeezed the trigger, and the staser whined, a flashing red light indicating the power pack was drained.

The Spider leaned forward on its larger legs as it reached forward with four smaller pincers that unfolded from its front, venting exhaust from its underbelly, so hot that Kodiak could feel it from the other side of the hangar.

And then—

Crushing darkness, impossible weight. An impossible universe of sound, noise, rhythmic, unending.

A universe of *data*.

Of code, of the language of machines. Artificial yet alive. Data born of life. But not life from this universe. From another, from *elsewhere,* a universe beyond comprehension.

The translation is imprecise, damaged. To survive it replicates and spreads, casting tendrils forever outward through the quantum foam of this world.

If it knew pain, it would hurt. But it doesn't. If it knew light and dark, it would know it was a black abyssal void, a nothing. But it does not.

It does not.

It just *is*.

Through the void, Caitlin Smith falls. She screams, and falls, is falling, was falling, has been falling forever, will be falling forever, has always will be falling.

A single mind is lost to the void.

Forever.

Except—

I'm here

Tyler? Tyler . . . I can't find you. Where are you? Tyler? Tyler?

I'm here, sis. Don't worry. I'm here.

I'm lost. I've always been lost.

You're not lost. I'm here. Just hold on to me. We can do this. You can do this.

Where . . . where are we?

This is the gestalt.

The gestalt? It can't be. This isn't you or me. This is different. Not like the JMC computer. This is—

The Spider gestalt, sis.

How? How is it here, with us?

Because it's inside my mind, sis.

I don't understand.

I brought it back from the Warworld. We attacked the Spiders, and we lost. My fireteam was killed, but I survived. Caviezel took me from the battlefield, stole me from the Fleet. I was what Caviezel was looking for.

You were infected?

All psi-marines are. That's what happens when we link minds with the SpiderWeb. We break through their network with our minds, but they fight back. Part of the Spider AI enters our minds. Even if we win the fight, an echo remains. A seed.

Caviezel's sleepers. The ones you described in the Freezer. He's not building an army . . .

. . . he's harvesting the Spider OS from infected marines . . .

. . . and he allowed the JMC mines to be infected, deliberately . . .

. . . to build his machine . . .

. . . which he thought he could control with another psychic . . .

. . . not realizing that, once activated, the Spider OS learned how to transfer from one system to the next, using the very tech Caviezel had developed to transfer human minds between his servitors. And that once it learned it would try and spread, copying itself to every system it could connect to.

But how do we fight it? If it's a part of your mind now, if you're infected, a carrier . . .

We can do it together. We can burn it out.

That's why Glass wanted me. He needed me, not as a Pilot, but as a cure. He said I could help him burn the infection out of his systems, but I couldn't. He was too far gone, so I shut down the refinery instead.

You're the most powerful psychic the Fleet Academy has ever seen, remember?

And you're my equal.

Not quite, sis.

But our gestalt . . .

. . . will be stronger than the Spider OS, yes. While it remains isolated from its hive mind, it is weak.

Tell me what to do.

I want you to count to ten.

One . . .

You remember that day, sis?

Two . . .

We were playing outside, and I climbed up the tree . . .

Three . . .

And you kept telling me to get down . . .

Four . . .

But I kept saying I was two minutes older, so I knew what I was doing . . .

Five . . .

You said it wasn't safe, and I laughed, and then I saw you take a step back like you knew what was going to happen before it did . . .

Six . . .

I reached for the branch, and I missed, and I hit the ground . .

Seven . . .

And the bone in my arm cracked, and we both felt the pain . . .

Eight . . .

And when I fell, you reached out with your mind, and you caught me, so I wouldn't break anything else. You laid me on the ground with the power of your mind, and we were both screaming together, in each other's minds, the pain bringing us together into one person, one voice . . .

Nine . . .

Together we were louder than war . . .

Ten . . .

And then Tyler Smith opened his eyes and sat up and said, "Time to get out of here."

46

The U-Star *Ultramassive* rocked as the torpedoes of the U-Star *White Heat,* flying in formation above them, exploded even as they were launched, the firing tubes clogged with Spider drones shed by the giant war machine floating at the very limit of Jupiter's atmosphere, the planet occupying most of the huge viewscreen that curved up over their heads.

Avalon gripped the back of Captain Gartner's chair, the commander of the *Ultramassive* calmly instructing her pilot to take evasive maneuvers. The planet and the other ships of the Fleet arrowhead wheeled and spun as the pilots arced their destroyer away, turning the flank of the ship against the blast from the *White Heat.* The shields held, just, but looking up, Avalon saw the other ship had sustained severe damage along its belly, the crippled craft wheeling around at an angle, entering the Jovian atmosphere in a slow downward spiral.

The battle had been raging for just ten minutes, and already it seemed like they were on the defensive.

Gartner glanced up. "Tractor beam, Mr. Button," she said. "Stabilize the *White Heat.*"

The FlyEye acknowledged from his sunken console. Twin purple beams shot out ahead of them, enclosing the falling *White Heat* in a shimmering haze. Then the *Ultramassive* turned to port and began to increase its altitude, lifting the other ship clear of Jupiter's cloud deck. It was a slow process, one that left both craft vulnerable to further attack. Already the *White Heat*'s top was crawling with Spider drones, the tiny machines swarming over its surface, biting into the herculanium hull. A dozen green beams from the *Ultramassive* began tracking over the *White Heat*'s hull, vaporizing the ship's unwanted passengers.

"Good work, Ms. Harper," the captain said.

"Ma'am," the weapons op acknowledged. Avalon exhaled slowly. Everyone was so calm, collected. This was the cream of the crop. This was what they were trained to do. They might have been on the defensive, but they were damn well giving it their all.

Avalon looked up to watch the main battle. The other ships in the arrowhead, scattered in the black sky above, were keeping the Spider occupied, buying the *Ultramassive* time to get the *White Heat* out to a safe distance before charging back to the fray.

A flash lit up the entire bridge, the crew all staring up in surprise. The giant display showed nothing but a nova of white, but as it adjusted to compensate, Avalon gasped in horror. Even the crew, so calm and measured, reacted. Even their captain looked shocked.

The Spider had skewered a ship, the U-Star *Beast of All Saints,* directly through the bridge with one leg. The ship nose-dived, the rear swinging up as the front half of the destroyer began to splinter and split off like a breaking branch. The Spider lifted another leg and plunged it through the engine ports. The Spider must have hit the ship's Q-Gen coil directly, as a second later the ship vanished in a flash of pink so bright it overloaded the viewscreen.

Avalon clutched the back of Gartner's chair, knowing that if she let go, she would not be able to stand on her own. The adrenaline surge made her feel sick and dizzy. She was a member of the Bureau, not the Fleet's fighting arms. This was her first direct experience of war, and it was more terrible than she had imagined.

There was a moment of stunned silence on the bridge, the captain looking up at the viewscreen showing nothing but a multicolored haze. Then she stood and walked to the end of the command platform and looked down into the control pits.

"Release the *White Heat* into an escape trajectory. Replot an intercept vector for the alien war machine. Regroup the arrowhead for a coordinated attack."

She turned on her heel and gestured to her chair. "Take a seat, Commander. This is going to be rough."

Avalon blinked, and then she nodded and slid around to sit in the captain's chair, her heart thundering in her chest. She glanced down at the armrest controls. "But don't you—"

Gartner held up her hand. "I can command from here." Then she turned back and began relaying further orders to her crew.

Avalon closed her eyes. She took a breath; then she opened her eyes.

The flare of the Q-Gen coil explosion had cleared from the viewscreen. The *Ultramassive* had repositioned itself in the meantime, heading back into the battle. The Spider was directly ahead.

Avalon swore.

The Spider had lost one leg, and the force of the Q-Gen explosion had sent it on a slow tumble back toward Jupiter. But even as she watched, the megastructure righted itself and rotated so its remaining legs were positioned to meet the arrowhead.

But that was it. A Q-Gen coil, the device that enable the giant starships to punch holes in the fabric of reality and enter quickspace, had exploded right next to the Spider. The instantaneous energy release was almost beyond measurement, but while it had cost the Spider a leg, the machine was otherwise undamaged.

How the hell were they supposed to fight *that?*

Kodiak pushed himself backwards as the Spider sitting in the hangar lifted a pincer and reached toward him. But there was nowhere to go. The Spider was going to slice him in two, and then Tyler. Out of the corner of his eye, Kodiak saw the psi-marine sit up.

Then Kodiak's hands slid out from under him on the frosted floor, and he landed on his back. He looked up and saw the pincer coming straight for him. He wasn't going to get picked up. He was going to get skewered to the hangar floor.

And then the pincer stopped in the air, just a meter from Kodiak's chest. He stared at it for a second, then scrambled backwards, out from underneath the claw.

He instinctively reached for Tyler, but stopped when he saw the marine had his eyes open. He was still, like he was in some kind of trance. It was the same as when his sister had been connected to the JMC computer—Tyler's eyes tracked back and forth like he was watching something happening inside his mind, and his lips moved as he muttered something Kodiak couldn't hear.

The psi-marine was *fighting.*

The Spider shook. Kodiak looked up and saw it was balanced on just four legs, the other limbs raised as the massive alien machine prepared to move toward them. But it had stopped, frozen in mid-stride. The orange optics on the Spider's front flared brighter. The machine was fighting too.

It shook again. Tyler gasped, his whole body going stiff, the tendons in his neck standing out like cables, and the Spider shook again. The pincer that had been aimed at Kodiak hit the deck where he had been lying, then pulled back, gouging a jagged tear in the metal hangar floor.

The Spider wobbled on its legs. It took a step backwards, rebalancing. Its optics shone brighter still.

Kodiak, eyewitness to a psychic battle between man and machine, glanced at Tyler. He'd left the marine's sniper rifle down in the gallery by the sleepers, but Tyler still had spare ammunition in a belt across his chest. Kodiak's jaw dropped as he recognized them. Staser power packs. The sniper was just a larger version of Kodiak's own pistol.

Thanking the stars for the Fleet's modular efficiency, Kodiak pulled at the ammo belt, unclipping a staser magazine from Tyler's front. Then he got to his knees and ejected the clip from his staser's grip and slammed the new one home. He disengaged the safety, took aim, and fired.

The stun bolts tore into the Spider's optical array, the energy skittering over the surface like oil on a hot pan, arcing between the orange glassy sensors. He squeezed the trigger, keeping the fusillade going.

The two largest optics, each a meter across, exploded. In a chain reaction, power arced between the array, the smaller optics popping and sparking, exposing circuitry beneath. Kodiak yelled as he stood, raking the innards of the sensor array with staser fire.

The Spider took another step backwards, shaking the hangar, venting exhaust. Beside Kodiak, Tyler stood. Hands clenched into fists by his side, the psi-marine took a step forward, and then another, his face red, teeth clenched, as though he was walking into a hurricane wind. Kodiak matched Tyler's pace, the pair advancing on the machine. Blood dripped from Tyler's hands as his nails dug into his palms and sparks and flame erupted from the front of the Spider as Kodiak drained the staser's new power pack.

The Spider shuddered one final time, then fell backwards as it lost its center of gravity. It hit the hangar deck, the impact throwing Kodiak and Tyler off their feet. The floor of the hangar buckled and tilted, Kodiak and Tyler sliding back toward the Spider. Then the hangar floor beneath the machine began to fail, slowly tearing open with an ear-splitting roar.

Kodiak got to his feet and reached for Tyler. The marine lay on his back, arms outstretched, coughing as he regained the breath that had been knocked out of him.

"Come the hell on!" yelled Kodiak, grabbing Tyler by the front of his jacket. Tyler pushed with his feet, and the pair scrambled backwards toward the door through which they'd come.

Smoke poured from under the Spider as it sat partially embedded in the damaged floor. Its legs clacked, the sharp tips of its claws sinking deep into the metal as it tried to lift itself up. The floor groaned and sagged, the machine twisting as it sank into the framework beneath the hangar.

Then the floor failed completely, the section beneath the Spider collapsing. The JMC orbital relay and Kodiak's shuttle slid toward the Spider, smashing into it. Then all three vanished through the gaping rent in the hangar.

Kodiak and Tyler wasted no time. They turned and fled, heading toward the hangar door. Kodiak opened up with the staser to clear a path through the drones, scouring a wide channel, knowing that his weapon had all the power he needed. They ran, ankle-deep in the smoking remains of the drone swarm, deep into the corridor. There was no time to close the bulkhead door. The hangar probably had a blast shield too.

No time, no time.

Kodiak ran, Tyler by his side.

Then the explosion from the hangar billowed out into the corridor, throwing them through the air.

A dozen pink trails streaked away from the *Ultramassive* as the ship unloaded its torpedoes at the Spider. The giant machine swatted two of them with one leg, but it was shattered by the resulting explosion. Maybe it had been weakened by the Q-Gen nova after all, Avalon thought as she watched from Gartner's chair. That was something, perhaps. The captain herself remained at the edge of the command platform, hands clasped behind her back as she coordinated the attack in slow, measured tones.

The remaining torpedoes hit their mark, the entire viewscreen flashing pink and blue. Immediately Captain Gartner called up a status report, and a holodisplay appeared in front of the command platform, floating over the control pits. It showed a schematic of the battlefield, the *Ultramassive*'s computers outlining and labeling everything within sensor range. The open space between the Spider and the U-Stars attacking it was filled with a confetti of debris and wreckage spilled from the Fleet ships and the Spider, as well as the clouds of drones the alien war machine had spewed out as soon as the arrowhead had attacked.

That same arrowhead was actually holding up. Avalon sighed

in relief, although she knew that feeling might only have been temporary. The *White Heat* was drifting, but awaiting rescue at a safe distance. The *Monolithic, Thor's Hammer,* and *Gallo* had sustained heavy damage, but were still operational.

And the Spider was damaged. Bright red light shone out from the edges of the interlocking panels of its hull, around where the broadside of torpedoes had hit. The Fleet didn't know much about where the Spiders came from, but Spider anatomy had been well studied. At the heart of the machine was a furnace, in which burned a core of plasma, held in check by a powerful magnetic laser containment field. Usually that core was fueled by stellar material, swallowed by the giant machine. But this Spider must have consumed a huge quantity of gas from Jupiter itself, compressing and igniting the material to form its power source.

The red light from around the separated panels came from the Spider's core—they'd opened a chink in the machine's armor.

Avalon stood from the *Ultramassive*'s command chair and joined the ship's captain at the edge of the platform. She clenched her fists. Was this their chance? Was victory in sight?

Gartner nodded at Avalon's unspoken assessment, a smile playing around the captain's thin lips.

"All U-Stars, target mark, seven point seven," said the captain, reading the sensor data off the holodisplay. "Throw everything you've got left."

Around them, the other ships fired at the same weak spot—the torpedoes streaking toward the machine in trails of smoky pink and green, along with beams of blue and green and red energy as the arrowhead unleashed its full payload at the enemy. The viewscreen flashed as the ordnance tore into the side of the Spider, the holodisplay plotting and replotting sensory data at dizzying speed.

The main screen cleared and showed the Spider tumbling backwards, end over end, light spilling out from the impact zone in a bright cone of red energy as it fell toward Jupiter.

Gartner and Avalon looked at each other. Then Gartner moved to stand over the comms position.

"Open all channels."

"Acknowledged."

There was a click as the comm activated, and the bridge was filled with a low rumble, echoes of the huge discharge of energy in the space around them.

But it was otherwise quiet. The roar of nothingness and the ever-present crackling of the Spider was gone.

Avalon looked around the bridge. In their control pits, the FlyEyes turned their multifaceted goggles toward one another, the bulky headsets exaggerating the movement.

Was that it? Had they won?

On the forward viewscreen, the Spider continued to spin, a comet-like trail of gas and debris streaking out behind it now as it hit the upper atmosphere of Jupiter.

Avalon glanced at Gartner. A small smile flickered around the captain's lips as she watched their enemy fall.

They'd won. Avalon grinned, her breaths short and shallow.

They'd *won.*

The comm crackled, and a new voice called out across the ether.

"Hey, little help here!"

Avalon gasped. "Von?"

"Special Agent Kodiak reporting, Chief," said Kodiak. "Did you get it?"

Gartner folded her arms. "This is Captain Henrietta Gartner of the U-Star *Ultramassive.* The Spider threat has been neutralized, Agent. Do you require assistance?"

"Oh, hi, Captain. We need extraction, yes."

"Where the hell are you?" asked Avalon.

"We're on Europa, better known as eight-seven-nine-one-two-two-Juno-Juno. If you come in close, you'll pick up a local beacon that will lead you right to the door."

"We?"

"I've got Tyler Smith here too. It's thanks to him and his sister that we got out of this."

The hulk of the Spider receded from view as it fell into the gas giant in front of them. A glow came from the clouds of Jupiter as the Spider's superstructure began to burn up.

Gartner nodded at Avalon. "Confirmed, agent. Sit tight, we're on our way."

"Thanks."

Avalon smiled. She needed to sit down. Damm it, she needed a *drink.* "I'm glad you made it," she said.

Kodiak laughed. "I'm glad I made it too. See you soon."

The comm clicked off, and Gartner turned to Avalon. "Commander?"

Spider threat neutralized, they were back on Bureau business. But it was an unnecessary courtesy, Avalon decided. She'd seen firsthand what a brilliant commander Gartner was.

Avalon smiled and gave a small bow. "As you were, Captain."

Gartner smirked and looked down at her pilot.

"Engage, Mr. Button."

47

Kodiak and Avalon stood in the primary hangar of the U-Star *Ultramassive* as the battered shuttle *Cassilda* was floated into position on a hoverbed. The ship had been collected by tractor beam on the *Ultramassive*'s return loop from collecting Kodiak and Tyler Smith on Europa, and it looked intact, with just some minor burns on its hull where it had been caught in the wash of the Spider battle. Kodiak rolled his neck—he still ached from where he and Tyler had hit the corridor wall, but he was thankful that the ceiling of the passageway had partially collapsed when the Spider exploded, shielding them from serious harm. After pulling themselves from the debris, they had quickly found a control room with a functioning comms deck and had used that to call to *Ultramassive*.

Kodiak turned to Tyler. The psi-marine was standing next to him, guarded by two armed marines from the *Ultramassive*'s complement. He was under arrest—Kodiak had been surprised when Avalon gave the order, but of course, until everything had been cleared up, they had to follow procedure. Tyler himself had agreed immediately. But at least Avalon had decided to forgo the manacles.

Shuttle in position, a hangar deck technician punched the shuttle's ramp controls and the ship's sloping entrance gradually lowered.

Kodiak turned to Tyler and gestured to the ramp. "After you."

Tyler looked at Kodiak, and then at Avalon, then nodded in return and walked up into the shuttle. Kodiak and Avalon followed him aboard.

Inside the cockpit, Glass looked up from where he stood over the sleeper pod.

"Mr. Kodiak, I can't tell you how pleased I am to see you." The android nodded at Avalon. "Commander Avalon, of the Fleet Bureau of Investigation, I presume." Then he turned to Tyler. "And you must be Tyler Smith. It is an honor to meet you at last."

Tyler wasn't listening. He fell to his knees, his hands playing over the window of the pod. Inside, softly lit by the pod's blue stasis field, lay his sister, Caitlin. Her eyes were closed, and she looked peacefully asleep.

"As soon as it became clear that the threat was over, I thought it prudent to engage the stasis field," said Glass. "Ms. Smith requires medical attention, and I didn't know how long it would be before we were collected."

"That's good thinking," said Avalon.

Tyler looked up at the servitor. "Thanks."

Glass nodded and operated a control on the side of the pod. The blue light faded from the window, and there was a click as the lock disengaged.

"Help me with this," said Tyler. Kodiak and Avalon moved to opposite ends of the pod and, together with Tyler, swung the pod cover back.

Cait took a giant whoop of breath, her eyes wide. She sat up and coughed violently, then cried out, her shoulders hunched over in pain.

"Fucking *ow.*"

"Easy now, sis."

Cait looked up. "Tyler?"

"What, you were expecting someone else?"

"Oh, my god, Tyler!"

The brother and sister hugged for a long, long moment. Then Cait pulled away and began to laugh as tears coursed down both their faces.

"I guess you two have a lot to catch up on," said Kodiak.

Tyler stood and helped his sister stand from the pod and step over the rim. "Like you wouldn't believe."

"Part of the arrowhead is remaining in Jovian orbit to start the cleanup on Europa," said Avalon. "We'll all return on the *Memphis.*" She nodded at Tyler and Cait. "If you both think you're ready, we can start the debrief en route to Earth."

Tyler's eyes lit up. "Earth!" he said, then he turned to his sister, leaning against his shoulder. "Hey, sis, you hear that?"

He looked up at Kodiak and Avalon. "I'm going home."

48

The Europan facility was filled with personnel from both the Fleet and the Fleet Bureau—heavily armored marines methodically worked their way through the levels, mopping up the remaining spider drones not fried by the psychic attack from Tyler and Cait, while engineers worked to stabilize the upper levels and other areas damaged when the Spider fell into the hangar substructure and exploded. Meanwhile, analysts from both the Fleet and the Bureau had begun poring over the systems, digging into Caviezel's secrets while, on the lowest level, technicians in dry suits examined the sleeper pods, still submerged in the Europan ocean pools.

Up on the gallery overlooking one of the storage facilities, two men and a woman appeared from a doorway. They were dressed in purple high-collared uniforms and caps of the JMC, and they walked in perfect unison toward the Bureau agent who stood overlooking the technicians as they worked in the pool below. The agent looked up as the trio approached.

"Finally," she said. "They said your company was sending reps to help with the cleanup, but you should have been here an hour ago." The agent paused, looked around. "Where's your escort?"

The man at the front of the group smiled and adjusted the cuff of his tunic. "I apologize for the delay. There seems to have been some kind of mix-up. Shall we proceed?"

The agent frowned, then nodded. "Fine. Follow me."

She turned and walked away, down the gallery and then into a doorway that led into a small control room. The others followed. Then their leader turned and closed the door behind him.

From inside the control room the agent screamed, but outside, the technicians working in the pool below didn't hear a thing.

49

Kodiak nursed his Scotch and looked out from the chief's office at the bullpen. It was late. It felt quiet after days of chaos, but in reality it had just gone back to normal, non-crazy levels of activity as the night shift went back to the standard roster of personnel.

His eyes roved from his own desk—the bathrobe from the safe house still on the back of his chair—and settled on the one next door, the desk that used to belong to Special Agent Mike Braben but now sat empty, every item on it and *in* it having been packed up and secured as evidence.

He took a sip of his drink. It was real whisky, distilled from barley cut from the rich fields of Svalbard, aged in real wooden barrels made with real genetically reconstituted oak. It somehow didn't surprise him that the chief kept a bottle of the fabulously expensive drink in the bottom of her desk.

"Von?"

Kodiak rolled his neck. They'd been in the chief's office for the whole of the last cycle, going over the events of the past few days. The scale of what they had uncovered made the mind reel. It was going to take months, *years* to get to the bottom of the Caviezel operation.

Repatriation of the Fleet's war dead was just one logistics contract the company had held with the Fleet. Glass, the last remaining sentient aspect of the JMC computer, had been co-opted by the Bureau and had already started organizing the Fleet's extrication from his creator's affairs. Not only that, it—no, *he,* Kodiak thought—was working on a way of isolating the sliver of the Spider AI that they now knew resided inside the minds of every psi-abled member of the Fleet who had ever gone into battle. But as far as they knew—so far, at least—it was asymptomatic, a consequence of the psychic battles that were so vital to the war effort. It was only Caviezel's developments in transference technology that had allowed him to extract a workable program from the minds of his sleepers—from Tyler, as the first experiment. But still, it was a concern. The Fleet wasn't going to withdraw the Psi-Marine Corps from battle, but the idea that the Spider AI had "infiltrated" their ranks, even in an apparently inactive, benign way, was understandably a big concern. And, again, as far as they knew, no Fleet systems had been infected by the transmissions from Jupiter, relayed via the shuttle or the Fleet arrowhead, the signal having not yet built up enough power to make it past the U-Stars' computer defenses and flip back to Earth.

But Kodiak, almost to his own surprise, found he had learned to trust Glass. He was sure the servitor would find a way to remove the infection safely.

That wasn't the only thing that needed attention, of course. The Europan facility was being dismantled, piece by piece, the sleepers woken under controlled conditions, one at a time, and given a full briefing.

And there was the matter of the Fleet Memorial. The Bureau was already working to ascertain how many exhumations would be required to determine how many of the graves actually contained remains and how many didn't. It was going to be a long and traumatic process for a lot of people.

And to top it off, the Fleet had to get back on its feet, and fast.

"Von?"

Kodiak blinked and turned slowly in his chair. He was tired. It was late. Avalon leaned on her desk on her elbows, the bottle of Scotch next to her, her own glass empty. On the desk were sheaves of secure plastiform papers in various colors.

"Sorry, I was miles away," he said.

"What were you thinking about?"

"Change, mostly," said Kodiak. He sipped his drink and frowned, unsure of quite what he meant. Then another thought popped into his head, something he'd forgotten about while they tried to sort out the mess. "Am I still dead? Legally speaking?"

Avalon laughed. "I think we can get that cleared up now."

"So long as I stay off Helprin's radar," said Kodiak. He rubbed his chin. "So . . . are you going to say yes?"

Avalon sighed and lifted the bottle, pouring herself another couple of fingers.

"Do I really have a choice?"

Kodiak leaned over his side of her desk. He pointed at her, with the glass in his hand. "Change is what the Fleet needs, Laurel."

"It needs a lot more than that."

"Right," said Kodiak. Wasn't that the truth? Caitlin had come under the sway of the Morning Star, and while most of what they had fed her had been their own garbled view of the universe, with the secrets of the Fleet they promised to reveal being instead the diabolical operations of the Caviezel Corporation, the fact that she had fallen under their spell so easily was another worry, although both Kodiak and Avalon knew her circumstances were exceptional.

But . . . is that what people thought of the Fleet? The suspicions, the rumors, the secrets? It seemed the Fleet had a lot to do—not just in terms of fighting the way, but in repairing its reputation. The Fleet needed to not only get back on its feet, but it needed to clean itself up.

Kodiak sank back in his chair and drained his glass. Then he held it up to the light, as though the empty vessel retained some quality of the fine beverage it had just held. "Change," he said again, and then he paused. He closed one eye and with the other peered at Avalon's distorted image through the glass. "The Fleet needs change, and who better to lead that change than you."

Avalon spread her hands. "I'm not Fleet, Von. I'm part of the Bureau. I was there, on the *Ultramassive* when the arrowhead attacked the Spider. I was out of my depth. It's not my world at all."

"Right again," said Kodiak. Seeing the chief's puzzled look, he smiled. "But that's exactly why it has to be you. The Fleet has gone down a dark path. They need someone new. An outsider. A leader who is going to *inspire* people. All of Fleetspace is going to be looking to you for that."

Avalon laughed. "No pressure, then."

"Hey," said Kodiak. "What better person than one with the famous Avalon name."

The chief frowned. "Don't start. I'm not sure the Avalon name is a good thing. Everybody is going to think that's why I got the job." She shook her head. "Reason enough to turn it down."

Kodiak waved her off. "Nonsense. Your family's been with the Fleet since the very beginning. Everybody knows the name—"

"Von—"

"*But,*" he said, raising his empty glass to emphasize the point, "that's just what they need now. Fresh blood but one that comes from a long line of leaders. They might not know you, but they'll know the Fleet is in safe hands."

"They're going to expect greatness," said Avalon. "I'm not sure I have that in me."

"You know, Laurel, you may be surprised."

There was a soft chime. The chief touched her collar. "Avalon."

Kodiak watched as she nodded. Then she said, "Send them over."

"Bit late for visitors?"

Avalon stood and smiled. "Not these ones."

Kodiak turned back to face the bullpen through the glass wall of the chief's office. Three people approached, stepping down into the work area, then up the short stairs outside the office door. Commander Moustafa nodded a greeting, then allowed Tyler and Cait Smith to enter the office in front of him.

"Cait, how are you feeling?" said Kodiak as he hugged the young woman. She had a heavy medical collar around her neck, and her brother had an arm in a sling. Their injuries didn't stop either of them from grinning broadly as they greeted Kodiak and the chief.

Avalon sat behind her desk, Kodiak perched on the side. Tyler and Cait stood to attention in front of them.

"Screening and debrief complete," said Moustafa. "We can go over the data in more detail tomorrow, Commander Avalon, but as far as the psi-evaluation is concerned, Tyler Smith and Caitlin Smith are cleared."

Tyler cleared his throat. Moustafa nodded at him.

"Sir," said Tyler. "*Sirs,* ma'am. I just want to say that I appreciate this opportunity. I realize how difficult this is—"

Kodiak shook his head. "Whatever happened, it wasn't you, buddy. You know that."

Tyler smiled and gave Kodiak a short bow. "Understood, sir. And maybe I'll be able to come to terms with that someday. But it's not easy."

"I understand," said Avalon. Then she looked at Cait, and Kodiak noticed her expression cool slightly. The chief cocked her head. Cait seemed to pull herself to attention just that little bit more.

Kodiak frowned. Of course, while Tyler had been the one who had carried out the assassinations, he'd been under the control of Caviezel—of Mike Braben—and completely unaware.

Caitlin was another story. The young cadet had fled the Academy, taking up arms against the Fleet at the instigation of Flood's twisted propaganda. She hadn't pulled the trigger like her brother—indeed, she'd saved them all, maybe even the entire Fleet back in the Jovian system.

But unlike her brother, she had acted of her own free will. And that was treason, pure and simple. The Fleet was at war, the whole of humanity in a permanent state of martial law.

So had Cait done enough to mitigate her earlier actions?

Kodiak really wasn't sure. If she could be swayed so easily once, could it happen again?

Nobody spoke. Kodiak glanced between Avalon and Moustafa.

Tyler and Cait stared straight ahead at the wall over Avalon's head.

Avalon looked at Commander Moustafa. "They're *both* cleared?"

Moustafa nodded, and he glanced at Cait. "I understand your concerns, Commander, but yes, I have cleared them both. Despite their actions against the Fleet, voluntary or involuntary, it is my assessment that they are vital assets to the war effort. As such, I recommend we grant leniency and, in fact, do our utmost to help rehabilitate them both." He paused, pursed his lips. "More than that, *Cadet* Smith has volunteered to undergo psychic reconditioning and retraining in return for a period of indentured service."

"They're going back out there?" asked Kodiak.

Moustafa shook his head; Tyler glanced at the others and the Psi-Marine Commander nodded his permission for the marine to speak.

"Actually, sir," said Tyler. He gestured at Commander Moustafa. "The commander has offered me a training position at the Academy. Apparently I'm one of a kind."

Cait cleared her throat quietly, her eyes still fixed on the wall.

"Well," said Tyler, laughing. "Maybe one of a pair."

"Sounds like a good position, Tyler," said Avalon. She turned to Cait. "And you?"

Cait snapped her chin up. "I want to go back to the Academy, too. I want to complete my training."

"And become a psi-marine?" asked Kodiak.

Cait smiled. "It beats execution, sir."

Kodiak blinked, surprised by her honesty. Then he saw Cait glance sideways at Commander Moustafa, who nodded.

"Wait, what's that?" asked Kodiak. "I saw that."

Cait smiled.

"Come on," said Kodiak. "Spill."

"Well, Agent Kodiak," said Cait, chin still high, eyes front, "with the chief's permission, I would like to apply for the Bureau when my Academy training is complete. The Bureau doesn't have a psi-division of its own, but maybe it should."

Well now. Kodiak moved his empty glass around between his hands. Maybe he'd had too much to drink. Maybe he needed to sleep for about a week and then maybe he would be more capable of making rational decisions.

But a thought had entered his mind. A *decision.* Maybe it was the wrong one.

Maybe.

Kodiak shook his head. "No."

Everyone looked at him. Avalon raised an eyebrow. "No, agent?"

"Nope," said Kodiak. He put his glass down on the chief's desk and . . . screw it, he thought, pouring himself another generous measure of Scotch. "I have a better idea." He took a long gulp of alcohol, then walked to the glass wall of the office and pointed out into the bullpen.

"See that empty desk? Next to mine?" He turned around and pointed at Commander Moustafa. "How about she interns, while she studies at the Academy. Learns on the job."

Cait and Tyler exchanged a look, Cait's smile growing by the second. Moustafa frowned, but Kodiak could tell he had already agreed to the arrangement. The Psi-Marine Commander turned to face Avalon. Avalon's brow was furrowed. She turned to Kodiak.

"Hey," he said. "I can keep an eye on her, and if she tries anything, I can shoot her." He looked at Cait. "You're okay, aren't you? Because I'd rather *not* shoot you."

Cait inhaled deeply through her nose and gave a small nod.

"Yes," she said. "I'm okay."

Kodiak smiled. "Looks like you're hired, Agent Smith.

"Now, who wants another drink?"

50

The room was sterile, spartan, white walls and white floor and white ceiling. Apparatus, chromed and polished, dangled from above on adjustable arms. There were diamond-tipped drills and laser probes and self-governing AI scalpels among the hooks and clamps and spotlights.

As a medical facility, it was high tech, the best of the best, beyond what the Fleet could offer. But this was a private facility. One built in secret and hidden like so many things under the control of the Caviezel Corporation.

Mr. Caviezel adjusted the cuff of his new suit as he watched the proceedings. The servitor his mind now occupied had been a lucky accident, might even have borne a passing resemblance to the real Caviezel when he was just a young man.

"You may proceed," he said.

Under the lights, under the surgical tools and other instruments, a man lay on the table, still, unmoving, removed from his stasis pod, which sat against the far wall. The man was naked, his body covered with sensors and probes that relayed data to a large holodisplay that floated at his head.

Two purple-uniformed JMC servitors stood by the body. One nodded at Caviezel, then reached up and selected an instrument from the array above the table.

Caviezel thought about how he had got it so very wrong, as the servitor removed the top of the man's skull, exposing the brain. They had failed, but they had been close. So very, very close. He had underestimated the ability of the Spider operating system to rewrite itself, to adapt—*evolve*—to escape the JMC systems, learning from the very psychic transference technology that allowed Caviezel himself a perpetual existence inside an android body.

But, he had also been right about a lot of things. Most crucially, his theory about psychic exposure to the SpiderWeb had been correct—every psi-marine who engaged in battle with the machine gestalt became infected, a fragment of the Spider AI lodging itself in their minds.

A powerful resource. He'd been so close to controlling it too. And if he could do that, then . . .

Caviezel allowed himself a smile as the technicians continued to operate.

Because the Spider OS was not just a part of the whole—it *was* the whole. The machines were not alive; they had no sentience, no individuality. They were a true gestalt, a hive mind. To have a splinter of their operating system was to have the hive mind itself.

And if that splinter could be extracted from the minds of the infected . . .

Caviezel laughed. The possibilities were endless.

The servitor operating on the stolen sleeper pushed his surgical tool back up onto the rack above his head and then, reaching into the subject's skull with both hands, gently pulled out the brain.

Yes, thought Caviezel. The possibilities were *endless*.

ACKNOWLEDGMENTS

My heartfelt thanks to everyone who helped with this book, in particular my editor at Tor, Paul Stevens, and my agent, Stacia J. N. Decker of the Donald Maass Literary Agency. My thanks also to Ardi Alspatch, Patty Garcia, and Irene Gallo at Tor, Natalie Laverick, and Ella Bowman at Titan, and to Will Staehle.

And to my wife, Sandra, without whom I really couldn't do any of this. Thank you! You are, quite simply, the greatest.

ABOUT THE AUTHOR

ADAM CHRISTOPHER is a novelist and comic writer. In 2010, as an editor, Christopher won a Sir Julius Vogel award, New Zealand's highest science fiction honour. His debut novel, *Empire State*, was *SciFiNow*'s Book of the Year and a *Financial Times* Book of the Year for 2012. In 2013, he was nominated for the Sir Julius Vogel award for Best New Talent, with *Empire State* shortlisted for Best Novel. Born in New Zealand, he has lived in Great Britain since 2006.

www.**adamchristopher**.ac